DK EYEWITNESS TRAVEL

Umbria

D1344212

Produced by Fabio Ratti Editoria Srl,
Milan, Italy

Project Editors Mattia Goffetti, Silvia Riboldi
Editor Marina Beretta
Designers Modi Artistici, Tiziano Perotto

Contributors
Giovanni Francesio, Marina Dragoni,
Patrizia Masnini

Photographer
Ghigo Roli

Illustrator
Elisabetta Mancini

Cartography
Laura Belletti

Dorling Kindersley Limited
Publishing Managers Fay Franklin,
Kate Poole
Senior Art Editor Marisa Renzullo
Translator Fiona Wild
Editor Emily Hatchwell
Consultant Jeffrey Kennedy
Factchecker Leonie Loudon
Production Sarah Dodd

Printed in China

First published in Great Britain in 2004 by
Dorling Kindersley Limited
80 Strand, London WC2R 0RL

17 18 19 20 10 9 8 7 6 5 4 3 2 1

**Reprinted with revisions 2006, 2008,
2011, 2015, 2017**

Madonna and Child fresco at the Palazzo
dei Consoli in Gubbio, Northern Umbria

Introducing Umbria

The scenic medieval city of Todi, in Southern Umbria

◀ **Title page** The medieval town of Assisi, crowned by the Basilica di San Francesco.   **Front cover main image** Rooftops of Trevi,
backed by lush Umbrian countryside.   **Back cover image** The Cascata delle Marmore, a man-made waterfall, near Terni.

Contents

Detail of the Palazzo Comunale in Narni, Southern Umbria

Apennine mountains overlooking the beautiful Piano Grande, Northern Umbria

Basilica di San Francesco, Assisi

HOW TO USE THIS GUIDE

This guide helps you to get the most out of your visit to Umbria by giving detailed descriptions of sights, practical information and expert advice. *Introducing Umbria* sets the region in its geographical, cultural as well as historical context.

Umbria Area by Area describes the main sightseeing areas, with maps, detailed illustrations and photographs. Hotels, restaurants and shops are covered in *Travellers' Needs*, while the *Survival Guide* contains invaluable practical advice.

Umbria Area by Area

Umbria has been divided into two sightseeing areas, each with its own colour-coded thumb tab: a key to the colours used is on the inside front cover. Each area has its own chapter, which opens with a Regional Map with a numbered list of the sights described. There is a Road Map and a key to symbols inside the back cover.

Each area has a colour-coded thumb tab.

1 Introduction

The landscape, history and character of each region is described here, showing how the area has developed over the centuries and what it offers to the visitor today.

A locator map shows the area in relation to the region as a whole. It is identified by its colour-coding.

Exploring Northern Umbria

2 Regional Map

This gives an illustrated overview of the whole area. All the sights covered in the chapter are numbered and there are also useful tips on getting around by car and public transport.

Features and story boxes highlight special aspects of an area or sight.

3 Detailed Information

All the important towns and other places of interest are described individually. They are listed in order, following the numbering on the Regional Map. Within each entry there are details on the important buildings and other major sights.

4 Major Towns

All the important towns are described individually. Within each entry there is further detailed information on all the main sights. The Town Map shows their location.

A Visitors' Checklist provides the practical details needed to plan a visit, including local transport and details for the local tourist office.

The Town Map shows all the key sights, along with train and bus stations, car parks, churches and tourist offices.

5 The Top Sights

All the most important sights have two or more pages devoted to them. Historic buildings and churches are dissected to reveal their interiors, and museums and galleries have colour-coded floorplans.

Stars indicate the features you should not miss.

6 Areas of Natural Beauty and National Parks

Parks and nature reserves are described in detail and illustrated with a pictorial map. Roads are shown, together with scenic routes, picnicking areas and campsites.

The scale bar makes it possible to judge distances. The compass shows due north.

Verification of the Stigmata, detail, Upper Chuch of the Basilica di San Francesco, Assisi ▶

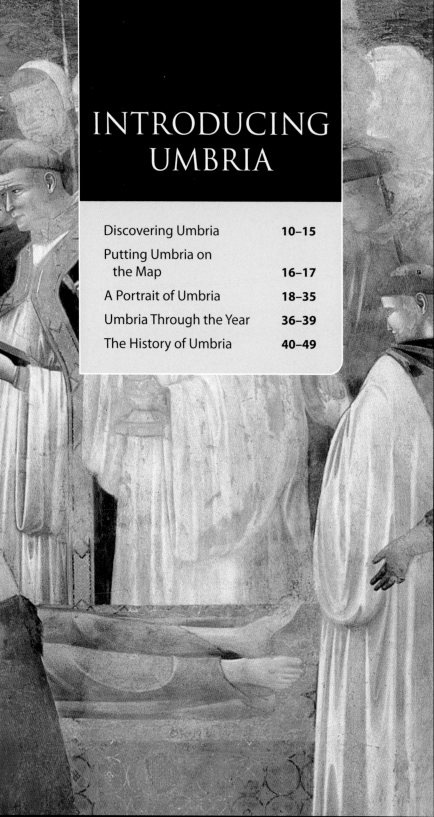

INTRODUCING UMBRIA

DISCOVERING UMBRIA

The following tours have been designed to take in as many of Umbria's highlights as possible, while keeping long-distance travel to a minimum. Our first tour covers two days in Perugia, followed by five days spent exploring Northern Umbria. These two itineraries can be followed individually or combined to form a week-long tour.

Next comes two days in Terni and its environs, and five days exploring Southern Umbria, which, again, can be combined to give a seven-day tour. Extra suggestions are provided for those who want to extend their stay. Pick, combine and follow your favourite tours, or simply dip in and out and be inspired.

Lake Trasimeno
The setting of the lake is idyllic, with a lush cypress belt and hills draped along the turquoise waters. This is Italy's fourth-largest lake and the spot where Hannibal destroyed the Roman army in 217 BC.

5 Days in Northern Umbria

- Be captivated by **Assisi**, its history and its wondrous buildings, like the **Duomo**.
- Marvel at the scenery of the **Parco Regionale del Monte Subasio**.
- Walk through Gubbio's **Via Gabrielli**, a street lined with gorgeous medieval houses.
- Visit **Città di Castello's Pinacoteca Comunale**, one of Umbria's finest art galleries.
- Take a leisurely boat trip from Castiglione del Lago on **Lake Trasimeno** to Isola Maggiore and Isola Polvese.
- Spend two days hiking along the **Franciscan Path of Peace** from Assisi to Gubbio.

Key

— 5 Days in Northern Umbria
— 5 Days in Southern Umbria

Città di Castello
Montone
Umbertide
Tevere
Isola Maggiore
Castiglione del Lago
Isola Polvese
Lago Trasimeno
Perugia
Torgiano
Deruta
Tevere
Chiani
Todi
Orvieto
Lugnano in Teverino
Amelia

Assisi
A picturesque view of the centre of the fascinating town of Assisi. This UNESCO World Heritage Site has a string of magnificent churches and timeless scenic beauty.

5 Days in Southern Umbria

- Visit the huge fortress sitting on top of a hill overlooking the ancient town of **Narni**.

- Explore **Amelia** with its ancient Mura Poligonali (Polygonal Walls).

- Head for the spectacular white and grey **Piazza del Duomo** in Orvieto.

- Admire **Pozzo di San Patrizio** in Orvieto, a deep well with a 248-step spiral staircase.

- Witness the well-preserved medieval architecture of **Palazzo dei Priori**, **Palazzo del Popolo** and **Palazzo del Capitano** in Todi.

- Enjoy dinner in one of **Spoleto**'s sophisticated restaurants in the buzzy **Piazza del Mercato**.

Amelia
Reconstructed in Baroque style in the 17th century, the cathedral in Amelia bears important works of art including a panel with *Madonna and Child* attributed to Antoniazzo Romano.

Parco Regionale del Monte Cucco

Gubbio

Gualdo Tadino

Nocera Umbra

Assisi
Eremo delle Carceri · Parco Regionale del Monte Subasio

ettona

Spello

Bevagna · Foligno

Montefalco · Trevi

Fonti del Clitunno

Parco Nazionale dei Monti Sibillini

Norcia

Spoleto · Cascia

Acquasparta

Carsulae
San Gemini · Ferentillo

Terni · Parco Fluviale del Nera

Narni

isciano

Nera

0 kilometres   15

0 miles   15

Narni
A typical old street in the unspoilt, medieval hill town of Narni.

Todi
Aerial view of red-tiled rooftops, Palazzo del Populo and Duomo in the centre of this well-preserved medieval town.

2 Days in Perugia

The largest city in Umbria, Perugia is notable for its Romanesque churches, monuments, museums and the famous Jazz Music Festival, Umbria Jazz.

- **Arriving** International and domestic flights arrive at the Aeroporto Regionale Umbro di Sant'Egidio daily. The airport is 12 km (7 miles) from Perugia and Assisi. Buses and taxis operate from outside the terminal.

- **Transport** The city's main sights can be visited on foot. There are buses around the city and to the suburbs.

Day 1

Morning A good place to begin touring **Perugia** *(pp88–95)* is **Piazzale Partigiani** *(p88)*, where the bus terminal and car park are located. Take the escalator to Piazza Italia and follow Perugia's elegant main street, the Corso Vannucci to **Palazzo dei Priori** *(pp90–91)*. This imposing 1293 building houses the splendid **Galleria Nazionale dell'Umbria** *(pp92–3)*. Spend a couple of hours here admiring exquisite masterpieces such as St Anthony Polyptych and the San Domenico of Fiesole Altarpiece. Don't miss Sala dei Notari and its fabulous frescoes. Take the stairs down to Piazza IV Novembre, stopping at Fontana Maggiore, one of Italy's most important Romanesque monuments.

People walking outside the main entrance of the Palazzo dei Priori

Afternoon Stop for lunch at a restaurant around Piazza IV Novembre, and move on to the Piazza Danti dominated by the **Duomo** *(p93)*. Visit the amazing engineering structure, **Etruscan Well** *(p94)*, in Palazzo Bourbon-Sorbello. Next, head for the Palazzo del Capitano del Popolo on **Piazza Matteotti** *(p94)* and look out for the covered market, where you can see the piazza's foundations. Explore the narrow streets of Porta Sole quarter until you reach the church of **San Severo** *(p94)*, home to one of Raphael's most famous frescoes, the *Holy Trinity and Saints* (1507–8). Follow the medieval Corso Garibaldi to see the 5th century church of **San Michele Arcangelo (Sant'Angelo)** *(p95)*.

Day 2

Morning The well-preserved Benedictine church of **San Pietro** *(p89)*, dating from the early Christian period (6th century AD), is your first port of call. Admire the splendour of its Romanesque and Renaissance styling. Head along Corso Cavour until you reach the huge church of **San Domenico** *(p89)*. Venture inside to see its magnificent stained-glass window, the second largest in Italy. Behind the church is the **Museo Archeologico Nazionale dell'Umbria** *(p88)*.

Afternoon After lunch around Corso Cavour, take the short walk to **Rocca Paolina** *(p88)* fortress and its striking Etruscan Porta Marzia archway before exploring Giardini Carducci and the Giardini del Campaccio gardens. Follow the city wall to **Oratorio di San Bernardino** *(pp94–5)*, known for its Renaissance architecture and sculptures, and its piazza dominated by the church of **San Francesco al Prato** *(p94)*.

> **To extend your trip…**
> Visit the ancient burial site, Ipogeo dei Volumni, 7 km (4 miles) southeast of **Perugia**, and the futuristic new district Fontivegge.

5 Days in Northern Umbria

- **Arriving** Assisi, like Perugia, is served by the Aeroporto Regionale Umbro di Sant'Egidio.

- **Transport** The main sights of Assisi can be visited on foot.

Day 1

Morning Assisi *(pp72–85)* is one of the best-preserved cities in the world. Start the day at the **Duomo (San Rufino)** *(pp74–5)* where St Francis was baptized. Spend some time admiring its magnificent 12th-century façade and rose windows. Next, make your way along Via San Rufino to the Corso Mazzini, and on to the **Basilica di Santa Chiara** *(p73)* to see its collection of frescoes. Head back to the **Piazza del Comune** *(p75)* for lunch with a little detour to the Santa Maria Maggiore *(p83)*, the city's first cathedral.

Fontana Maggiore flanked by the Palazzo dei Priori and the Duomo, Perugia

A grand view of Basilica di San Francesco, Assisi

Afternoon Walk down **Piazza del Comune** (p75), a handsome square lined with palazzos. In the middle is the **Temple of Minerva** (p75), which once marked the heart of the city. Continue on to **Basilica di San Francesco** (pp76–7), a 13th-century structure built to celebrate the life of St Francis. Inside, you will see important frescoes and the tomb of the saint. Spend the night in **Assisi**.

Day 2
Morning Take the road from Assisi (pp72–85) to **Nocera Umbra** (p69), but not before taking a short detour to **Parco Regionale del Monte Subasio** (pp70–71) to see the centuries-old friars' hermitage, the **Eremo delle Carceri** (p70). Stop a while to admire the park's natural scenery. From Nocera Umbra, continue on to the ancient town of **Gualdo Tadino** (pp68–9). Tour its churches and palazzos.

Afternoon Visit the **Rocca Flea** (p68), a hilltop fortress dominating **Gualdo Tadino** (pp68–9). It has an interesting small museum and an art and ceramics gallery. Later, take the road to **Gubbio** (pp62–5), your overnight stop, which passes through the scenic **Parco Regionale del Monte Cucco** (pp66–7).

Day 3
Morning Explore the ancient city of **Gubbio** (pp62–5), at the foot of Monte Ingino. Start with the **Roman Ruins** (p62) and

then follow the city wall to Porto Castello gate, where you can enter Gubbio's old quarter. Look out for **Via Gabrielli** (p63), a street lined with gorgeous medieval houses, the church of **San Domenico** (p63) and **Palazzo dei Consoli** (p64), one of Gubbio's most impressive buildings housing Museo Civico.

Afternoon A leisurely lunch in the old quarter might precede a visit to the **Duomo** (p65) and the restored **Palazzo Ducale** (p65). Don't miss the Ducale's archaeological area on its lower level, where ancient remains can be seen. Other attractions include the Gothic **San Giovanni Battista** (pp62–3), the medieval Porta Romana and the shop-lined **Corso Garibaldi** (p65), all worthy of a visit.

Day 4
Morning Leaving **Gubbio** (pp62–5), head for **Città di Castello** (pp58–9). Take the scenic route through mountains and valleys, or opt for a faster road, both routes pass through the ancient towns of **Montone** (p60) and **Umbertide** (p61) .

Afternoon Explore **Città di Castello** (pp58–9), including its 11th-century **Duomo** (p58), its museum and the **Palazzo Comunale** (p58), or town hall. The **Pinacoteca Comunale** (p59), one of Umbria's finest art galleries, will occupy you until the evening. You can enjoy dinner as busy Città di Castello unwinds.

Detail of fresco of *Madonna of the Quercia*, Church of San Giovanni Battista

Day 5
Morning Leaving Città di Castello, make your way to **Lake Trasimeno** (pp96–7) via Perugia or by following a scenic mountain route. Explore the perimeter of the lake until you reach **Castiglione del Lago** (p98), from where you can bring your tour of Northern Umbria to a close with a leisurely boat trip to the islands, **Isola Maggoire** (p96) and **Isola Polvese** (p97).

To extend your trip…
Explore Umbria's villages and small towns: **Torgiano** (p86), **Bettona** (pp86–7) and **Deruta** (p87), or hike along the Franciscan Path of Peace from Assisi to Gubbio (2 days).

Beautiful frescoes above the entrance to Duomo Santa Maria Assunta

2 Days in Terni

Terni, with a compact historic centre, has many famous sights to visit that include Roman ruins, churches and museums.

- **Arriving** Terni is served by the Aeroporto Regionale Umbro di Sant'Egidio on the outskirts of Perugia. The A1 and S204 motorways, along with a good rail network, link the two capital cities.
- **Transport** The main sights of Terni can be visited on foot, while its environs are served by bus and road.

Day 1
Morning Begin your tour of **Terni** (pp122–3) with a visit to Piazza Duomo, a busy square dominated by the 17th-century **Duomo (Santa Maria Assunta)** (pp122–3). Look out for the intricate animal and bird reliefs on the main door. You can see the **Roman Amphitheatre** (p123) here. Next, make your way to the Romanesque church of **Sant'Alò** (p122), and on to the church of **San Salvatore** (p123) in Piazza Europa. Refresh yourself with coffee and delicious *pan nociato*, a sweet bread roll filled with pecorino cheese, walnuts and raisins.

Afternoon Head for the 14th-century church of **San Pietro** (p123) adorned with colourful frescoes. Walk down to

the **Centro Arti Opificio SIRI (CAOS)** (p123), where you can admire works by artists such as Picasso and Chagall. If studying fossils is your passion, visit the **Mostra Permanente di Paleontologia** (p123). Its exhibits tell Umbria's ancient history through mammals' remains.

Day 2
Morning Begin your day early with a visit to the **San Francesco** church (p122) before driving to Marmore, around 8 km (5 miles) away. Marvel at the spectacular **Cascata delle Marmore** (p126), the highest man-made waterfalls in Europe. You are now in Terni's **Parco Fluviale del Nera** (p127), which is a natural park that follows the valley of the River Nera. Continue along the road to **Montefranco** (p127) and on to the attractive town of **Ferentillo** (p127) for lunch. Many restaurants here have stunning views of its medieval castle.

Afternoon The Benedictine abbey of **San Pietro in Valle** (p119), 20 km (12 miles) from **Ferentillo** (p127), is breathtaking. The abbey, one of the most powerful in the land, contains frescoes considered among the finest in Italy. Don't miss the elaborate tomb of Faroaldo. Return to Terni for dinner.

To extend your trip...
The **Parco Fluviale del Nera** (p127) is famous for its excellent rafting, nature trails and rock climbing.

---

5 Days in Southern Umbria

- **Arriving** Southern Umbria is served by the Aeroporto Regionale Umbro di Sant'Egidio on the outskirts of Perugia.
- **Transport** The main sights of Southern Umbria can be explored by road.

Day 1
Morning Begin your tour of Southern Umbria in the unspoilt, ancient hill town of **Narni** (pp124–5). Its main sights, including its **Duomo** (p124), dedicated to its patron saint San Giovenale, can be found around Via Garibaldi. Don't miss its huge fortress that sits on top of the hill overlooking Narni. Continue until you reach the highway and follow signs to **Orvieto** (pp138–43), your overnight stop. There are a number of detours you might like to consider along the way. **Visciano** (p125) with its heavily frescoed church, the walled town of **Lugnano in Teverina** (p131) or **Amelia** (p130–31) with its ancient **Mura Poligonali** (p130).

Afternoon Orvieto (pp138–43) has a wealth of attractions so waste no time. Visit the spectacular white and grey structure that dominates this city, the **Duomo** (pp140–41). Inside, there is a breathtaking collection of paintings and frescoes, including the **Cappella della Madonna di San Brizio**

(p141). Around the piazza are a number of museums: **Museo Archeologico Nazionale** (p138), **Museo dell'Opera del Duomo** (pp138–9), **Palazzo Soliano and Museo Emilio Greco** (p139), and **Palazzo Faina** (p139), which houses Museo Civico and Museo Claudio Faina.

Day 2
Morning Start your day with a visit to **Sant'Andrea** (p142), one of the oldest structures in Orvieto (pp138–43). Look out for its unusual 12-sided tower. Next, head for the **Piazza dei Popolo** (p142), passing the **Torre del Moro** (p142), and on to the **Pozzo di San Patrizio** (pp142–3), a deep well with a 248-step spiral staircase. Before leaving Orvieto, take a little time to admire the **Rocca dell'Albornoz** (p143) castle.

Afternoon Head for **Todi** (pp134–7), passing through the Parco Fluviale del Tevere. Wander around its medieval square, the Piazza del Popolo. Here, you can see three palaces, **Palazzo dei Priori** (p134), **Palazzo del Popolo** (p134) and the **Palazzo del Capitano** (pp134–5), which are remarkable for their authentic, well-preserved architecture. The square also has the impressive Gothic-style **Duomo** (p135). Join locals for a stroll along the **Corso Cavour** (p136).

Day 3
Morning Leaving **Todi** (pp134–7), your next stop is **Spoleto** (pp114–17). En route take a short detour to the medieval towns of **Acquasparta** (p133) and **San Gemini** (p132), or the ruined Roman town of **Carsulae** (pp132–3). In Spoleto, begin your tour in the Piazza Garibaldi, which is dominated by the church of **San Gregorio Maggiore** (p114), and take the Via dell'Anfiteatro to the historic centre.

Afternoon Around the elevated Piazza del Duomo in Spoleto, you will discover the **Santi Giovanni e Paolo** (p115) church, famed for its frescoes, along with the **Palazzo**

The steep, spice sellers' street, Corso Cavour in medieval Todi

Arcivescovile (p116) that tells the story of the city, and the **Duomo** (p117) itself, which has a lavish Baroque interior. Don't miss its frescoes by Pinturicchio and views of the La Rocca d'Albornoziana. Enjoy dinner in **Piazza del Mercato** (p116).

Day 4
Morning An early start could see you visiting Spoleto's restored 1st century AD **Teatro Romano** (p115) theatre, followed by an hour or two in the Museo Archeologico before heading to the ancient town of **Trevi** (p110) for lunch, via the **Fonti del Clitunno** (p111) springs.

Afternoon Trevi's historic centre sits atop a hill with roads spiralling down to more modern quarters. At the

summit is the cathedral of **Sant'Emiliano** (p110) with the super **Palazzo Lucarini Contemporary** (p110) exhibiting contemporary Italian paintings.

Day 5
Morning Drive 16 km (10 miles) or so to **Spello** (pp104–5), passing by the charming old towns of **Foligno** (pp106–7), **Bevagna** (p108) and the hilltop wine-producing centre of **Montefalco** (pp108–9). Once in Spello, take Via Centrale Umbria to the archaeological site where you can see the ruins of this once prosperous Roman city. Nearby, is the city's amphitheatre, along with **San Claudio** (p105), one of Spello's most charming churches.

Afternoon Explore the medieval part of **Spello** (pp104–5). Enter the city through the Roman gate, the **Porta dell'Arce** (p105), and ascend to the **Piazza della Repubblica** (p104). Here, both within walking distance, is the **Pinacoteca Civica** (p104) art gallery and the splendid church of **Santa Maria Maggiore** (p104) with its frescoes by Pinturicchio. Round off your stay with dinner in the medieval heart of the Spello.

> **To extend your trip...**
> Explore **Parco Nazionale dei Monti Sibillini** (pp112–13), along with the nearby ancient towns of **Norcia** (p120) and **Cascia** (p121).

Ruins of the ancient Roman town, Carsulae

Putting Umbria on the Map

Of all the regions that make up the Italian peninsula, Umbria is the only one to be totally landlocked. The region covers 8,450 sq km (3,260 sq miles), of which three-quarters belongs to the province of Perugia and one-quarter to the province of Terni. Plains make up less than one-tenth of the total area, the rest being taken up with hills and mountains. The main river is the Tiber (il Tevere) and the highest peak is Monte Redentore, at 2,450 m (8,050 ft). Lake Trasimeno, west of Perugia, is the largest inland lake in central Italy.

SWITZERLAND

San Bernardino

Chiav

Locarno

Colico

Verbania

Como

Lecco

Aosta

Bergamo

VALLE D'AOSTA

Biella

Monza

Ivrea

Grenoble

Modane

Novara

Milano (Milan)

LOMBARDI

Lodi

Susa

Torino (Turin)

PIEMONTE

Pavia

A1

Briançon

Asti

S211

Carmagnola

Alessandria

Piacenza

Gap

Alba

Tortona

Marsaglia

Barcelonnette

Argentera

Cuneo

Carcare

LIGURIA

Genova (Genoa)

Pontremol

Digne-les-Bains

Mondovi

Calizzano

Savona

Tende

S1

La Spezia

Entrevaux

Albenga

FRANCE

Escragnolles

Imperia

Nice

Sanremo

Monaco

Antibes

Cannes

Fréjus

Ligurian Sea

Toulon

Isola di Gorgona

Barcelona, Tangier, Tunis

Isol d' Elb

Centuri

0 kilometres 100

0 miles 100

Bastia

Calvi

L'Ile-Rousse

Key

━━ Motorway

▰▰▰ Motorway under construction

━━ Main road

─── Railway

─── Regional boundary

━━ International boundary

– – Ferry route

Corsica

Porto

Corte

Ajaccio

Ghisonaccia

For keys to symbols *see back flap*

Solenzara

Sardinia, Sicily ↓

Europe

NORWAY
SWEDEN
North Sea
DENMARK
REP. OF IRELAND
UNITED KINGDOM
NETHERLANDS
POLAND
BELGIUM
GERMANY
CZECH REPUBLIC
UKRAINE
Atlantic Ocean
FRANCE
SWITZ.
AUSTRIA
SLOVAKIA
HUNGARY
SLOV.
ROMANIA
CROATIA
ITALY
BOSNIA HERZ.
SERBIA
Perugia
MONTEN.
KOS
MAC.
PORTUGAL
SPAIN
ALBANIA
GREECE
ALGERIA

Strengen
Prutz
AUSTRIA
avos
Scuol
S40
A22
Spondigna
Bressanone
Brunico
Bormio
Merano
S38
Bolzano
S38
S42
Cles
Canazei
S48
ndrio
Edolo
TRENTINO-
ALTO ADIGE
Predazzo
Darfo
Riva
del Garda
Trento
S47
Feltre
Rovereto
Bassano
del Grappa
Iseo
A22
S12
A31
S53
Brescia
Vicenza
A4
Verona
A57
S236
VENETO
Padova
(Padua)
Venezia
(Venice)
CROATIA
emona
Mantova
S434
Ostiglia
Rovigo
Chioggia
Poreč
A22
Rovinj
rma
A1
Ferrara
Mesola
Pula
Reggio
Emilia
A13
RA8
EMILIA-
ROMAGNA
Modena
Comacchio
Adriatic
Sea
Bologna
Alfonsine
S309
Pievepelago
Imola
Ravenna
S9
S64
Faenza
S71
assa
S65
A1
Forlì
S12
Pistoia
Cesena
Lucca
Prato
S67
Rimini
S16
Pesaro
A11
Firenze
(Florence)
San Marino
Fano
a
Cascina
A1
S3b
Urbino
S73b
Croatia,
Greece
Livorno
5429
RA3
S73b
A14
Certaldo
Sansepolcro
Cagli
MARCHE
Ancona
Volterra
TOSCANA
Arezzo
Città di
Castello
Cecina
Siena
S73
Cortona
S76
Macerata
Civitanova Marche
Massa
Marittima
S73
Sinalunga
S3b
Perugia
S3
S77
Tolentino
A14
Porto
San Giorgio
mbino
S1
Roccastrada
Castiglione
del Lago
S75
Foligno
Ascoli
Piceno
S16
Follonica
S223
S2
UMBRIA
Giulianova
Grosseto
S71
Todi
Spoleto
S4
Teramo
Pineto
Orvieto
S2
A1
S3b
S4
A24
scano
S74
Terni
Rieti
ABRUZZO
Pescara
Orbetello
Viterbo
L'Aquila
A14
Isola del
Giglio
S1
Vetralla
Civita
Castellana
S4
Chieti
Tarquinia
A25
Tyrrhenian
Sea
Civitavecchia
S2
S3
LAZIO
A24
Sulmona
S84
A12
S5
Avezzano
S17
Rome
Sardinia, Sicily

A PORTRAIT OF UMBRIA

Umbria is a land apart, with its own singular character and identity.
At the geographical centre of Italy, it is known, thanks to its lushness, as
the peninsula's "Green Heart"; its rolling hills and fertile plains are studded
with picturesque towns, castles and monasteries, recalling millennia of
human habitation.

Small in comparison to its neighbouring regions, at just 8,450 sq km (3,260 sq miles), with barely a million inhabitants, Umbria nevertheless radiates a powerful image, both in Italy and abroad. Elemental features of its reputation are its unspoilt landscape, its inimitable art and architecture, and, perhaps most significantly, its deeply mystical heritage. Add to that the region's famously fine cuisine and exuberant festivals and it is no wonder that Umbria has developed a cachet all its own.

Recent decades have witnessed the arrival of a breed of "New Umbrians", neo-settlers who have migrated here, maybe from Milan, Manchester or Manhattan. It is not unusual, while exploring the region's splendidly scenic roads and byways, to come across American couples enjoying the view, European travellers looking for rural escapism, or Italian ex-urbanites who have chosen a new, more relaxed way of life in this idyllic, largely rural setting.

Timeless Landscapes

Umbria's pristine natural loveliness is certainly a major enticement. The landscape ranges from the great green slopes and peaks of the Monti Sibillini and the mountain chains that border Le Marche to the gentle hills and plains around Assisi and Perugia; from the roaring waters of the Cascata delle Marmore to the subtle sibilance of the

Picturesque Assisi, with typical Umbrian countryside in the background

◀ People taking part in La Corsa dei Ceri or Race of the Candles, an exciting candle race festival held in Gubbio

Piece of traditional Umbrian fabric

wind among the reeds on the shores of Lake Trasimeno. Green – the colour which has, in effect, become the region's popular "trademark" – is very much a reality here and dominates the scenery. However, the beauty of the environment alone could never fully account for Umbria's undeniable mystique. The fields, the olive groves, the forests of beech, holm oak and chestnut are inevitably set off by evocative vestiges of a long-standing human presence.

Umbrian potter at work

Sublime Architecture and Art

Whether in the form of a town, a village or a medieval monastery, an ancient farmhouse, a dry-stone wall or a ruined church, architecture is essential to the region's spirit. Whether grand or rustic, Roman, Romanesque or Renaissance, such architectural heritage conveys a timeless feel that is distinctively Umbrian. It evokes a symbiosis of man and nature that has flourished since the days of the primordial Umbri and Etruscans, and later the Romans, right down to modern Italians.

Umbria's cities and towns are among Italy's most gorgeous. Perugia, Assisi, Gubbio, Orvieto, Spoleto, Todi – the very names are synonymous with the perfection of the medieval hill town. They are approachable, human in scale, but also filled with world-class masterpieces of architecture and art in recognizably Umbrian style. Some of Italy's finest palaces and civic structures are here, as well as some of its most resplendent churches, while Umbrian painters such as Perugino helped set the standard for sheer beauty in the High Renaissance.

Lying at the crossroads between Rome and Florence, the region has been embellished by the works of many renowned artists, including Cimabue, Giotto, Piero della Francesca, Simone Martini, Fra Angelico, Filippo Lippi, Luca Signorelli, Ghirlandaio, Raphael and Gian Lorenzo Bernini. At the same time, venerable Umbrian crafts, especially ceramics and textiles, have been famous for centuries.

Nor should the ancient remains be overlooked. Throughout Umbria, the Romans left behind superb gates, towers, bridges and even a still-functioning

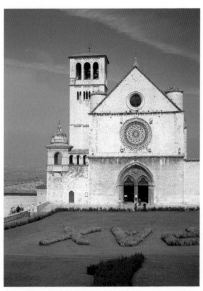

The renowned Basilica di San Francesco in Assisi

An antiques market in Città di Castello, one of the most significant towns in Umbria

theatre or two, while the archaeological finds dating back to Etruscan times and beyond are immensely rich and displayed in beautifully appointed museums.

One insightful observer of Italian life wrote, "With its millennia of infiltration, art has saturated the soul – everyone here lives art, whether they know it or not." This is nowhere more true than in Umbria.

A Place of Spirituality

Most appealing to many modern new-comers is Umbria's glowing spiritual legacy. The birthplace of St Francis, St Clare and Jacopone da Todi has become the home of many spiritual centres and teachers of every persuasion. Retreats here are not only Christian, but are affiliated with all beliefs, everyone apparently drawn by the ineffable meditative power of the place. Over-whelmingly, it is a venue of peace, as embodied in the Marcia per la Pace (Walk of Peace) from Perugia to Assisi, which takes place every other autumn. Many global spiritual leaders have promoted greater understanding here, including the Dalai Lama.

Inviting Hospitality

Visitors attracted more by earthly pleasures are well satisfied, too. Umbria's robust and tasty cuisine consists of dishes that combine the best of local culinary traditions, while taking full advantage of the produce and game of the region – highlighting wild mushrooms, black truffles and wild boar *(cinghiale)*.

Hospitality is an art form here, too. Every city, town or village proudly rivals its neighbours with its age-old festivals, as well as its gastronomic specialities. In the countryside, *agriturismi* (farm lodgings) have become a reliable alter-native to standard hotel accommodation, offering a delightful first-hand taste of authentic Umbrian life.

Decades of modernization have tested the traditional values of the region, and disastrous earthquakes, one in 1997 and another in 2016, have left their mark, but the quintessential allure of Umbria remains intact.

Apparition at Arles, Upper Church, Assisi

The Landscape of Umbria

The mountains of Umbria are of comparatively recent origin. The fact that the region's topography developed relatively late, together with the presence of still-active powerful tectonic forces, means that there is a heightened risk of earthquakes in Umbria. Once cultivated up to fairly high altitudes, the mountains have now been largely abandoned by farmers. Rolling hills made up of fertile but often fragile terrain border the highest peaks; centuries of cultivation have given them their current shape. In Umbria's southwestern corner, and around Orvieto, the land is of volcanic origin. Lake Trasimeno, in the northwest, is the most important lake in central Italy.

A bright field of sunflowers, widely cultivated in Umbria

The Mountains

The average height of the mountains in Umbria is around 1,000 m (3,280 ft). Most of the range consists of karst limestone and is riddled with caves and subterranean galleries and rivers. The vegetation most characteristic of this environment is beech forest and upland pasture. Among the wildlife found in the mountains are birds of prey, wildcats and several kinds of wolf.

The Hills

The climate in the hills is milder than that at higher altitudes, and is also less polluted than on the plain. For this reason, the hills of Umbria have been settled and cultivated since ancient times. In areas not given over to farmland and olive groves there are oaks, holm oaks and, lower down, mixed woodland and scrub.

Wolves became extinct in Umbria in the 18th century but have reappeared in the protected Monti Sibillini. There is a greater chance of seeing them in winter, when they come down to the valley.

This Apennine edelweiss lives on calcareous crags. Similar to alpine edelweiss, it is distinguished by its spathulate leaves (that is, wide at the tip and narrow at the base).

The wild boar is one of the most common mammals in the hills. Its meat is prized.

Acorns

The olive is one of the most important agricultural products in Umbria. Olives produced in the area around Trevi *(see p110)* are especially highly regarded.

Cultivation of the Plains

The few areas of plain found in Umbria lie along river courses and include the Valle Umbra (between Assisi and Spoleto), the Valle del Paglia (in the southwest), and the plains of Terni and Gubbio. Reclamation in these areas in the years after World War II has created very fertile land, where farming is now carried out on an industrial scale (where possible, producing forced and cash crops), although man has been present here since ancient times. The plants found are those commonly seen in cultivated fields.

The corn cockle
(*Agrostemma githago*) was once widespread on cultivated land. It is now rare, owing to the use of herbicides by farmers. It's also poisonous.

Lapwings form flocks in cultivated fields and in pastureland during the winter season.

The Plains

In general, every area of flat ground in Umbria occupies the site of an ancient lake or marsh, and is therefore especially fertile. These plains are now primarily given over to cultivation (grapevines and olives, for example). As a consequence, the land is not known for its varied wildlife, although rodents and small predators, such as foxes, are common.

Lakes, Rivers and Marshland

Lake Trasimeno is a place that has a fascinating history, with a tradition of fishing going back to ancient times. Rivers in Umbria include the Tiber (il Tevere), the Velino and the Nera; the last boasts the spectacular manmade waterfall, the Cascata delle Marmore, and some particularly fine scenery. Freshwater fish and other species abound in the wild.

Grain was once grown as animal fodder, while today, increasingly, it is grown in industrial quantities.

A trout is camouflaged among the stones on the riverbed thanks to its marbled colouring.

The fox is a highly adaptable mammal which manages to live in all kinds of habitat. In cultivated fields, foxes find shelter among the hedgerows.

Freshwater crabs live in reedbeds and are active mainly at night. Their presence indicates good water quality.

Nature Reserves in Umbria

Although nature plays a fundamental role in the overall image of the region, Umbria has been rather slow to set up protected parks and reserves. The creation of parks has frequently been opposed at a local level (the inhabitants are exceedingly passionate about hunting), and their establishment has been achieved largely by balancing the demands of nature with those of the development of the economy and the tourist trade.

Together with the Umbrian portion of the Parco Nazionale dei Monti Sibillini (part of a great series of protected areas in the Apennines, safeguarding the principal mountain masses in the chain), Umbrian parks today protect around seven per cent of the terrain in the region. These parks can be divided into two categories: "mountain parks", which are those along the border with Le Marche, and "water parks", which are focused around the lakes and watercourses of the region.

The Parco Regionale del Lago Trasimeno *(see pp96–7)* covers 13,200 ha (32,600 acres) and includes the lake shores – thereby safeguarding the water and banks – but not the tourist resorts around the lake. The perimeter of Lake Trasimeno measures around 60 km (37 miles).

Lago di Alviano *(see p131)* is an ecosystem that serves as a breeding ground for numerous species of water birds, as well as an important source of food for rare birds such as cranes, wild geese and ospreys.

The Parco Fluviale del Tevere *(see p137)* extends from the gates of Todi as far as Alviano, along the banks of the longest river in central Italy, the Tiber. The park protects some 7,925 ha (19,585 acres), over a length of 50 km (31 miles).

Città di Castello
Umbertide
Lake Trasimeno
Perugia
Todi
Orvieto
Lago di Corbara
Alviano
Narni

S221 · S257 · S219 · S3bis · S75bis · S599 · S220 · S317 · S71 · S397 · S3bis · S79bis · S448 · S205

0 kilometres   15
0 miles   15

Key

■ Regional Park
■ National Park

The Parco Regionale del Monte Subasio *(see pp70–71)* separates but also links Assisi, Spello and Nocera Umbra, and covers an area of 7,440 ha (18,390 acres). For centuries, Monte Subasio has been a favourite destination among mystics and hermits. St Francis lived here with his fellow brothers in the Eremo delle Carceri, in the shade of a forest of ancient holm oaks.

The Parco Regionale del Monte Cucco *(see pp66–7)* is in the northeast area of the province of Perugia. It extends over more than 10,000 ha (24,700 acres), and was created in 1995 to protect the peak (1,555 m/ 5,100 ft) made famous by the subterranean cave system of the Grotta di Monte Cucco; the latter is 920 m (3,017 ft) deep and extends for tens of kilometres.

The Parco Regionale di Colfiorito *(see p107)*, not far from Foligno and Nocera Umbra, protects a beautiful landscape of upland plain and marshland. The area consists of a series of drained depressions, once ancient expanses of water, and a lake that has been declared a Waterfowl Habitat and is home to amphibians and many species of bird.

The Parco Nazionale dei Monti Sibillini *(see pp112–13)* extends over more than 70,000 ha (173,000 acres), crossing regional borders. The Umbrian side of the park, along the border with Le Marche, is a typical Apennine environment. The countryside is characterized by peaks of varying height (the highest, at 2,475 m/ 8,120 ft, is Monte Vettore), large areas of upland pasture, river valleys and beech forests. Wolves, wildcats and porcupines live at ground level, while golden eagles and peregrine falcons circle in the sky.

The Parco Fluviale del Nera *(see pp126–7)* is famous for the abundance of its waters and for the magnificent Cascata delle Marmore. The course of the Nera is protected by this 2,120-ha (5,240-acre) park, which includes the lower reaches of the river for 18 km (11 miles), as far as the famous cascade.

Gubbio

S298

S147
Assisi
S75

Topino

Foligno

S3

Spoleto
S209
S418
Nera

S3

S3bis

S204
Terni
S3

S396
Norcia

S320

Outdoor Activities

Given the beauty of the landscape in Umbria, nature and the great outdoors should feature in every visitor's trip to the region. Furthermore, open-air sports are increasingly well catered for, and in every part of the region. Just as pilgrims flock to Assisi from all four corners of the globe, it is equally easy to encounter a whole range of languages among a crowd of canoeists sweeping its way down the Nera or the Tiber, or among the hang-gliding community taking off from Monte Cucco or from the windswept uplands of the Monti Sibillini.

More everyday activities should not be forgotten either, particularly as they constitute one of the best ways of seeing and appreciating this beautiful region: consider going on a long bicycle ride through the hills, past farms and ancient abbeys, or on a gentle horse-ride through one of the greenest, most fascinating and relaxing landscapes in Italy.

Hiking is a popular activity in Umbria, and affords beautiful views

Horse-riding around the village of Castelluccio, Southern Umbria

Horse-riding

In Umbria there are many stables and farm holiday (*agriturismo*) businesses that can organize horse-riding trips. As well as being an enjoyable sport, riding offers a closer and more natural view of the countryside than is possible with conventional means of transport.

Many Umbrian horse-riding stables belong to national associations, such as ANTE (Associazione Nazionale Turismo Equestre), and can offer trekking in all the most beautiful areas of the region, including the hills around Assisi, Città della Pieve and Bettona, the shores of Lake Trasimeno, the slopes of Monte Subasio and the steep bridle paths of the Valnerina. Treks that last for several days or more are available from various equestrian clubs, or you can apply directly to ANTE.

Walking and Cycling

No equipment is required to enjoy walking: all you need is a good view, decent weather, paths to follow and a destination, whether it be historical or natural.

The Monti Sibillini national park, to present the most enticing example, has always been one of the best-loved destinations among walkers in Umbria (along with the neighbouring park areas in the nearby region of Le Marche). In the colder seasons, however, it is also possible to find routes at lower altitudes, such as the bridle paths that link the towns and villages.

The routes that connect Umbria's most famous towns and villages are very popular with cyclists: the gradients are not excessive and the varied landscape provides plenty of interest along the way. Bridle paths and footpaths at higher altitudes are also used by mountain bikers. There are now more than 600 km (373 miles) of mountain-biking trails in the region. Brochures and information about walking and cycling are available from tourist offices.

Rock Climbing, Caves and Gorges

Not all that long ago, all that one had to choose from was mountaineering. Today, various rock-climbing sports are popular in Italy, and there are all kinds of cliff faces to use. In Umbria, any visitor in search of a vertical cliff face will feel at home on certain cliffs in the Monti Sibillini and in the village of Ferentillo, where there are numerous suitable sites: rock climbing is such a big thing here that there is even a climbing guide dedicated to the area.

A PORTRAIT OF UMBRIA | **27**

Umbria is also a place that finds much favour among speleologists. The biggest attraction is the cave system beneath Monte Cucco, on the border with Le Marche (not far from that region's famous caves, the Grotte di Frasassi). There are also caves worth visiting in the mountains near Terni.

A sport that has taken hold in Umbria, which developed out of speleology – the equipment used is much the same – is "torrentismo", or canyoning, the sport of navigating steep-sided gorges. The most famous and popular sites are found in the Valnerina (Fosso di Rocca Gelli and Forra del Casco), on Monte Cucco (Forra di Riofreddo), and in the hills surrounding Lake Corbara (Gole di Prodo).

It is important to make clear that all of the above are extreme sports, and that they can all be exceedingly dangerous. Anyone trying them out for the first time should ensure that they are accompanied by an expert.

Hang-gliding and Cross-country Skiing

Wind, unlimited vistas and serious gradients are the three ingredients necessary for hang-gliding and paragliding. Umbria has plenty of all three. Famous locations for this exciting but daredevil sport are Monte Cucco and the Monti Sibillini, where the isolated, high-altitude village of Castelluccio di Norcia is now one of the most popular destinations for hang-gliding aficionados, who come here from all over the world.

The topography of the Umbrian mountains does not much favour downhill skiing, however; few of the slopes are steep enough, and the lower altitudes are not suitable for the building of ski lifts or ski resorts of any great size. To compensate, the great Apennine uplands provide perfect cross-country territory. Skiers can follow the beaten tracks or, better still, ski along snow-covered bridle paths and footpaths.

Shooting Rapids

In spring, the many rivers and watercourses that cross Umbria, almost all of them torrential, are an irresistible attraction for canoeists from all over Europe. As the water rises and the rapids swell, canoes, kayaks and rubber rafts appear as if from nowhere along the banks of the rivers Nera and Tiber.

The Nera offers a range of experiences and caters to various levels of difficulty, up to the highest level, requiring considerable skill and expertise. This river also offers the extraordinary sight of the Cascata delle Marmore (*see pp126–7*), which is the principal starting point for rafting trips. The stretch of the Tiber below Todi is one of the most popular routes for river rafting and other excursions, but you can also join the Tiber further north, at Città di Castello, allowing you to cross virtually the entire region.

A non-competitive descent from Todi to Rome takes place every year from the end of April to early May. It is open to everyone and is very popular. There are also good river-rafting sites from the Monti Sibillini down to the Valnerina.

Sailing boats on Lake Trasimeno, Nothern Umbria

Sailing on the Lakes

Lake Trasimeno is clearly the most obvious place for holidaymakers in landlocked Umbria to go sailing and windsurfing. Visitors can bring their own boats or make use of the craft available for hire. There are numerous regattas. Other stretches of water that are at least partially equipped for sailing, windsurfing and other watersports include Lago di Piediluco and Lago di Corbara, both in southern Umbria.

You can also go water-skiing on Lake Trasimeno, but you must first apply for a permit from the office of the Provincia di Perugia.

Hang-gliding in Castelluccio during the winter

In the Footsteps of St Francis

Francis was born in Assisi in 1181–82, and grew up to be a bright, cultured and even ambitious youth. A military career was chosen as the means by which he could rise up through the social hierarchy, and he enrolled in the army that Walter of Brienne was preparing for the Crusades. However, illness brought Francis back to Assisi, where he experienced his conversion and where he began his charity work. The story of his life, marvellously illustrated in the frescoes in the Upper Church at Assisi, provides us with a picture of the patron saint of nature and ecology, a man drawn to the natural world, charity and prayer. They also inspire us to explore the many places in Umbria that retain the memory of St Francis's power and presence.

Francis found refuge with the Spadalonga family of Gubbio after his departure from his father's house. The saint also spent time in the small monastery of the Vittorina (*see p85*), along the road between Gubbio and Assisi. It was here, according to historians, that he tamed a wolf.

Isola Maggiore, on Lake Trasimeno, was the home of one of the first communities of the Friars Minor at the beginning of the 13th century. St Francis spent a long Lenten period with them here.

Santa Maria degli Angeli was erected in the 15th century, in order to shelter the old monastery of the Porziuncola (*see p84*), in whose infirmary St Francis died on 4 October 1226. What is left of that room is kept in the Cappella del Transito. Above, *The Poor Clares mourn the dead saint.*

One of the most famous episodes in the life of the saint is undoubtedly his preaching to the birds. The stone on which the scene is said to have taken place is in the church of San Francesco in Bevagna (*see p108*). Right, *Francis preaches to the birds.*

Città di Castello

Tiber

Gubb

S3bis

Arezzo

Tiber

Lake Trasimeno

S298

S75b

Sar Ma dei An

Perugia

Nestore

Cannara

Tiber

Beva

Chiani

Paglia

Lake Corbara

Lake Alviano

S204

On Monte Subasio *(see pp70–71)*, cloaked in holm oaks, the monastery of the Eremo delle Carceri was built around the little church and the caves where Francis and his companions would gather in prayer. A trail from the hermitage goes through the surrounding woods and passes a series of sites dear to the saint's tradition because they were places of prayer and meditation.

Every church, every corner of Assisi bears traces of the life of the saint. He was baptized in the font in the cathedral of San Rufino; next to the church of San Giorgio was his school; and the Chiesa Nuova was constructed on the very spot where Francis is thought to have been born. Right, *St Francis gives his cloak to a poor man*, with a view of Assisi in the background.

At Vecciano, not far from Montefalco *(see pp108–9)*, is the small church of San Rocco. Under the name of Santa Maria della Selvetta, this was the first seat of the Franciscan Order. To the left, *Innocent III approves the saint's Order.*

0 kilometres 20
0 miles 20

The monastery of Sacro Speco *(see p125)*, near Narni, was founded by St Francis in 1213. You can still see the small hollow where the saint used to pray.

Near the Fonti del Clitunno *(see p111)*, in the church of San Pietro di Bovara, is a Crucifix which spoke to St Francis. (The more famous talking Crucifix is in the Basilica di Santa Chiara, *(see p74)*. Above, *The Saint in Ecstasy*.

Key

 Trail of St Francis

Other roads

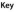 River

Art in Umbria

The region of Umbria as it is defined today was established only after the unification of Italy in 1861. In the preceding centuries, Umbria's towns and cities formed part of a political and artistic mosaic which extended from Tuscany to the Adriatic coast, without precise boundaries. In art, as in politics, there was plenty of opportunity for contacts and exchanges with other regions. Two crucial highlights stand out in the long history of art in Umbria: the founding and construction of the Basilica of St Francis in Assisi – with the contribution of great artists, from Umbria and from other parts of Italy – and the golden age of the city of Perugia. UNESCO has recognized various sites and structures in the towns of Assisi and Spoleto, with splendid artistic presence, as World Heritage Sites.

Tempietto del Clitunno, detail of the front

Cast of stone with Umbrian inscription, 2nd century BC

Origins

Umbria was populated from the sixth millennium BC. Interesting ceramic finds from that time have been discovered near Norcia and Parrano (outside Orvieto). With the passing of the millennia, a community of shepherds – part of what scholars describe as the Apennine civilization – developed in the mountains. Around the 16th century BC, they started to produce elegant pottery, decorated with geometrical motifs. The burial site at Monteleone di Spoleto dates back to these very early civilizations. Archaeologists discovered a bronze cart here, and this is now in the Metropolitan Museum in New York. During the first millennium BC, Umbrian land was divided between two very different peoples: the Etruscans, who settled on the west bank of the Tiber, with the key towns of Perugia and Orvieto, and the Umbri, about whom little is still known, who were on the Tiber's east bank and in the Apennine mountains.

The Romans

The Roman conquest of Umbria was slow but inexorable. If one had to choose a symbolic historical date for the arrival of the Romans in Umbria, it would be 219 BC, the year in which the Via Flaminia was opened. This Roman road became the main communication route through the region for centuries. The presence of the Romans led to a great push in building and civil engineering: theatres, public works as well as roads were built. In terms of sculpture dating from the Roman age, many marble and some bronze statues survive. The latter include the extraordinary statue of Germanicus, found in Amelia and returned there only recently after

Male statue, 1st century AD

a long and controversial residence in Perugia (see p130). One can also see well-preserved Roman buildings, such as the amphitheatre in Gubbio (see p62) and the Temple of Minerva in Assisi (see p75).

Christianity reached Umbria in around the 3rd and 4th centuries AD. Of particular interest from this period are the church of San Salvatore in Spoleto (see p119) and the little temple at the Fonti di Clitunno (see p111), both of which show clearly how early Christian architecture was inspired by the Roman and classical traditions. Another important church from the Early Christian era in Umbria is San Michele Archangelo, or Sant'Angelo, in Perugia (see p95), which was influenced by Byzantine architecture.

The Middle Ages

Politically split between Byzantium (on the west bank of the Tiber) and the Lombard dominion (on the east bank), Umbria was subject to a range of influences in the field of art. Even though few works of art have survived from the second half of the first millennium, and even though the buildings that remain have often been extensively remodelled, it is known that the 9th century was a period of significant development in Umbria. Cathedrals were founded all over the region and were often adorned with great pictorial cycles (now mostly lost). The main centre for this boom was the Lombard stronghold of Spoleto *(see pp114–19)*, where even today you can admire the reliefs on the façade of San Pietro and the frescoes in the churches of San Gregorio and San Paolo inter Vineas.

The cloister of the abbey of Sassovivo, near Foligno, was built using Roman columns and arches.

Detail of the façade of San Pietro in Spoleto

Assisi

In 1228, less than two years after the death of St Francis, and at the wishes of Frate Elia (who took it upon himself to hide the body of the saint), construction of the Basilica of San Francesco in Assisi *(see pp76–7)* began. This was a truly crucial moment, since the work on the basilica was to influence the art and architecture of both Umbria and nearby regions for centuries to come. The Basilica in Assisi is still one of the most important monuments of Western art today.

The first frescoes were commissioned in 1254 from an anonymous Umbrian artist, known as the Maestro di San Francesco, who is regarded as having operated a workshop of the highest quality. Then,

Giotto

Born in 1267, Giotto di Bondone probably trained at the Florentine workshop of Cimabue. It was accepted that the cycle of the *Life of St Francis* was not Giotto's work but that of Roman painters, but restored frescoes in the basilica of St Francis in Assisi beared his initials. Giotto's great works include a *Last Judgment* and *Stories from the Life of the Virgin* in the Cappella degli Scrovegni in Padua and the bell tower for the Duomo in Florence, a project that he directed up to his death in 1337.

Presumed self-portrait

from the end of the 13th century, great masters were summoned from outside the region – among them Cimabue and Giotto – to decorate the walls of the upper and lower churches. Their work would become a model for Umbrian painters later on. Work on the two basilicas continued for more than two centuries, with contributions by other great names from the history of Italian art, including Simone Martini and Pietro Lorenzetti. In parallel with the spreading of the Franciscan faith, so too the pictorial style created in Assisi gained ground, and was imitated and reproduced in many new Franciscan churches all over Italy. On 26 September 1997 this immense inheritance risked being lost forever. The entire complex was badly damaged by a violent earthquake, and parts of the vault in the upper church collapsed. Through the extraordinarily hard work of restorers, fragments of frescoes were saved and reinstalled where possible. The basilica remains magnificent but tarnished.

Painted Cross, Maestro di San Francesco, 1272

Vault of the Evangelists, Cimabue (1240–1302), Basilica of Assisi

Perugino

Pietro Vannucci, or Perugino, was born in Città della Pieve in 1452 and died in Fontignano in 1523. He was influenced by the work of Piero della Francesca and Verrocchio, in whose workshop the painter trained early on. Works in Rome include *Handing the Keys to St Peter* in the Sistine Chapel (1481), in the Vatican. In Florence are a *Lamentation* (Palazzo Pitti, 1494) and a *Crucifixion* (Santa Maddalena de' Pazzi, 1493). He also painted frescoes

Epiphany, 1475–8, detail

in the Sala dell'Udienza in the Collegio del Cambio, Perugia. His work can be found in several of the smaller towns of Umbria, particularly near Lake Trasimeno *(see p99)*. While still young, Raphael was apprenticed to Perugino, who exerted great influence over the former's works.

came here, including: Piero della Francesca, Fra Angelico (who contributed to the decoration of the cathedral in Orvieto), Filippo Lippi (who would later be called to Spoleto to fresco the cathedral apse), and also Agostino di Duccio. A cycle of frescoes (1498–1500) painted by Perugino in the Collegio del Cambio was to exert a great influence over painters such as Pinturicchio and the young Raphael, who produced some of his early work in Perugia.

In this same period – in Perugia as well as in other cities in Umbria – a new style of architecture began to change the look of the old medieval city spaces, with new palaces being erected for noble merchant families. Influences in this field came from Rome, Urbino or from the great cities of nearby Tuscany.

An example of Umbrian art by the Maestro di Città di Castello

Perugia's Golden Age

The position of Perugia, on the Via Flaminia and Via Amerina, at the junction of routes of communication between Rome and the Adriatic coast, made the city vulnerable to conquest. After invasions by the Goths and Lombards, the foundation of the cathedral (by the 10th century) marked the first stage in Perugia's rebirth in the Middle Ages.

For around three centuries, the commune of Perugia grew in power, riches and possessions. Signs of the prosperity of this age are the thick walls and city gates, though an even greater indication is the aqueduct, which brought water to

the city centre and was one of the first of its kind to be built in Italy. To celebrate this magnificent achievement a fountain was built in Piazza IV Novembre, featuring sculptures by Nicola and Giovanni Pisano *(see p91)*.

The 16th Century in Perugia

Towards the middle of the 15th century, the city of Perugia was rich and cosmopolitan. The great Italian painters of the age

The Umbrian School

It was because of the influence of the great artists who were attracted to Umbria in the second half of the 15th century

Polyptych, Niccolò di Liberatore known as l'Alunno, 1471

that a regional school developed in its own right, liberated from the Gothic models that had influenced art in the previous centuries. The principal artists to learn lessons from the Florentine Renaissance were, besides Perugino, Niccolò Alunno, Antonio Mezzastris, Matteo da Gualdo, from around Foligno, and Benedetto Bonfigli, of Perugia. In the first half of the 16th century, the most representative name is that of Giovanni di Pietro, or Spagna. The Umbrian school lost its originality and died out rapidly with the advent of Mannerism.

Coronation of the Virgin,
1511, Spagna

The Domination of Rome

When the power of the communes *(see pp46–7)* gave way to papal rule, great military structures were built: Antonio da Sangallo the Younger designed Perugia's Rocca Paolina *(see p88)* and the Pozzo di San Patrizio in Orvieto *(see p142)*. Vignola worked on the Castellina in Norcia *(see p120)*.

By the end of the 16th century all the major artists of the time were working in Rome – not only Italians, but also Flemish artists such as Van Mander and Stellaert. Umbrian towns were totally dependent on the Church. In Todi, the construction of Santa Maria della Consolazione *(see pp136–7)*, worked on

by Baldassarre Peruzzi, Vignola and Ippolito Scalza, inaugurated a new concept of religious architecture. In 1569, on the plain below Assisi, work began on the great church of Santa Maria degli Angeli *(see p84)*, intended as a home for the Franciscan chapel of the Porziuncola. Designed by Galeazzo Alessi with Vignola as consultant, it was finished only in 1679.

Umbria's noble families, often important figures in administration and in the ranks of Roman power, built palazzi and villas in their native cities.

Statue in Santa Maria della Consolazione

18th–19th Centuries

The following centuries, dominated by papal rule right up to the unification of Italy in 1861, did not really produce great works of art

in Umbria. The dominant influence was Rome, and the examples of Baroque and Rococo in the region are not of great importance. A moment of regional pride came with the brief period of splendour of Perugia's Accademia di Belle Arti, which championed the Neo-Classical style. It is certainly no coincidence that the artist Canova, who stayed at San Gemini (near Todi), took up contact with the great families of Perugia.

The 19th century saw the cities of Umbria becoming stages on the set routes followed by travellers on the Grand Tour. Admiration for the art of the Middle Ages became the cult of the time and *medievalismo* took hold in Perugia and led to the restoration – sometimes rather ingenuously – of ancient buildings.

Applied Arts

Along with most of Italy, Umbria has long been famous as a treasure trove of art, sculpture and architecture. However, it has also produced a great many master craftsmen of skill and stature. In the many museums in Umbria's towns, old and new, one can find pieces of rare beauty, in particular ceramics and textiles, worked by hand over the centuries. The production of these objects continues today, and no tourist in Umbria should miss the opportunity to visit one of the numerous handicrafts workshops in the region. Besides ceramics, for which Deruta *(see p87)* is particularly renowned, and fabrics, which are still woven by hand, look out for the embroidered tulle of Panicale (near Lake Trasimeno) and the delicate lace of Assisi, as well as painted stuccoes and woodcarving.

Majolica jug, 16th century

Antique fabric, manufactured in Todi in the 14th century

Architecture in Umbria

Even though the most significant impact on the towns of Umbria occurred during the centuries of the Middle Ages and the Renaissance, monuments from all periods of history are found in the region. From the time of the Etruscan city state to the era of Roman domination, from the rise of Romanesque architecture to the advent of Neo-Classicism, every people, every era, every architectural style and every artistic movement has left its traces, thanks to the work of the major artists of the time. The influence of the Roman Catholic Church, however, has been a constant and is prevalent today.

A bas-relief, frequently used to decorate churches and palazzi

Roof covered with turf

The chambers were placed according to the terrain.

Walls in local stone

Architrave, often bearing the name of the deceased.

The necropolises are the most tangible sign of the Etruscan presence in Umbria. In general, they consisted of a series of tomb chambers lined up along cemetery roads. Inside, the deceased lay on a funeral bench.

Antiquity

While the Umbri left few traces of the form of their cities, the imposing polygonal walls of Amelia and Spoleto owe their existence to this Italic people. The Etruscans left necropolises and tombs, such as those near Orvieto (Necropoli del Crocifisso del Tufo) or the extraordinary monumental burial site of the Ipogeo dei Volumni at Perugia. There are impressive Roman monuments such as the Temple of Minerva in Assisi, the theatres of Gubbio, Spoleto and Terni, the great cisterns of Amelia and Todi, and the city gates of Spello and Todi. Not forgetting the Via Flaminia, which still links Rome with the Adriatic coast, as it did 2,300 years ago.

The Middle Ages and the Renaissance

After a period of Byzantine and Lombard domination, architecture was rejuvenated by the birth of the Romanesque style. Town squares lined with public buildings – a sign of temporal and communal power – were being built, as were cathedrals, a tangible and potent symbol of spiritual power.

The building of commercial towns in contact with outside markets brought about the arrival of the Gothic style during the 14th century. Especially fine examples of this style are Orvieto cathedral (see pp140–41) and the decoration in the Sala delle Arti Liberali e dei Pianeti in Palazzo Trinci in Foligno (see p106), from the early years of the 15th century.

Palazzo dei Priori

Duomo

Fontana Maggiore

Piazza IV Novembre in Perugia (see p90) is overlooked by both the duomo (cathedral) and the Palazzo dei Priori, a sign of the political power of the medieval commune. Between the two stands the Fontana Maggiore, decorated between 1275 and 1278 by Nicola Pisano and his son, Giovanni.

Multi-sided tower

Powerful walls, often with battlements and equipped with a communication trench.

Circular keep

The Rocca Maggiore at Assisi *(see p83)* was rebuilt in 1356 on the foundations of a feudal fortification built by Frederick Barbarossa. Its restoration was the work of Cardinal Albornoz, the papal legate who studded Central Italy with these strongholds of the faith.

The Age of the Fortresses

The conquest of Umbrian towns by the papacy brought about profound changes in the urban layout. The new power, aiming to increase military control and to diminish the importance of the traditional social space of the town square, commissioned a series of imposing fortresses which, although they have been modified over the centuries, have come down to us today virtually intact. These include the fortresses of Orvieto (begun in 1364 and then rebuilt in 1450), Narni (built from 1367–78), Assisi (rebuilt in 1356) and Spoleto (built in 1359).

Tympanum in classical style

Mirrored windows

Colonnade inspired by the entrance to a classical temple.

Palazzo della Regione *(see p94)*, in the Fontivegge quarter of Perugia, was part of a town plan by the architect Aldo Rossi. From 1982 to 1989 he rebuilt this area of the regional capital in Post-Modern style, with classical references.

Modern Architecture

Outside the encircling walls of Umbria's medieval towns, large and small, modern suburbs have developed, usually on the flat land just below the hilltop towns. Building styles have not always been particularly respectful of the artistic beauty of the old town, but there are some successful examples of modern architecture, such as the quarter of Fontivegge in Perugia. The countryside, too, has had to accept change. Many medieval groups of houses and farms have been converted for modern use, for example as hotels.

Romanesque Churches in Umbria

Around the 11th century, when medieval society was developing and the Church was re-creating its own autonomy, a style of religious architecture developed which, with simple linear forms, attempted a direct link with local cultures. In the 19th century, this style was defined as "Romanesque", after its derivation from the Christian basilica of the Roman era. The Romanesque church presents a harmonious façade, featuring arches and one or more rose windows. From the three doorways access is gained to the three-aisled interior, at the end of which is a presbytery, raised to allow the construction of a crypt. Examples of the style, since reworked, are San Lorenzo di Arari in Orvieto and the cathedrals of Spoleto, Assisi and Todi.

Three-mullioned window in a square frame

Large rose window (13th century)

San Michele (1195) in Bevagna has a beautiful doorway in which Romanesque elements and Roman finds are combined.

UMBRIA THROUGH THE YEAR

All year round in Umbria there are feast days, religious celebrations and pagan festivals linked to the farming year, including the harvest, or to popular and historical traditions of the ancient communes. Some of these events are famous worldwide, but every small village in Umbria has its own festival or saint's day worthy of wider renown. Besides the traditional events that have taken place for decades or centuries, there is also a full calendar of cultural events, such as the Festival of Spoleto and Umbria Jazz, not to mention historical re-enactments, and cinema and theatre seasons.

Spring

Umbria has no sea coast. As a result, the spring climate can be cool and windy. On higher ground, the snow may remain until March or April, while on the hills and high plains spring flowers are emerging. The main religious events during this season are those that fall during the Easter period, but there are also important feast days in May.

Women in medieval costume at the Calendimaggio in Assisi

March

Benedictine celebrations, Norcia (*third week of Mar*). Includes a torchlit procession and a crossbow competition.

April

Antiques fair, Todi (*mid- to late Apr*). Held in the Palazzo delle Arti.
Wine week, Montefalco (*Easter*). Large trade fair of DOC wines.
La Desolata, Perugia (*Holy Week*). Exciting staging of the Passion.
Tableaux Vivants, Città della Pieve (*Holy Week*). Scenes from the Passion.

Processione del Cristo Morto, Assisi, Tuoro sul Trasimeno and Norcia (*Holy Week*).
Via Crucis, Alviano and Amelia (*Good Friday*).
Processione della Rinchinata, Bastia Umbra and Cannara (*Easter*). Staging the meeting of Christ and the Madonna.
Coloriamo i Cieli, Castiglione del Lago (*late Apr to early May*). A colourful biennial kite festival.
Corsa all'Anello, Narni (*late Apr to mid-May*). Costumed knights spear a ring (*anello*) with a lance.

May

Cantamaggio, Terni (*May*). Folk festival celebrating the advent of spring. Parade of floats with allegorical scenes.
Festa del Calendimaggio, Assisi (*first week*). Three days of fun, including a costumed re-enactment of medieval stories, in which two of the town's districts compete.
Corsa dei Ceri, Gubbio (*15 May*). Three guilds challenge each other to carry towering candlesticks (*ceri*) on their shoulders up to the basilica of Sant'Ubaldo.
Palio della Balestra, Gubbio (*last Sun*). In Piazza della Signoria, the crossbowmen of Gubbio and Sansepolcro (Tuscany) challenge each other in a Palio.
Festa di Santa Rita, Cascia (*21–22 May*). A torchlit procession towards the Santa Rita basilica, then a historical procession with the saint's remains and the staging of scenes from her life.
Festa della Palombella, Orvieto (*Pentecost*). Similar to the Scoppio del Carro in Florence, in which an artificial "dove" sets light to a cart of fireworks.

Opening of the Corsa all'Anello festival in Narni

Average Daily Hours of Sunshine

Sunshine
In summer the days are long and sunny, and it can become very hot in the towns. In September and October the days are still sunny, and often pleasantly warm, as they are also in the spring – perhaps the best time to visit Umbria.

Summer

Umbria can be very hot and humid in July and August, so many summer events are held outside, and in the evening. Festivals take place in squares, parks and gardens, and attract locals and tourists alike.

June
Festa della Fioritura, Castelluccio di Norcia. Ancient feast marking the return of flocks of sheep to the mountains.
Mercato delle Gaite, Bevagna *(second half of Jun)*. Medieval fair with splendid costumes and stalls.
Infiorata, Spello *(Corpus Christi)*. Procession along a flower-strewn route. Floral carpet competition.
Procession, Orvieto *(Corpus Christi)*. Procession in historical costume.
Festa del Voto, Assisi *(22 Jun)*. Re-enactment of the expulsion of the Saracens.

A band performing at Umbria Jazz in Perugia

Rockin' Umbria, Perugia and Umbertide *(last ten days of Jun)*. Rock music festival, with up-and-coming bands, as well as photography and comic exhibitions.
Biennale di Scultura, Gubbio. A biennial exhibition of works by contemporary Italian artists.
Festa delle Acque, Piediluco and at the Cascata delle Marmore *(late Jun)*. Processions of boats, canoe races and fireworks.

July
Festival di Spoleto *(end Jun to mid-Jul)*. A major international event dedicated to theatre, dance and music.
Umbria Jazz, Perugia *(mid-Jul)*. Theatres, gardens and squares are taken over by some of the world's great jazz artists.
Gubbio Summer Festival *(Jul–Aug)*. Chamber and symphony music in the open air.

Palio delle Barche, Passignano sul Trasimeno *(last week in Jul)*. Town districts compete in a boat race, for which participants wear medieval costume.

Historical costume

August
Palio dei Terzieri, Città della Pieve. Archery competition and all manner of street entertainment, including acrobats and a procession featuring costumes derived from the works of Perugino.
Palio dei Quartieri, Nocera Umbra. Popular historical re-enactment in costume.
Palio di San Rufino, Assisi. Crossbow competition.
Rassegna Internazionale del Folklore, Castiglione del Lago. Folklore festival.
Festival delle Nazioni *(late Aug to early Sep)*, Città di Castello. Festival of chamber music.

Floral decorations in the street during the Infiorata, Spello

Average Monthly Rainfall

Rainfall
Late autumn is the time of year when rainfall is at its heaviest. In winter heavy snow-falls are common in the Apennines, while storms may occur in spring and late summer.

A procession led by men in costumes during Giostra della Quintana, Foligno

Autumn

The end of the summer heralds the grape harvest, followed by the olive harvest. These are two very important occasions for the customs and culture of the region. Summer festivals and tourist events are usually over by this stage, and this is the start of a season of festivals linked to the gastronomy and history of the region.

September
Cavalcata di Satriano, Nocera Umbra *(first Sun)*. Knights in medieval costume retrace the last journey of St Francis, from the hermitage at Nocera to his native Assisi.
Giostra della Quintana, Foligno *(second Sun)*. In this joust, competing knights attempt to spear a ring held by a wooden puppet. The streets are filled with historical processions.
Giochi delle Porte, Gualdo Tadino *(last week of Sep)*. Includes archery and catapult competitions, donkey and donkey cart races all around the town. There are also historical re-enactments.

Festa dell'Uva *(end Sep)*, Montefalco. Celebration of the grape harvest.
Segni Barocchi, Foligno *(Sep–Oct)*. Musical and theatrical performances, all with a Baroque theme.

October
Giostra dell'Arme, San Gemini *(late Sep to mid-Oct)*. Costumed knights from two town districts compete in a historical jousting tournament.
I Primi d'Italia, Foligno *(late Sep to early Oct)*. National food festival celebrating the first dishes of Italy.
Palio dei Terzieri, Trevi *(first Sun of Oct)*. Cart race and historical parade.
Festival Eurochocolate, Perugia *(mid- to late Oct)*. Chocolate stands and superb chocolate sculptures fill the historic centre.
Festa di San Francesco, Assisi *(2–4 Oct)*. Important religious celebration on the anniversary of Francis's death.
Marcia per la Pace, Perugia to Assisi *(biennial)*. Groups and movements from around the world participate in an international march for peace.

Rassegna Antiquaria, Perugia *(end Oct to early Nov)*. Antiques fair. Includes displays of antique textiles.
Ottobre Trevano, Trevi. Gastronomic feasts and historical re-enactments performed in costume.
Mostra del Tartufo, Città di Castello *(late Oct to early Nov)*. Taste white truffles and all sorts of other woodland delicacies.

November
Festa dell Olio Nuovo, Trevi *(early Nov)*. Celebration of the olive oil harvest.
Fiera dei Cavalli, Città di Castello *(third Sun of Nov)*. Cattle markets and horse fairs.
Wine Tasting, Torgiano *(late Nov)*. World-famous wine-tasting competition of Umbrian and other Italian wines.
Festa dei Ceramisti, Deruta *(25 Nov)*. Festival for Deruta's older ceramicists, plus displays of ceramics. Dedicated to Santa Caterina d'Alessandria, patron saint of ceramicists.
Rassegna Cinematografica di Assisi *(Oct/Nov/Dec)*. Film festival dedicated to Italian cinema.

Revellers celebrating the grape harvest during Festa dell'Uva, Montefalco

Average Monthly Temperature

Temperature

The Umbrian climate is temperate, though temperatures are much cooler in the Apennines. Autumn and spring, when the days are not too hot, are the most pleasant seasons. The summer months are hot and humid, especially in the towns.

A recreation of the birth of Christ at a Living Nativity in Assisi

Winter

This season can be very cold and windy, and snow often falls at higher mountain altitudes. There are festivals celebrating the chestnut harvest, for instance, but Christmas is the focus of the season. At Christmas, living nativity scenes are staged, a popular tradition dating from the Middle Ages.

National Holidays

New Year (1 Jan)

Epiphany (6 Jan)

Easter Sunday

Anniversary of Liberation (25 Apr)

Labour Day (1 May)

Festa della Repubblica (2 Jun)

Ferragosto (15 Aug)

All Saints (1 Nov)

Immaculate Conception (8 Dec)

Christmas (25 Dec)

Santo Stefano (26 Dec)

December

Ri Fauni or Festa delle Campane *(9 Dec)*. Commemorating the transporting of the Madonna of Nazareth to Loreto (9 December 1921).

World's largest Christmas tree, Gubbio *(from 7 Dec)*. Lights transform Monte Ingino into a giant Christmas tree.

Living Nativity, Attigliano, Alviano, Acquasparta, Calvi, Giove, Monteleone, Petrignano, Lugnano in Teverina, Perugia and Rocca Sant'Angelo *(24 Dec)*.

Christmas in Assisi. Concerts and formal celebrations take place in the basilica and other churches.

Monumental nativity, Città della Pieve *(Christmas to Epiphany)*. This is displayed in the Palazzo della Corgna.

January

Umbria Jazz Winter, Orvieto *(end Dec to early Jan)*. Winter version of the Perugia jazz festival. Concerts and musical events.

February

Carnevale. Parades and events throughout Umbria.

Festa dell'Olivo and **Sagra della Bruschetta**, Spello *(penultimate Sun of Carnevale)*. Olive and bruschetta festivals, with parades, feasts and music.

Mascherata, San Leo di Bastia *(first Sun of Carnevale)*. A masked procession through the village.

Festa di San Valentino, Terni *(Feb)*. Events all month, but 14 Feb is the focus. Betrothed couples exchange vows of love in the basilica of St Valentine.

Sagra del Tartufo Nero e dei Prodotti Tipici della Valnerina, Norcia *(Feb)*. Tastings and sales of produce, including truffles.

The world's largest Christmas tree, illuminated on the slopes of Gubbio's Mount Ingino

THE HISTORY OF UMBRIA

Wedged between powerful neighbours like Tuscany, Le Marche and Lazio (especially Rome), the territory of Umbria has been an area of conquest, transit and trade for millennia. Its regional identity today dates back to the creation of a unified Italy in the 19th century, although the towns and cities of Umbria nonetheless have many characteristics in common.

The first populations date back to the Neolithic age – evidence remains of ceramics from the 6th and 5th millennia BC. Later, the Apennine civilization occupied Umbria's hills and mountains, and lived off agriculture and stock raising. They left behind decorated vases and tools of stone, bone and metal.

The golden age of prehistory in central Italy coincided with the development of the Villanovan culture in the 9th and 8th centuries BC. These people used iron for tools and arms, and had complex funerary rituals. The cities of many Italic peoples developed from the settlements of this era. They had a turbulent relationship with the emerging economic and military powers of the Etruscans and the Romans, and would manage to remain independent for only a few more centuries.

Until the Romans arrived, the Umbrian territory was divided into two areas of control: on the west bank of the Tiber was a series of rich Etruscan cities, while on the east bank the Umbri held control. The little that is known about the Umbri comes from the famous Eugubine Tablets *(see p64)*. Discovered in 1444, these seven bronze slabs were written in the 2nd century BC in the Umbrian language, using the Etruscan and then the Latin alphabet. The text describes religious rites and also Gubbio's political system. Other cities founded by the Umbri include Todi, Assisi, Spello and Gualdo Tadino.

Confrontation between Rome and the Etruscans reached crisis point in 295 BC, when Roman legions defeated the Umbri, the Sannites, Gauls and Etruscans, opening up territory for conquest. The cities changed sides quickly, and the opening in 219 of the Via Flaminia from Rome to the Adriatic confirmed Rome's power. Rome suffered one of its most bitter defeats, however, on the shores of Lake Trasimeno. In 217 BC the Roman army clashed with Hannibal and the Carthaginians to the west of the lake. The Carthaginians laid a trap to surprise the enemy on the lake shore and Hannibal's army wiped out two-thirds of the Roman forces.

8th century Etruscan city of Velzna (Orvieto) established

Funerary object

672 Traditional date for the founding of Terni

219 Opening of the Via Flaminia, from Rome to Fano and Rimini

1500 BC	1000	800	600	400	200

16th century Apennine civilization (geometric ceramics)

Inscription in the Umbrian language from the 4th century BC

4th century Building of Spoleto city walls

295 Roman victory at Sentinum against Sannites, Gauls, Umbri and Etruscans

◀ *Fortitude and Temperance*, Perugino (1448–1523), Collegio del Cambio in Perugia (detail)

Roman Umbria

After the defeat of the Etruscans and the Italic peoples allied to the Umbri, Rome consolidated its domination of Umbria in the 1st century BC, when Emperor Augustus created Region VI (Umbria), which included all the cities and municipal towns on the west bank of the River Tiber. Region VII (Etruria) took in territory and settlements on the east bank of the river. The Romans, who were great civil engineers, undertook a series of urban projects in the 1st and 2nd centuries AD, including aqueducts, cisterns, theatres and walls that would feature in the lives of Umbrian towns for centuries. Via Flaminia and Via Amerina would become the main communication routes in the region for hundreds of years to come.

The Villa di Plinio (Pliny's Villa) at San Giustino would have been very grand at one time. This shows one of many hypothetical reconstructions.

San Giustino

Tifernum Tiberinum (Città di Castello)

VIA TIBERINA

Lake Trasimeno was the scene of a battle between the Romans and Carthaginians *(see p97)*. Today, there is little to be seen of the encounter: just the names of a river and a hill – Rio Sanguineto (bloody river) and Monte Sanguigno (Mount Blood) – and several ditches dug to cremate the corpses of Hannibal's soldiers.

Tuoro al Trasimeno

Lake Trasimeno

Perusia (Perugia)

Region VII

VIA ORVIETANA

VIA AMERINA

Roman Umbria

This map shows the administrative shape of Umbria under the Romans, as well as the busy network of Roman roads planned and built over the centuries. The Via Flaminia was of particular importance to Umbria. Construction began at the end of the 3rd century BC, and a number of towns of importance developed along its length, among them Spoleto. The road maintained its role in the centuries following Roman domination.

VIA CASSIA

VIA NOA TRAIANA

Tuder (Todi)

Carsula

Volsinii Veteres (Orvieto)

River Tiber

Paglia

Ameria (Amelia)

The site of Carsulae *(see p132)* is one of the most important in Umbria, and many of the objects discovered here now feature in the museums of the region. The site was abandoned in 27 BC, when commercial traffic moved to the eastern side of the Via Flaminia.

Via Amerina was the second main artery road.

Narnia (Nar

The baths at Otricoli were built on the site of natural springs. Baths were an important feature of Roman civilization.

Ocriculum (Otricoli)

The Mausoleum of Pomponio Grecino, near Gubbio, demonstrates that the city was an important political and religious place at the time of Region VI.

The Via Flaminia was the main route through Umbria, built along the axis of the towns of Narnia, Spoletium, Carsulae and Fulginiae. Traces of the original paving stones can be seen in many towns.

The Temple of Minerva (see p75) in Assisi was built in the 1st century AD, on a set of terraces representing the centre of the Roman city. The temple performed different functions over the centuries until, in 1456, it finally became the church of Santa Maria sopra Minerva.

The bronze statue of Germanicus, found near Amelia, is now on view in the town's archaeological museum (see p130). For a long time the famous statue was held in Perugia's Museo Archeologico Nazionale dell'Umbria (see p88), which is probably the best in Umbria for the wealth and importance of its Roman and Etruscan collections.

The paving of Roman roads was famous for its solid construction. Various stretches are still visible today, including at Spoleto.

Chiascio

uvium
ubbio)

Region VI

Asisium (Assisi)

Hispellum (Spello)

Fulginiae (Foligno)

Tribiae (Trevi)

Region IV Nursia (Norcia)

Spoletium (Spoleto)

Nera

Interamna Nahars (Terni)

Theatres and amphitheatres were built by the Romans in Umbria. They can be seen in many parts of the region, several still in good condition, such as the one at Spoleto (see p115), from which the above mosaic comes. It is now used for events and concerts.

Norcia was a prefecture and then a municipium of Region IV.

0 kilometres 10
0 miles 10

Cisterns were large underground reservoirs for storing water, built by the Romans and still visible today in some towns, along with their wells. Amelia's reservoirs are particularly impressive; they consist of ten parallel tanks with a capacity of four and a half million litres.

Key

–·– Today's regional boundary

— Roman boundary

The Late Middle Ages

The ending of Roman rule in Umbria was a heavy blow to a region that depended on trade and agriculture. Communication routes ceased to be secure, apart from the road linking Rome with Amelia, Narni, Perugia and Gubbio. The townspeople had built houses on the plain in the quest for more space during the years of the *pax romana* (as can still be seen today in Gubbio), but they were forced to return to the hills to protect themselves from the aggressive barbarians – the Goths and Huns – coming from the north. The towns became crowded and unsanitary, plague and famine wrought havoc in many areas. The Umbrian population declined noticeably and the ordered farms of the Roman era rapidly became fragmented into numerous small plots of land. Feudal power held sway virtually everywhere, typically dominated by local families who ruled over small areas from a castle or a fortress.

In 553, a narrow strip of Umbrian land passed into Byzantine hands, but of far greater significance was the arrival of the Lombards, who set up a principality that included much of Umbria. From the 570s onwards, the so-called Duchy of Spoleto developed into a political entity of some weight. When either historians or geographers referred to

Frederick Barbarossa flanked by his sons Enrico il Severo and Frederick, 12th-century miniature

Lombard sword hilt

"Umbria" at this time, and indeed for centuries to come, they generally meant the lands of the Duchy of Spoleto and therefore only the east bank of the Tiber. In the centuries prior to the year 1000, small monasteries and convents appeared all over the region, albeit scattered and often in inaccessible places. Under the Lombards, who adopted many of the customs of the local people, there was a flowering of art and architecture.

The end of the first millennium signalled a change in the tendency to build hill fortresses. During this phase, lower, flat ground gradually began to be reoccupied, as trade became more significant. New towns (which sometimes kept Roman elements in their names, such as Villa Nova) were built,

4th century Construction of the basilica of San Salvatore in Spoleto	**553** End of the war with the Goths: part of Umbria comes under Byzantine domination		**756** Pepin the Short gives Perugia and the Duchy of Spoleto to Pope Stephen II

300 A.D.	400	500	600	700	800

c.480 Birth of St Benedict (San Benedetto) in Norcia		**6th–7th centuries** Invasion of the Lombards. The Duchy of Spoleto includes Terni, Foligno, Spello and Assisi 00
St Benedict in a miniature		

populated by ordinary peasants, now freed from their feudal obligations. This led to the birth of early forms of self-government, which would later develop into the communes of the 11th and 12th centuries.

At the request of the papacy, the Franks (under Pepin the Short and then Charlemagne), drove the Lombards and the Byzantines out of Umbria. Charlemagne won the title of Holy Roman Emperor from the papacy in exchange for territory, but relations soured. When Barbarossa, Holy Roman Emperor, arrived in Italy in the 1150s, he destroyed Spoleto and a number of other towns.

Artisans and farm labourers at work in the era of the communes

The Rise of the Communes

Eventually, economic progress and demographic growth made it essential to expand the towns, too restricted now inside their old walls. In 1244 construction began of the new walls in Todi, and in 1296 Spoleto enlarged its city walls. The emphasis on ambitious public works, such as town halls and cathedrals, demonstrated a lively spirit of initiative on the part of the town populations. It was certainly no coincidence that they elected to adopt a form of autonomy in the 11th and 12th centuries, leading to the rise of the communes *(see pp46–7)*. By 1111, Pope Pasquale II was complaining that Umbrian towns did not recognize the authority of the Church of Rome. In Umbria, meanwhile, the communes flourished: Perugia's Palazzo dei Priori, Orvieto cathedral and the basilica in Assisi date from this time. In addition, the Franciscan influence started to spread from Assisi, encouraging the use of the Gothic style in new churches. The years of architectural, social and political triumph of these autonomous towns were, however, also years of constant battles for regional or local domination, and plagues and earthquakes badly affected the towns and countryside. The end of the era of the communes coincided with a push by the papacy to regain control. Between 1350 and 1370 the figure that the Umbrians feared most was Egidio Albornoz, cardinal and papal legate, creator of the great fortresses which were to watch over Umbrian towns on behalf of Rome for the next five centuries.

Montefalco, an example of a fortified city commune, in a painting by Benozzo Gozzoli (1420–1497)

Pasquale II, pope from 1099 to 1118

1155 Frederick Barbarossa destroys Spoleto

1277 Cimabue starts work on the frescoes in the basilica of Assisi

1290 Orvieto: Nicholas IV blesses the first stone laid in the building of the cathedral

900   **1000**   **1100**   **1200**   **1300**

11th–12th centuries The Umbrian communes are set up: in 1111 Pasquale II realizes that none of the Umbrian towns respect the authority of the pope

1226 On 4 October, St Francis of Assisi dies

1354 Beginning of the papal campaign to reconquer Umbria

The Communes of Umbria

The communes *(comuni)*, or independent city states, and their organizational structures spread rapidly throughout central Italy in the 11th–12th centuries. The independence of the communes – which were frequently at war with one another – developed at a time when central power was weakening. Despite the reaction of the papacy and of the Holy Roman Empire, the 12th century marked the rise of the commune, asserting the autonomy of the city-state and enabling the arts and economy to flourish. The political master was no longer a feudal lord but an urban bourgeoisie growing rich through manufacturing and trade. Textile industries were established, as were the first banks (which later led to the creation of the great Italian banks of subsequent centuries). In the meantime, merchants from the communes developed trade relationships with the rest of Europe and the Mediterranean, and, thanks to the Crusades, with the Far East, too.

Palazzi Comunali (town halls), symbols of the communes, were built in Umbria during the 13th and 14th centuries. In many towns and cities, they are still the seat of the town hall.

The Torre del Popolo remains a landmark in Assisi's Piazza del Comune.

St Francis was the subject of a book by St Bonaventure, written in the same century that the saint died.

The Temple of Minerva, still visible in Assisi's Piazza del Comune, is clearly recognizable, even in this stylized rendering.

One of the first signs of the birth of communal civilization was population growth, which required cities to increase available housing. City walls were enlarged and rebuilt in all the main town centres in Umbria, among them Spello, shown above.

Increasingly imposing cathedrals (left is the cathedral of Foligno) were often built facing the centres of temporal power. After centuries of fortified towns criss-crossed with narrow streets, the era of the commune saw the building of town squares that functioned as meeting places as well as centres of power.

The town fountain was a celebration of the wealth of a city – the years when the communes flourished signalled the return of water supplies to many towns. After centuries of abandonment, ancient aqueducts were restored and rebuilt. This is the famous Fontana Maggiore in Perugia (*see p91*).

Population growth meant that urban centres were forced to expand upwards as well as outwards. This is how multi-storey houses and porticoes arose.

Homage of a Simple Man

St Bonaventure, a 13th-century Franciscan monk, tells the story that one day, in Assisi, Francis met "a simple man". Inspired by God, the man laid his own cloak down before the saint. This episode begins the story of the life of St Francis in the cycle of frescoes in the Basilica in Assisi. The work is of great importance because, with great attention to detail and careful observation, the artist, Giotti, has created a perfect picture of the medieval centre of Assisi at the end of the 13th century. A picture that is not so different from that visible in Piazza del Comune today.

Clashes and battles between the Umbrian communes were continual. Some cities had troops of soldiers, such as the crossbowmen, that formed exclusive companies. They are commemorated today in numerous historical processions.

The citizen in the era of the communes, like the one present in this scene, was expected to maintain a dignified demeanour in public squares; swords should never be unsheathed. Crimes committed in this place were severely punished.

Impressive fortresses, like the one at Spoleto, pictured here, dominate Umbrian towns. They were built by the papacy, from the end of the 14th century, in order to consolidate the power of the Church. The construction of such strongholds, often under the watchful eye of Cardinal Albornoz, heralded the end of communal power.

Perugia, as depicted in a fresco by Benedetto Bonfigli in the mid-15th century

The Centuries of Decline

The conquest of Umbria by the papacy coincided with the effects of the great plague that had devastated Europe in 1348.

At the end of the 15th century, the term "Umbria" began to appear in the works of scholars and academics: the clergyman Innocenzo Malvasia, in his *Italia Illustrata* drawn up for Pope Sixtus V, defined Umbria as the land of the Duchy of Spoleto, while he described the remainder of the region as being part of Etruria, and Gualdo and Gubbio as dependencies of the Duchy of Urbino.

Following centuries of development, 16th-century Umbria found itself in a tricky situation. The cities, peripheral dominions of the state gravitating around Rome, were declining, while craftsmen and industries were diminishing in number and quality. The heads of the great aristocratic families abandoned the cities and returned to the land and agriculture.

Town and Countryside

A fundamental instrument in the development of the new Umbrian economy was the "*mezzadria*", or sharecropping system, and the gradual colonization of the hills and plains, on partly reclaimed land in some cases. One very noticeable effect of the agricultural revival was the gradual depopulation of the cities. The historian Cipriano Piccolpasso wrote of Assisi: "…it is a badly composed city, with many derelict and unoccupied houses next to inhabited ones, so that it seems more like the residue of a city than a completed one…". The move to the country was not the only factor to alter the appearance of the cities: during the 16th and 17th centuries, nobles invested some of the profits from their farms in town projects.

Politically, the 17th century saw important new developments: in 1624 the della Rovere family ceded the Duchy of Urbino to the pope, and the following year Pope Urban VIII put the University of Perugia under episcopal control.

From Papal Rule to the Unification of Italy

By now an agricultural, rural region, Umbria became one of Rome's "bread baskets" and a major producer of olive oil. Mills multiplied, as did the frequency of country fairs, which took the place of town markets in the economy of the countryside. With the end of the 18th century came the Napoleonic revolution. As part of the Roman Republic created in 1798, Umbria was divided into the two departments of Trasimeno and Clitunno. In the imperial era the division was dissolved, and Umbria

1416–24 Braccio da Montone becomes lord of Perugia

1472 In Foligno, 300 copies of The *Divine Comedy* are printed: the first book published in Italian in Italy

Paul III, pope from 1534 to 1549

1400   **1500**   **1600**   **1700**

1444 The Eugubine Tablets are discovered

1508 Building begins on Santa Maria della Consolazione, near Todi

1540 Perugia comes under the papal rule of Paul III

1656–1701 The population of Umbria falls from 317,000 to 280,000

Perugia's Rocca Paolina, destroyed on 14 September 1860

became a single territory, with Spoleto as its capital. This confirmation of a common identity would be returned to without much alteration by the unified state after 1860.

In line with the Romantic movement elsewhere, the 19th century saw a rise in interest in the Middle Ages. The discovery of the remains of St Francis (1818) and Santa Chiara (1850) caused a sensation. In 1859, a great popular uprising in Perugia against the papal troops resulted in a brutal massacre, which became known as the "Stragi di Perugia". In September 1860 soldiers entered the town, and the local population immediately set about destroying the Rocca Paolina fortress, which had become a much detested symbol of the power of the Roman Catholic Church.

The Making of a Region

Following a plebiscite, the province of Umbria was created in 1861, as part of a unified Kingdom of Italy. It included all the current provinces (plus Rieti), with a population of 500,000. The economic situation in the closing decades of

Santa Chiara in Assisi, which holds the remains of Santa Chiara

the 19th century was, however, woeful: agriculture was languishing and farmers were increasingly forced into seasonal migration towards the Maremma and the countryside around Rome. Even so, the Industrial Revolution did not leave Umbria behind: in 1866 the railway line that links Rome, Terni and Foligno was completed, and between 1875 and 1887 arms factories and the Terni steelworks (the first – and only – really major employer in the region) were founded. In 1881 the population of Umbria numbered 611,000; in 1911 it was 767,000.

Modern Umbria

World War II saw the bombing of Umbria's industries, and recovery in the postwar period was slow. The development of light industry, cottage industries and especially tourism has since helped boost the region's fortunes, though the earthquakes that strike periodically have affected certain areas of Umbria badly. The worst was in 1979, in Valnerina, but the quakes that struck Assisi, Foligno and Nocera Umbra in 1997, and Norcia in 2016, received broader coverage around the world because of the damage to culturally important sites, such as the art-packed St Francis basilica in Assisi and the monasteries and churches of Norcia. In 2000, Assisi was recognized as a UNESCO World Heritage site, thus highlighting the region's cultural importance.

1798 During Napoleonic domination Umbria is divided into two departments: Trasimeno and Clitunno

1875 The steelworks of Terni built

1923 Rieti becomes part of Lazio

1997 26 September: an earthquake devastates Umbria

2000 Assisi recognized as a UNESCO World Heritage Site

2016 30 October: earthquake destroys many churches in Norcia

1800

1900

2000

2020

1859 Uprising in Perugia and sacking by the papal troops

1861 The province of Perugia is established as part of the Kingdom of Italy

1958 First Festival dei Due Mondi in Spoleto

Poster for Festival dei Due Mondi, Spoleto

2013 Pope Francis visits Assisi, the birthplace of St Francis

2006 The Galleria Nazionale dell'Umbria completes its renovation work, more artwork goes on show

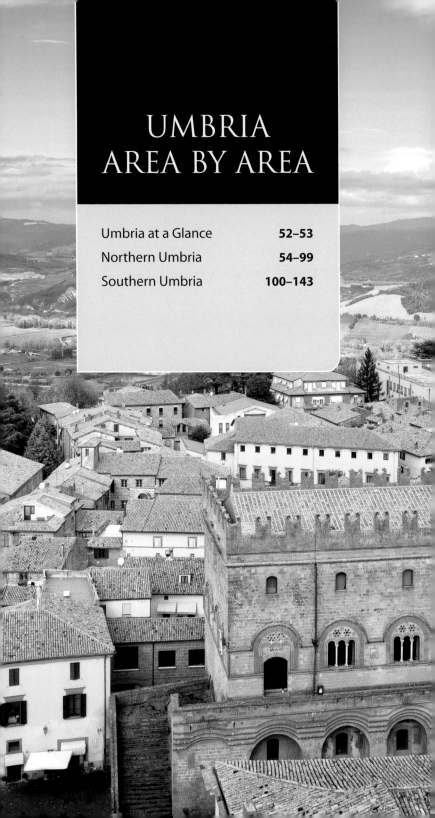

UMBRIA AREA BY AREA

Umbria at a Glance

The region of Umbria is not particularly large, but it has numerous towns, villages, parks and other places of great interest. Northern Umbria includes the upper valley of the River Tiber (Alta Val Tiberina), the Apennine regional parks (Monte Subasio and Monte Cucco), the medieval towns of Perugia, Assisi and Gubbio and the great expanse of Lake Trasimeno. The southern half of the region revolves around the towns of Todi, Narni, Terni and Orvieto, on the border with Tuscany, within the area once occupied by the Etruscans. Completing this picture of southern Umbria are the great mountains of the Monti Sibillini national park and the Valnerina (the valley of the Nera River), with its famous waterfalls, the Cascata delle Marmore.

Città della Pieve
Famous as the birthplace of the artist Perugino (some of his works are here), this small town near the Tuscan border is a good departure point for visiting the area south of Lake Trasimeno.

0 kilometres   15
0 miles   15

Selci
Fraccano
Città di Castello
Trestina
Umbertide
Tevere
Cascata

NORTHERN UMBRI
(see pp54–99)

Lago Trasimeno
Magione
Castiglione del Lago
Perugia
Tavernelle
Nestore
Città della Pieve
Carnaiola
Marsciano
Ficulle
Colonnetta
Todi
Tevere
Lago di Corbara
Castel Giorgio
Orvieto
Amelia

Todi
Perched on a hill above the Tiber, Todi was for centuries a border town between the land of the Etruscans and territory occupied by the Umbri. It has a lovely historic quarter, centred around Piazza del Popolo.

◀ Panoramic view of the medieval town of Orvieto

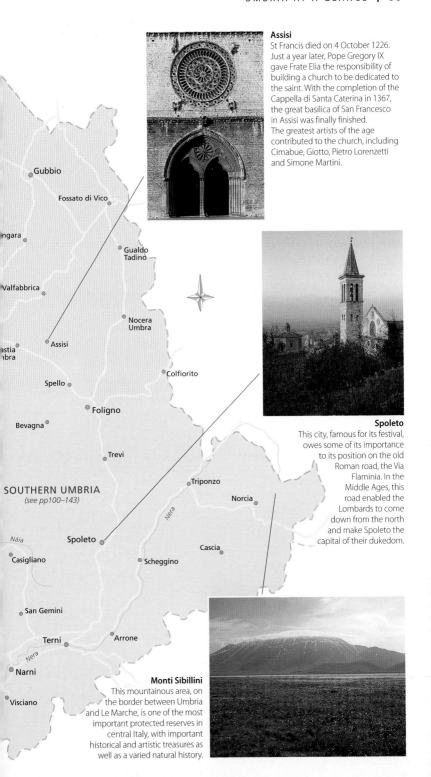

Assisi

St Francis died on 4 October 1226. Just a year later, Pope Gregory IX gave Frate Elia the responsibility of building a church to be dedicated to the saint. With the completion of the Cappella di Santa Caterina in 1367, the great basilica of San Francesco in Assisi was finally finished. The greatest artists of the age contributed to the church, including Cimabue, Giotto, Pietro Lorenzetti and Simone Martini.

Spoleto

This city, famous for its festival, owes some of its importance to its position on the old Roman road, the Via Flaminia. In the Middle Ages, this road enabled the Lombards to come down from the north and make Spoleto the capital of their dukedom.

Monti Sibillini

This mountainous area, on the border between Umbria and Le Marche, is one of the most important protected reserves in central Italy, with important historical and artistic treasures as well as a varied natural history.

Gubbio

Fossato di Vico

ngara

Gualdo Tadino

Valfabbrica

Nocera Umbra

astia
bra

Assisi

Colfiorito

Spello

Foligno

Bevagna

Trevi

SOUTHERN UMBRIA
(see pp100–143)

Triponzo

Norcia

Nera

Nàia

Spoleto

Cascia

Casigliano

Scheggino

San Gemini

Terni

Arrone

Nera

Narni

Visciano

NORTHERN UMBRIA

Northern Umbria consists of three distinct geographical areas:
the first is the Alta Val Tiberina (the Upper Tiber Valley), the second
is the area around Lake Trasimeno, and the third is the easterly
Apennine region around Gubbio and the Via Flaminia. These three
regions, laden with history and culture, meet at northern Umbria's
two most important towns, Perugia and Assisi.

Perugia is the capital of the region and one of the main cities in central Italy, both culturally and economically. Assisi is visited every year by thousands of tourists and pilgrims, who come to retrace the steps of St Francis and admire the fresco cycles in the basilica.

The three aforementioned areas have differing histories. The Alta Val Tiberina, as well as delineating the border between the Etruscans (to the west) and the Umbri (to the east), has long been of commercial importance, with its direct lines of communication with the north. The entire area of Lake Trasimeno, on the other hand, has always been of great strategic and military significance, as can still be seen today from the many fortifications scattered around the lake. The lakeshore was the setting for one of the battles of the Second Punic Wars (217 BC), which culminated in the victory of Hannibal over the Romans. To the east, in contrast, hermitages that

were refuges for entire populations in the time of barbaric invasions cling to the Apennines. Northern Umbria's fortunes became allied to those of the rest of the region with the ending of the Duchy of Spoleto.

Despite the bombardments of World War II and the earthquake of 1997, which struck the area along the border with Le Marche, splendid testimony remains to the region's history, including Etruscan and Roman buildings and finds. The legacy of the Middle Ages and the Renaissance can be seen in churches, palazzi, town halls and castles, as well as in works by the great artists of the day, among them Perugino, a native of Città della Pieve.

The varied and well-preserved landscape of the northern region includes two national parks, Monte Cucco and Monte Subasio, where the "song of nature" that so struck St Francis of Assisi can still be sensed.

A patchwork of ordered fields carpeting the hillsides of northern Umbria

◀ San Girolamo Monastery in Monte Cucco Park

Exploring Northern Umbria

Città di Castello is the first main town on the road into Umbria from neighbouring Emilia-Romagna, along the old trade route which then continues down through the Upper Tiber Valley. At Umbertide, a road heads off eastwards to Gubbio and beyond to the Via Flaminia, which skirts the Apennines on its route south towards Assisi. West of Assisi lies the province of Perugia and the regional capital itself. Further west again, bordering Tuscany, is Lake Trasimeno and the homeland of Perugino.

The town of Assisi, a UNESCO World Heritage Site

Sights at a Glance

For hotels and restaurants see pp148–50 and pp156–61

Sansepolcro
Monte Valmeronte 977m
S73b
San Giustino
Tevere
Selci
Fraccano
Arezzo
S221
S257
Lerchi
1 CITTÀ DI CASTELLO
Monte Santa Maria Tiberina
Santa Lucia
Monte Favalto 1082m
S3b
Morra
Fabrecce
MONTONE 2
Niccone
La Dogana
UMBERTIDE
Romeggio
Lisciano Niccone
Polgeto
San Giuliana
Preggio
Tuoro sul Trasimeno
Pantano
RA6
Passignano sul Trasimeno
Maestrello
Monte Tezio 961m
Isola Maggiore
LAKE TRASIMENO
Magione
Corciano
CASTIGLIONE DEL LAGO 16
15
Isola Polvese
San Savino
RA6
Sant' Arcangelo
Monte Sperello
Panicarola
S599
18
Mugnano
Strozzacappo
Paciano
SOUTHERN LAKE TRASIMENO
Panicale
Pietráia
Sant 'Enea
Po Bandino
S220
Tavernelle
Piegaro
S71
Nestore
Spina
S317
CITTÀ DELLA PIEVE 17
Montarale 845m
Monteleone d'Orvieto
Montegabbione
Marsciano
S39
A1
Orvieto

0 kilometres   10
0 miles   10

The azure waters of Lake Trasimeno

Getting Around

Lake Trasimeno and Perugia can be reached from the Autostrada del Sole (A1) by following Superstrada 75bis, a motorway spur that heads east from the exit Val di Chiana, Bettole-Sinalunga. Further south, the Fabro exit from the A1 is just a few kilometres from Città della Pieve. The state roads 3 and 3bis, which link Umbria with Le Marche and Emilia-Romagna, are also major routes. Two railway lines run from Perugia: north to Sansepolcro and northwest to Florence, with trains running at least daily. Coach and bus services are good, in particular around Lake Trasimeno (where there are also ferry services) and in and around Perugia.

Key

▬▬ Motorway

▬▬ Major road

═══ Major road under contruction

▬ Secondary road

═══ Minor road

▬ Scenic route

╌╌ Main railway

── Minor railway

▬ Regional border

△ Summit

Ruins of the Roman amphitheatre in Gubbio

For keys to symbols *see back flap*

❶ Città di Castello

The town that is today the most important centre in the Upper Tiber Valley, the gateway to Umbria for anyone approaching from the north, was originally a settlement of the ancient Umbri. Situated as it was between Le Marche and Tuscany, and not far from Emilia-Romagna, the town was in a perfect position as far as trade was concerned. It became a commune in the Middle Ages, when it was in almost perpetual conflict with the nearby city-states. Even so, the former "Civitas Castelli" grew in power and riches, thanks to the flourishing commercial activity, including printing, which is still an important part of the city's economic fabric today. Following a period of rule by nobles installed by the Church, Città di Castello was completely redesigned under the rule of the Vitelli family, in the 16th century, as can be seen by the various palazzi bearing its name.

Exploring Città di Castello
The town is built on the right bank of the River Tiber, at the northernmost edge of Umbria. The architecture displays Tuscan influences, thanks to the work of the Florentine architects Antonio da Sangallo and Giorgio Vasari, brought in by the Vitelli family in the 16th century.

The tour described here begins in Piazza Gabriotti. Visitors are advised to leave their cars in the car park in Viale Nazario Sauro and then take the escalator up to the piazza. The monuments seen at the beginning of the tour date from the period prior to that of the Vitelli.

⛪ Duomo
Piazza Gabriotti. **Open** daily.
It is immediately apparent that the cathedral exterior has undergone more than one remodelling. The round bell tower formed part of the original 11th-century building, but the body of the church reveals two successive rebuildings, in the 14th and then the 15th–16th centuries. The unfinished Baroque façade dates from 1632–46. The interior has a single nave and contains a wooden choir and a *Resurrection* by Rosso Fiorentino (1529), in the chapel on the right-hand side. In the **Museo del Duomo**, objects on display map the evolution of the church in the Middle Ages.

⛪ Museo del Duomo
Piazza Gabriotti 3a.
Tel 075 855 4705.
Open Apr–Sep: 10am–1pm, 3.30–6pm Tue–Sun; Oct–Mar: 10am–12.30pm, 3–5pm Tue–Sun. ♿

⛪ Palazzo Comunale
Piazza Gabriotti.
In the same piazza as the Duomo (typical of a medieval town) is the Palazzo Comunale, or town hall. This 14th-century building is the work of Angelo da Orvieto and shows how the Florentine influence on the town's architecture pre-dates the arrival of the Vitelli family: in particular, the use of rusticated stone echoes the style of the Palazzo Vecchio in Florence.

Paliotto, c.1144, Museo del Duomo

In front of the palazzo, on the other side of the piazza, stands the Torre Civica, also 14th-century and once called "del Vescovo" (the bishop's), because it stood next to the bishop's palace (Palazzo Vescovile). From the top of the tower (open daily, entrance fee), there are good views over the town and the surrounding countryside.

⛪ Palazzo del Podestà
Corso Cavour.
From the east of the piazza runs Corso Cavour, home to the Palazzo del Podestà. The façade facing the street dates from the same era as the Palazzo Comunale, and it may be that the original design was also by Angelo da Orvieto. The eastern side is Baroque and leads on to Piazza Matteotti, where Palazzo Vitelli "in Piazza" stands.

The 14th-century Torre Civica

⛪ San Francesco
Via D Albizzini. **Open** daily.
The street that cuts the city in half from north to south is made up of Via XX Settembre, Via Angeloni and Corso Vittorio Emanuele. Halfway along Via Angeloni, near the corner of Via Albizzini, stands the church of St Francis, of 13th-century origin, to which the famous Florentine painter and architect Giorgio Vasari contributed in the 1500s. He was responsible for the Cappella Vitelli as well as an altar with a *Coronation of the Virgin* (1564).

⛪ Palazzo Vitelli a Porta Sant'Egidio
Piazza Garibaldi.
A short distance from San Francesco is this Vitelli palace (1540), one of many that the family had built in the town in an effort to impose some stylistic unity. The façade is symmetrical and there is a pretty garden inside.

The Work of Alberto Burri

Alberto Burri, a major figure in 20th-century Italian art and known all over the world, was born in Città di Castello in 1915 (he died in Nice in 1995). A doctor by profession, he turned to art during World War II. His work is often large-scale and makes use of innovative materials: particularly famous is the *Cretto* at Gibellina Vecchia, in Sicily, a huge carpet of white cement covering the ruins left by the 1968 earthquake. Città di Castello has a good collection of his work in Palazzo Albizzini and the former tobacco drying house, Ex Seccatoi del Tabacco.

Great Iron Sextant, 1982, on show in Città di Castello

Collezioni Burri: **Tel** 075 855 46 49. Palazzo Albizzini: Via Albizzini. Ex Seccatoi del Tabacco: Via Pierucci. **Open** 9:30am–12:30pm, 2:30–6:30pm Tue–Fri; 10am–1pm, 3–6pm Sat & Sun (check website for details). **Tel** 075 855 9848. **Closed** Mon, 1 Jan, 25 Dec. 🖼
🌐 **fondazioneburri.org**

VISITORS' CHECKLIST

Practical Information
Perugia. **Road Map** B2.
🏠 41,000. 🛈 IAT Alta Valle del Tevere, Corso Cavour 5e, 075 855 4922. 🌐 **cittadicastelloturismo.it**

Transport
🚆 FCU Perugia–Sansepolcro line, 075 575 401. 🚌 from Arezzo, 800 512 141.

🏛 San Domenico
Largo Monsignor Muzi.
Open daily.
Between Piazza Garibaldi and the Pinacoteca is the church of San Domenico, the largest in the town. It was built by the Dominicans in the 15th century and later reworked, although the façade remains unfinished. Frescoes from the 15th century line the nave.

🏛 Pinacoteca Comunale
Via della Cannoniera 22.
Tel 075 855 4202.
Open 10am–1pm, 2:30–6:30pm Tue–Sun. 🖼 📷 🏠

The Pinacoteca, one of the region's top art galleries, is housed in the Palazzo Vitelli alla Cannoniera, the most notable of the various Vitelli palazzi. It was built by Antonio da Sangallo (1521–32) with the assistance of Vasari, who was responsible for part of the frescoed friezes.

Among the many works are an *Enthroned Madonna and Child* by the Maestro di Città di Castello (early 14th century); a *Martyrdom of St Sebastian* by Luca Signorelli (1497–8); a *Gonfalone della Santissima Trinità* by Raphael (1499); and a *Coronation of the Virgin* attributed to the workshop of Ghirlandaio (early 1500s). There is, also, a remarkable *Assumption of the Virgin* in terracotta from the workshop of Andrea della Robbia (early 16th century).

Coronation of the Virgin, detail, Ghirlandaio workshop

Città di Castello Town Centre

① Duomo
② Palazzo Comunale
③ Palazzo del Podestà
④ San Francesco
⑤ Palazzo Vitelli a Porta Sant'Egidio
⑥ San Domenico
⑦ Pinacoteca Comunale

0 metres   250
0 yards   250

The verdant Upper Tiber Valley as seen from the medieval village of Montone

❷ Montone

Perugia. **Road Map** C2. 🅰️ 1,500.
🚆 Umbertide, 13 km (8 miles), FCU
Perugia–Sansepolcro line. 🚌 ℹ️ Pro
Loco, Piazza Fortebraccio 1, 075 930
7019. 🆆 comunemontone.it

Montone, 10 km (6 miles) from
Città di Castello, is one of the
most beautiful villages in Italy.
Built on two hilltops on the left
bank of the Tiber, it is the first
town of historical interest on the
road running south through
the Upper Tiber Valley. Founded
as a fortified site in the Middle
Ages (probably in the 11th
century), Montone is still enclosed
within a powerful circle of walls.
These are pierced by three gates:
Porta del Verziere, Porta di Borgo
Vecchio and Porta del Monte.
The names correspond to the
districts into which the castle
was once divided.

Montone was the birthplace
of Braccio Fortebraccio, better
known as Braccio da Montone
(1368–1424), who became
perhaps Umbria's greatest
condottiere (leader of a mercenary
army). He created a genuine
state, with Perugia as its capital.

The medieval village is beautifully preserved and, furthermore,
offers superb views. There are
several buildings of interest. On
the road leading up to the centre
of Montone from the south is
the church of the Madonna
delle Grazie (16th century), as
well as the oldest church in the
village, the Romanesque Pieve
di San Gregorio, dating from the
11th century.

Beyond the walls, it is worth
visiting the Gothic church of San
Francesco (14th century), at the
top of the village. Along with the
attached monastery, this is now
home to the **Museo Comunale**.
The fine doorway is made of
inlaid wood (1519). Inside, the
single-nave building contains
several valuable works of art by
Bartolomeo Caporali. Above
the votive altar are frescoes of
the Fortebraccio family and
also a painting depicting the
Madonna del Soccorso.

The church, which contains a
splendid wooden choir dating
from the 16th century, once
housed a *Madonna in Gloria* by
Luca Signorelli. This is now in the
National Gallery in London. The
former monastery also houses an
ethnographic museum.

Students of Italian history
should consider visiting the
Archivio Storico Comunale, one of
the most important historical
archives in Umbria, with papal
bulls and other important
documents. It is housed in the
former convent of Santa Caterina,
at the southern end of the village.

🏛️ Museo Comunale &
Museo Etnografico

Ex Convento di San Francesco.
Tel 075 930 6535. **Open** Apr–Sep:
10:30am–1pm, 3:30–6pm Fri–Sun
(Jun–Sep: from 4pm); Oct–Mar:
10:30am–1pm, 3–5:30pm Sat & Sun.
Closed 1 Jan, 25 Dec 🐾 🎥 ♿ 📷

Environs

The countryside around
Montone offers plenty of
opportunities for walking,
particularly along the course
of the Torrente Carpina, which
skirts the village to the east and
joins the Tiber at Umbertide.
On its banks, 4 km (2 miles)
northwest of Montone, is the
splendid Rocca d'Aries, a fortress
with Byzantine origins. It was
renovated in the Renaissance
era and restored in the 1990s,
and is now open for concerts
and exhibitions. It offers
marvellous views over the
Valle del Carpina.

A narrow, paved street in the heart of Montone

❾ Umbertide

Perugia. **Road Map** C2. 🏚 17,000.
🚂 FCU Perugia–Sansepolcro line.
🚌 ℹ️ IAT Alta Valle del Tevere, Via
Cibo 26, 075 941 7099.
🌐 **umbertideturismo.it**

One of the principal centres
of the Upper Tiber Valley,
Umbertide is of ancient origin,
dating back to the 6th century
BC, and was probably founded
by the Etruscans. The town,
skirted to the west by the
Tiber, frequently found itself
at the centre of wars and
suffered the resulting
destruction and sackings.
In 1863, the town's traditional
name of Fratta was replaced
by the name Umbertide in
honour of the sons of Umberto
Ranieri, who rebuilt the city
after the devastation caused
by the Lombard invasions of
AD 790.

Much more recently,
the centre of the old
town was badly
damaged by
bombardments
during World War II
(1944). Even so,
many important
buildings survive.
Two of these
overlook the vast
Piazza Mazzini, northwest of the
town centre: La Rocca (1385), a
fortress inserted into the walls
and now a centre for contemporary
art, and the church of
Santa Maria della Reggia, begun
in the second half of the
16th century and built on an
octagonal plan. The design
was by Galeazzo Alessi and
Giulio Danti. Inside, among
the canvases that decorate the

The square and circular towers of the Rocca of Umbertide

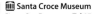
The octagonal Santa Maria
della Reggia

tambour (the wall below the
dome), note the one above the
organ, an *Ascension to Heaven*
by Pomarancio (1578).

Other important works to
be found in the town's
churches include a fresco
by Pinturicchio (1504), in
the lunette of the
doorway to the church
of Santa Maria della
Pietà (north of the
old town, outside
the walls), and,
in particular, a
Deposition by Luca
Signorelli in the
Baroque church
of **Santa Croce**, in
the southern (and
oldest) part of the town, in
Piazza San Francesco. Due
to the importance of the
Signorelli painting – it is the
only one by the Cortona
artist still to be found in its
original setting – the church is
now a museum. In the same
square are two other churches:
San Francesco (13th–14th
centuries) and San Bernardino
(18th century).

🏛️ **Santa Croce Museum**
Piazza San Francesco. **Tel** 075 942
0147. **Open** 10:30am–1pm, 3–5:30pm
Fri–Sun. **Closed** 1 Jan, 25 Dec. 🔲 🔲

Environs
The countryside around
Umbertide is scattered with
fortifications, lasting evidence
of the region's great strategic
military importance. Along the
road to Preggio, 15 km (9 miles)
southwest of Umbertide, is
the Rocca di Preggio, one of
the principal strongholds in
the area, dating from the
10th century. Also of note
along this route are the castles
of Romeggio and Polgeto.

A short distance east of
Umbertide, towards Gubbio,
look out for the privately-
owned Castello di Civitella
Ranieri (15th century), which
is one of the most complete
and best-preserved examples
of military architecture in the
area. Nearby, but higher up,
is the splendid Castello di
Serra Partucci.

Just north of Umbertide,
along the Città di Castello road,
you can see the tall tower of
another castle, the Castello
di Montalto.

A couple of kilometres
south of town, along the River
Tiber, a road climbs up to
the Badia Monte Corona, a
Romanesque abbey with
a beautiful underground crypt.
Climbing still higher, you reach
the 16th-century hermitage
and pretty village of San
Giuliana, set in a panoramic
position, and restored to its
medieval appearance.

Santa Croce and San Francesco churches in Umbertide

❹ Gubbio

The sight of Gubbio, built from local stone at the foot of Monte Ingino, is one of the most famous images of medieval Umbria. Founded by the Umbri, the town holds the famous Eugubine Tablets, seven bronze slabs that survived from the ancient city of Iguvium; they were engraved in the 2nd century BC with text in the local language describing rites and sacred sites. Under the Romans the town spread onto the plain, but after the Lombards invaded the people returned to the slopes, where they could defend themselves more effectively. A walled city, including the monumental Palazzo dei Consoli, was built here in the Middle Ages. At the end of the 14th century, the city, by now powerful and rich, passed to the Montefeltro of Urbino. In 1624 Gubbio, like the Duchy of Urbino, came under papal rule.

The well-preserved 1st-century arcades of the Roman theatre

Exploring Gubbio

The easiest route into Gubbio is by the road from the south, which also provides a chance to admire the town as a whole, as it spreads out in horizontal swathes against the slopes of Monte Ingino. Before climbing up to explore one of the best-preserved medieval cities in the world, take a look at the ruins of the Roman city, which, during the stability of the *pax romana*, developed on the flat land below the slopes.

🏛 Roman Ruins

Via del Teatro Romano.
The first Roman monument that you see as you arrive in Gubbio from the south is a mausoleum, a monumental tomb of which the burial chamber has survived with its barrel vault. Further on, not far from Piazza Quaranta Martiri, are the ruins of the Roman theatre (Teatro Romano), which dates from the 1st

century. It could accommodate around 6,000 spectators, and was faced in squared and rusticated blocks. Among other works uncovered over the last two centuries of excavations are some beautiful mosaics.

🏛 Piazza Quaranta Martiri

This broad square is the principal point of arrival in Gubbio, as well as the best place to leave a car. It is dedicated to the 40 local people executed by the Germans in 1944 in an act of vengeance against the partisans. The lowest point in Gubbio, the piazza is a good place from which to gaze upwards to admire the full extent of the town.

Gubbio's finest church, San Francesco, dominates the piazza. Its construction was begun in the mid-1200s and continued at least until the end of that century (though the façade was never finished). Inside are three aisles without a transept.

There is a fresco cycle by Ottaviano Nelli in the apse chapel on the left (*Scenes from the Life of Mary*, c.1408–13). The frescoes in the central apse, by an unknown artist, can be dated to around 1275, but they are badly damaged.

On the opposite side of the piazza is the Antico Ospedale (Old Hospital) of Santa Maria della Misericordia, a 14th-century building, with a long portico in front, surmounted by a loggia, added in the 17th century by the wool merchants' guild, which used the premises for some of its processing. Nearby stands the church of Santa Maria dei Laici, dating back to 1313 and now restored.

🏛 San Giovanni Battista

Via della Repubblica. **Open** daily.
From Piazza Quaranta Martiri, the steep Via della Repubblica leads to the base of the great structure supporting Piazza Grande (*see p65*). Heading up this street, visitors enter the oldest part of the medieval city, where the first cathedral, dedicated to San Mariano, is believed to have stood. What is now the church dedicated to San Giovanni Battista (St John the Baptist) probably occupies the site of the old cathedral.

This church, built in the 13th and 14th centuries, has a Gothic façade with a Romanesque bell tower. The Gothic style continues inside, with characteristic coupled

Gubbio, clinging to the lower slopes of Monte Ingino

The church of San Giovanni Battista, with Palazzo dei Consoli behind

VISITORS' CHECKLIST

Practical Information
Perugia. **Road Map** D2.
32,000. Via della Repubblica 15, 075 922 0693. Corsa dei Ceri, 15 May; Palio della Balestra, last Sun in May.
comune.gubbio.pg.it

Transport
Fossato di Vico, 20 km (12 miles), Roma–Ancona line, 892 021.

columns and great arches in stone. The single-nave church culminates in a squared apse.

San Domenico
Piazza G. Bruno. **Open** daily.
Returning to Piazza Quaranta Martiri, turn into Via Cavour to enter the old quarter of San Martino, which is built on both sides of the River Camignano.

At the heart of this district, in Piazza Bruno, is the church of San Domenico, which was built by the Dominicans in the 14th century on the site of a 12th-century church dedicated to San Martino. The appearance of the interior dates primarily from a period of restoration during the 18th century, but 16th-century frescoes from the Gubbio school remain; there is also a fine lectern decorated with inlaid wood.

Via Gabrielli
This street, lined with medieval houses, runs north from Piazza Bruno to Porta Metauro. Near the end is the small but impressive Palazzo del Capitano del Popolo, whose façade curves in line with the road. Adorned with a series of small Gothic windows, the palazzo is a typical Gubbio construction from the late 13th century. Nearby is the park attached to the Palazzo Ranghiaschi Brancaleoni. Laid out in the mid-1800s, the garden extends south along the slopes of Monte Ingino as far as the Palazzo Ducale. There is a Neo-Classical temple here.

Sculpture on the tower of Palazzo Ranghiaschi Brancaleoni

Gubbio Town Centre

1. Roman Ruins
2. Piazza Quaranta Martiri
3. San Giovanni Battista
4. San Domenico
5. Via Gabrielli
6. Largo del Bargello
7. *Palazzo dei Consoli*
8. Palazzo Pretorio
9. Duomo
10. Palazzo Ducale
11. Via XX Settembre
12. Corso Garibaldi

0 metres 250
0 yards 250

For keys to symbols *see back flap*

Gubbio: Palazzo dei Consoli

This superb building, begun in 1332, looks over Piazza Grande and is supported on the west side by an impressive row of arched buttresses. The entrance doorway, approached by a fan-shaped flight of steps, is a masterly example of the Gothic style and is decorated with a lunette representing the *Madonna and Saints John the Baptist and Ubaldo*, patron saint of the city. The palazzo houses the Museo Civico and an art gallery. From the loggia there are fine views over the city and countryside around.

VISITORS' CHECKLIST

Practical Information
Piazza Grande. **Tel** 075 927 4298.
Open 10am–1pm, 3–6pm (Nov–Mar: 10am–1pm, 2–5pm) daily.
Closed 1 Jan, 13–15 May,
25 Dec. 🅿

The tower is crowned with battlements and has four apertures echoing the form of the windows below.

Madonna and Child
This fresco by Mello da Gubbio from 1340–50 is one of the works on display in the Pinacoteca Civica (art gallery) on the first floor.

Arches, supporting the palazzo on the hill

The windows are set in pairs and decorated with a toothed cornice, which runs above the arches and unifies them.

Museo Civico, situated on the ground floor

In the Sala dell'Arengo, a magnificent room which occupies the entire floor area of the building, popular assemblies were held in the 14th century. Today fragments and stone tablets are displayed below.

Eugubine Tablets
These inscriptions in the old Umbrian language are on display in the Museo Civico. They provide crucial evidence of life in the region before the Roman conquest.

The Fontana dei Matti in Largo del Bargello

Largo del Bargello

About halfway along Via dei Consoli, which connects the San Martino quarter and Piazza Grande, the street broadens out to form Largo del Bargello, the centre of the ancient quarter of San Giuliano. In front of the 14th-century palazzo, after which the square is named, is the small Fontana dei Matti: tradition has it that in order to be defined as mad (*matto*), people had to run around the fountain three times bathing themselves in the water.

Piazza Grande

Via dei Consoli follows the route of the old Umbrian fortifications before suddenly opening out into Piazza Grande. Quite apart from the importance of the buildings found here, the square

is an extremely impressive piece of engineering: it is, in fact, an artificial space supported by walls and embankments.

In front of the more famous and much larger Palazzo dei Consoli is the Palazzo Pretorio (closed to the public), which was erected in the mid-14th century and designed by the same architect, Gattapone. On the last Sunday in May the traditional Palio della Balestra (involving the crossbowmen of Gubbio and Sansepolcro, over the border in Tuscany), takes place between the two buildings.

Duomo

Via Galeotti. **Open** daily.
From Piazza Grande, Via Galeotti climbs in a series of steps to the cathedral. This was founded in 1229 and enlarged around a century later. The façade has an entrance with an ogival arch and an oculus with bas-reliefs which belonged to the previous church on the site. Inside, the single nave is covered by a very high and distinctive stone "wagon vault", a local architectural speciality. There are many frescoes and other paintings, as well as some fine stained-glass windows.

The medieval Porta Romana

Palazzo Ducale

Via Federico di Montefeltro.
Tel 075 927 5872. **Open** 8:30am–7:30pm Tue–Sun. **Closed** 1 Jan, 25 Dec.

The restored Palazzo Ducale stands right in front of the cathedral. Locally known as the Corte Nuova, it was built by the Montefeltro family after they had taken possession of the town. The palazzo has an interesting archaeological area underground (where it is possible to see traces of the piazza that was here before the palazzo was built) as well as several rooms used for temporary exhibitions.

Via XX Settembre

From Piazza Grande, Via XX Settembre leads past palazzi and churches to the quarter of Sant'Andrea and the Porta Romana. This medieval town gate, with its high tower, houses a collection of majolica pottery and other pieces in various materials, as well as weaponry, maps and so on. Nearby, outside the walls, is the church of Sant'Agostino, which retains traces of frescoes dating back to the church's foundation (1294), as well as several works dating from the 14th century.

A short walk east of the church is the terminal for the funicular up to the Basilica di Sant'Ubaldo, which lies high above the town on Monte Ingino. The ride takes 8 minutes and offers lovely views on the way; there is also a path, if you prefer to go up on foot.

Corso Garibaldi

This street runs parallel with the quarter of Sant'Andrea and is the main thoroughfare through the San Pietro quarter, the busy centre of Gubbio. The narrow streets retain a village atmosphere and are lined with shops. On Corso Garibaldi itself look out for the churches of Santissima Trinità and of San Pietro, of 13th-century origin and built close to a large monastery complex.

The Festa Dei Ceri

The Corsa dei Ceri (candle race), considered within Umbria almost as great a spectacle as Siena's Palio, takes place every year on 15 May. The finishing line is the hilltop basilica of Sant'Ubaldo. The "candles" in question, three in all, are heavy wooden and papier-mâché structures in the form of superimposed prisms, 10 m (33 ft) high and 200 kg (440 lb) in weight. They bear the effigies of Sant'Ubaldo, St George and St Anthony Abbot, patron saints of masons and stonecutters, craftsmen and peasants respectively. The first drumroll is heard at dawn, but the *ceri* are not brought out until noon. The actual race, which attracts huge crowds, takes place in the evening.

Heavy wooden "candles" carried aloft over the crowd

❺ Parco Regionale del Monte Cucco

On the border with the neighbouring region of Le Marche, Monte Cucco is one of the most fascinating peaks in central Italy. Below ground are miles and miles of galleries and caverns, which form one of the most impressive cave systems in Italy: the Grotta di Monte Cucco. The higher altitudes can be reached from the village of Costacciaro, and the windswept terrain attracts devoted fans of hang-gliding. Within the park, which is centred around the village of Sigillo, various hiking trails have been marked out. There are also facilities for various open-air sports. Besides paragliding, the park can arrange exploration of the Forra di Riofreddo gorge (for experts only), and there are also mountain-bike trails and tracks for runners. Many palaeontological and archaeological finds have been discovered in the park, as well as ancient Roman settlements.

Scheggia
From this village of Roman origin it is possible to enter and explore the northern part of the park, with its Benedictine abbeys – in particular, Sant'Emiliano at Isola Fossara and the Hermitage of San Girolamo a Pascelupo.

Costacciaro
Unlike the other villages that surround the park, which are almost all of Roman origin, Costacciaro was built in 1250 by the citizens of Gubbio as a fortified town.

The "Natives" of Monte Cucco

Besides all kinds of opportunities for sport, the Parco Regionale del Monte Cucco is also one of the best places in the Apennines for observing wildlife. In fact, as well as being home to typically Apennine species (such as deer, wild boar, porcupines and martens), the park also harbours other species that are increasingly rare in central Italy, including the wolf, wildcat and golden eagle. Among other birds that can be seen in the park are partridges, quails, eagle owls and kingfishers. Crayfish can also be found in the rivers.

Wildcat

Golden eagle

0 kilometres 2
0 miles 1

Urbino

Aiale

Ponte Calcara

S360

Scheggia

Gubbio

Campitello

S3

Costa San Savino

Caprile

Costacciaro

Scirca

Summit of Monte Cucco
At 1,566m (5,136ft), Monte Cucco is one of the highest peaks in Umbria. It can be reached fairly easily along the scenic Via del Ranco, which leads out of Sigillo.

Key

▨ Major road

▨ Minor road

▨ Scenic route

Grotta di Monte Cucco
This cave can be reached on foot from the car park just beyond Val di Ranco. The cave reaches the record depth of 922 m (3,024 ft) and the water that gathers within the mountain emerges, after a lengthy subterranean journey, at the Scirca spring near Sigillo.

KEY

① **At Scirca**, ruins of a large Roman settlement have been uncovered. In the village, the old church of Santa Maria Assunta is decorated with frescoes by Matteo da Gualdo.

② **La Valdorbia**

③ **The Badia di Sitria** is an abbey with an interesting Romanesque church (Santa Maria) with a single nave and a barrel vault. The crypt is held up at the centre by a Roman column with a Corinthian capital.

④ **The Forra di Riofreddo**, is a deep, narrow gorge, which can only be tackled by experienced climbers. It was formed after many centuries of erosion by streams coming down from the mountain top.

Sigillo
Home to the park administration, this village has visible Roman origins, in the bridges on the Via Flaminia and over the Scirca torrent. Of note are the church of Sant'Agostino, in the heart of the village, and Sant'Anna, near the cemetery, with frescoes by Matteo da Gualdo.

For keys to symbols *see back flap*

❻ Gualdo Tadino

Perugia. **Road Map** D3. 🔼 15,000.
🚊 Foligno–Ancona line. 🚌 Piazza
Orti Mavarelli. 🛈 Associazione Pro
Tadino, Piazza Martiri della Libertà,
075 9150 263. 🌐 **protadino.it**

Gualdo Tadino, a town
of ancient Umbrian and
Roman origins, endured
a tormented history of
defeats, destruction
and emigration until
the 12th century, when
it was resettled on its
present site. The name
is a combination of the
Roman name *Tadinum*
and the Lombard word
wald, meaning forest.

As a commune, the
village took shape in
the Middle Ages, but
was heavily modified
over the course of the
centuries and today
bears only a few traces of its
centuries-old history. Gualdo
suffered terrible damage during
the 1997 earthquake, but
has now been almost totally
restored. The town is still, as
it was in the Middle Ages and
later centuries, one of the
principal centres of majolica
manufacture in Umbria.

The only ancient gate to
survive in Gualdo is that of
San Benedetto, on the eastern
side: from here, Corso Italia
(which becomes Corso Piave)
cuts through the whole of the
historic centre. Walking along
this street, you reach Piazza XX
Settembre, home to the
churches of San Donato (12th
century) and Santa Maria dei
Raccomandati (13th century).
The latter contains a fine
triptych by Matteo da Gualdo
of the *Madonna with Child and
saints Sebastian and Roch*, but
is closed to the public.

Further along, on Corso Piave,
is the church of San Francesco,
built by the Franciscans in the
13th and 14th centuries. It has
a beautiful façade, with an
elegant Gothic doorway, and
inside are many frescoes, most
of which are the work of Matteo
da Gualdo (1435–1507), the
best-known artist native to
Gualdo Tadino, whose works

**Fresco on a palazzo
in the centre
of Gualdo**

can also be seen in Assisi and
Spoleto. The fresco on the first
pilaster on the left, of *St Anne,
the Virgin and Child*, is said to
be the oldest work by the artist.
You soon arrive at the central
Piazza Martiri della Libertà, better
known to the residents of
Gualdo as Piazza Grande,
and where the town's
most important
buildings are found.
Lording it over the
space is the Palazzo
Comunale. The original,
12th-century palazzo
was rebuilt after a
terrible earthquake in
1751, so what is seen
now is its 18th-century
form. Most of the
town's medieval
buildings collapsed
during the same
earthquake, and the
Palazzo del Podestà
(13th century), in front of the
Palazzo Comunale, was
also badly damaged.
An international
ceramics exhibition
and competition is
held annually in the
Palazzo del Podestà,
which brings dozens
of ceramic workers
back to Gualdo, a centre
for the manufacture
of lustreware.

The cathedral of San
Benedetto stands on the
eastern side of Piazza Martiri.
The façade, dating from the
13th century but carefully
restored after the earthquake,
has three doors – one for each
of the aisles inside – and a
beautiful rose window. The
interior was entirely rebuilt in
the 19th century, and has

**Detail of a
fountain**

20th-century frescoes.
Outside, to the left, stands a
lovely Renaissance fountain.
The only building that
remained intact after the
earthquake, and that is still
visible in the piazza today,
is the Torre Civica.

In common with many other
villages in this part of Umbria,
Gualdo Tadino has a fortress at
the top of the hill. The origins
of the **Rocca Flea** date back to
the 10th century, when the
construction of fortifications
began on the site of a church,
of which several frescoes have
been uncovered. Today, the
sizeable fortress has more than
40 rooms – the result of a series
of enlargements and restoration
work carried out over the
centuries. In particular, the
buildings show the influence
of Frederick II, who restored
and made improvements to
the castle during the 13th
century, and also of the
Perugians, who made
changes in the
following century.
The Rocca, which
has reopened after
several years of closure,
houses a Pinacoteca
(art gallery), a ceramics
gallery and a collection
of archaeological finds.
The former has on display
detached frescoes by Matteo da
Gualdo as well as works by
Jacopo Palma, Antonio da
Fabriano and Niccolò Alunno.

🏛 Rocca Flea

Piazza della Rocca. **Tel** 075 914
2445. **Open** Jun–Sep: 10am–1pm,
3–7pm; Oct–May: 10am–1pm,
3–6pm. **Closed** 1 Jan, 25 Dec.
🈲 📷

The fortified bulk of Rocca Flea, guarding the town

Environs

About 7 km (4 miles) north of Gualdo Tadino is Fossato di Vico, a town that is divided into two parts: Fossato Basso, the largely modern town along the road, and Fossato Alto, the remnants of a major medieval settlement perched on a rocky spur. It is worth stopping off along the road between the two parts, at the church of San Benedetto, in order to see the frescoes by Matteo da Gualdo.

In the heart of Fossato Basso are covered walkways and the Cappella della Piaggiola, with frescoes by Ottaviano Nelli and his school (early 15th century).

Nocera Umbra, largely rebuilt after the 1997 earthquake

Porta Vecchia, ancient entrance to the old centre of Nocera Umbra

❼ Nocera Umbra

Perugia. **Road Map** D3. 🔼 6,000.
🚉 Nocera Scalo, 3 km (2 miles),
Rome–Ancona line. ℹ️ Pro Loco, Via
San Rinaldo 9, 334 845 0320. 🎭 Palio
dei Quartieri, first Tue in Aug.
🅆 nocerainumbria.it

The collapse of the Torre di Nocera Umbra, now rebuilt, during the earthquake of 1997 was an enduring image of that tragic natural disaster. The town has been hit by earthquakes on a number of occasions, but never with such ferocity. The structural damage affected the whole of the historic centre, formerly one of the best-preserved in the region. Even now, only a small number of inhabitants have returned. Yet Nocera Umbra is a hive of activity – houses are being

rebuilt, while historic buildings are gradually being restored. The symbolic tower has already been reconstructed.

High on a rocky outcrop that looms over fertile valleys drained by the Topino and Caldognola rivers, Nocera Umbra has always occupied a strategically significant location, thanks partly to the town's position on the border of Le Marche and to its proximity to the Adriatic Sea. Originally an ancient Umbrian town (called Nuokria), it was an important settlement under both the Romans and the Lombards. The waters that gush from the many springs in the area are known for their curative properties.

Most of the important buildings in Nocera Umbra are still closed for safety reasons, including the Duomo, on the top of the hill. The same is true of the historic centre, although visitors are allowed access to the heart of the old town, Piazza Caprera. The former church of

San Francesco, now home to the Pinacoteca Comunale and Museo Civico, can be found on this square at No. 5. It is open Tuesdays to Sundays from April to September, and at weekends during the rest of the year. It is also worth going as far as the western walls to the church of San Filippo, a Neo-Gothic structure from the late 19th century. This marks the start of the Portici di San Filippo, a covered walkway within the walls, which has apertures and arrow-slits that enable visitors to admire the views.

Environs

The peak of Monte Pennino (1,571 m/5,155 ft), on the Le Marche border, is reachable from Nocera Umbra by car along 20 km (12 miles) of tortuous road (asphalted, apart from the last stretch). This mountain, as well as being a very scenic place to visit, has facilities for hiking and skiing.

The Waters of Nocera

The therapeutic quality of the mineral water springs in the Nocera area has been known since the 16th century; in the 18th century the water was used as a benchmark for measuring the purity of other waters. However, it wasn't until the 20th century that the spring waters began to be exploited for economic and industrial use, through the building of bottling plants and spas. The two main springs are at Bagni di Nocera and at Schiagni (Fonte del Cacciatore). Their curative powers derive from the combination of a water that is particularly pure and mineral-rich in itself, and the clay typical of this terrain.

The modern spa at Bagni di Nocera

❽ Parco Regionale del Monte Subasio

In outline, Monte Subasio (1,290 m/4,230 ft) has a distinctively rounded form. It rises, isolated, between the historic centres of Assisi, Spello and Nocera Umbra and, since 1995, has formed the southern margin of a 7,442-ha (18,390-acre) regional park. As well as its own natural beauty, Monte Subasio offers superb views across to the high Appenines in the east. The park also includes many places of historic and religious significance. Subasio's distinctive rose-coloured stone was used to build much of Assisi, which lies right on the fringes of the park. The mountain was regarded as a sacred place in the 10th century BC, and its importance endured during the life of St Francis, who perhaps drew inspiration from these magical and mystical surroundings.

Monte Subasio
The summit of Monte Subasio is easily reached and seems to offer a view of the whole of Umbria. To the southeast are the sink-holes known as "*mortaro grande*" and "*mortaro piccolo*", cavities which were once used for collecting ice.

Eremo delle Carceri
Around 4 km (2 miles) from Assisi, this small and peaceful hermitage is surrounded by dense woodland. The name (Hermitage of the Prisons) derives from the fact that Franciscan friars used to "lock themselves away" here in order to pray: there is still a 15th-century church here, as well as a cave where St Francis would go to rest. Beyond the hermitage is a bridge that leads to a wood containing a series of caves and hermitages used in the Middle Ages by the devout and by friars.

KEY

① **I Prati degli Stazzi**, on the road between the Eremo delle Carceri and the peak, offer fine views over Assisi. In May, the fields are carpeted in flowers.

② **The northern road**, leaves Assisi near Cà Piombino, base for the park administration. Before winding its way south towards Spello, the road goes through the small historic centres of Armenzano, San Giovanni and Collepino.

③ **The Abbey of San Silvestro**, dates from the 11th century. According to tradition, it was built by San Romualdo, founder of the Camaldolese order.

Piano di Pieve

Téscio

S444

Assisi •

S147

Perugia

Montesubasio 1,290m

San Damiano

San Vitale

Road to the summit
Between Assisi and Spello the road retraces the route of an ancient cart track. A lovely scenic road, it leads almost to the peak of Monte Subasio. On the descent towards Spello, the road passes the sanctuary of the Madonna della Spella.

0 kilometres   2

0 miles   2

Key

▨ Minor road

▨ Scenic route

Rocca di Postignano

Within the park is the ancient fortification of Rocca Postignano, as well as several churches that were built on the site of places where hermits once prayed.

VISITORS' CHECKLIST

Practical Information
Perugia. **Road Map** C2. *i* Loc Cà Piombino, 06081 Assisi, 075 815 5290. Fax: 075 815 307. **w** parks.it or **montesubasio.it**

Transport
FS Santa Maria degli Angeli, Assisi, Foligno–Terontola line, 892021.
APM Assisi–Eremo delle Carceri, 800 512 141.

Wildlife on Monte Subasio

A pair of porcupines

The slopes of the mountain are today covered with three different kinds of vegetation. Olive trees are grown on land stretching from Assisi as far as Spello. Other areas support mixed woodland, including oak, black hornbeam, ash, maple, beech and holm oak. Forests of resiniferous trees, the result of replanting, characterize the third type of vegetation, along with meadow pasture. This range of natural habitats does not support a wide variety of wildlife, however, despite a ban on hunting lasting several decades: the golden eagle has not been seen since the 1960s. Current wildlife sightings include the partridge, wood pigeon, magpie, jay, wildcat, squirrel, porcupine, badger, wolf, weasel, stone marten and wild boar. Birds of prey seen here include the buzzard and goshawk.

Bandita Cilleni

Santa Maria Lignano

Castello di Armenzano

During the Middle Ages, this place was fortified because it occupied a strategic position. Today, the village offers peace and fine views.

Armenzano •

Nocera Umbra

San Giovanni •

③

Madonna della Spella

Collepino •

Spello

Collepino

About 10 km (6 miles) from the peak of Monte Subasio, this walled medieval village stands isolated near the source of the river Chiona.

For keys to symbols *see back flap*

❾ Assisi

Even without the churches, extraordinary frescoes and associations with St Francis, it would be worth coming to Assisi simply to witness a sunset. As the sun sinks, the medieval centre of Assisi, one of the best-preserved in the world, is bathed in a warm glow. Founded by the Umbrians, Assisi was prominent during the Roman era, but the town achieved greatest fame and importance during the era of the communes in the Middle Ages. By the time the Basilica of San Francesco was founded in the 13th century, Assisi, built using the reddish stone of Monte Subasio to which the town owes its distinctive coloration, had already taken shape. In the 14th century, when Assisi came under papal rule, two fortresses were built. Over the following centuries, the city changed little. Even today, the town has a timeless fascination.

Façade of the Basilica di San Francesco

Palazzo del Capitano del Popolo

Temple of Minerva

Basilica of San Francesco
(see pp76–7)

VIA PORTICA

PIAZZA D
COMUN

Monastery of San Giuseppe

VIA BANDA DA QUINTAVAL

VIA PORTA MOIAN

VIA PORTA MOIANC

Santa Maria Maggiore
This church was Assisi's first cathedral. Its Romanesque origins are clear from its formal simplicity.

Porta Moiano

Palazzo Vescovile is where Francis renounced all worldly goods. The bishop's palace was entirely rebuilt in the 17th century.

Piazza del Comune
This square has always been the heart of Assisi. Around the piazza are the Temple of Minerva (1st century BC), Palazzo del Capitano del Popolo (13th century), the Torre del Popolo (13th–14th century) and Palazzo dei Priori (14th century).

VISITORS' CHECKLIST

Practical Information
Perugia. **Road Map** D4.
🗺 29,000. ℹ️ Piazza del Comune 10, 075 813 8680.
🎭 Calendimaggio, 4–6 May.

Transport
🚉 Assisi (Piazza Matteotti); Santa Maria degli Angeli (Piazza Garibaldi), Foligno–Terontola line, 892 021 🚌 APM, 800 512 141.

Santa Maria delle Rose

VIA SANTA MARIA DELLE ROSE

VIA SAN RUFINO

CORSO MAZZINI

VIA SAN GABRIELE DELL'ADDOLORATA

★ **Duomo**
The present building was begun in the 12th century. The beautiful Romanesque façade, with its rose windows, dates from this time. It was here that saints Francis and Clare were baptized, and perhaps Emperor Frederick II, too.

At the base of the cathedral apse and bell tower, courses of Roman blocks are visible.

| 0 metres | 100 |
| 0 yards | 100 |

The Chiesa Nuova (17th century) was built where the house of the father of St Francis, Pietro di Bernardone, is thought to have stood.

PIAZZA SANTA CHIARA

Porta Nuova

The convent alongside the basilica still contains the crypt of the ancient little church of San Giorgio, in the cloister.

★ **Basilica di Santa Chiara**
This church was built shortly after the Basilica di San Francesco. As well as the remains of St Clare, it contains prized works of art and the famous Byzantine Crucifix of San Damiano.

Exploring Assisi

The draw of Assisi's famous Basilica can be overpowering, but there is much else to explore in the town. Motorists would do best to leave their car in the huge car park in Largo Properzio, just outside the walls, and to enter the historic centre through Porta Nuova, on the southeastern side of town. From here, Via Borgo Aretino leads to Assisi's first great building, the basilica of Santa Chiara. This lies in the heart of a medieval quarter, which is linked by steep streets to the upper town, dating from Roman times and home to the Duomo and Piazza del Comune. From this central piazza, continue along Via Seminario and Via San Francesco, lined with medieval buildings, to reach the great basilica of St Francis *(see pp76–7)*.

Baptismal font in the cathedral of San Rufino

The door and rose window of the basilica of Santa Chiara

⬆ Santa Chiara

Piazza Santa Chiara. **Tel** 075 812 282. **Open** 6:30am–noon, 2–7pm (6pm in winter).

Assisi's second great church was begun in 1257, and consecrated eight years later by Pope Clement IV: the body of St Clare (declared a saint in 1255), founder of the order of the Poor Clares, was buried here in 1260.

The façade has a simple doorway with a rose window above, while the side that faces the street is supported by three vast buttresses. The church is distinctive because of the use of alternating layers of white and red stone, as seen in some Tuscan churches.

The interior is in the form of a Latin cross, simple and spare. In the right transept there is a cycle of frescoes depicting *Scenes from the Life of St Clare*, by an unknown artist called the

Master of Santa Chiara (late 13th century). Other interesting frescoes, from the 14th century, can be found on the left wall, while on the right, in the Oratorio delle Reliquie, there is the late 12th-century wooden Crucifix of San Damiano. According to the hagiography, this is the crucifix that famously spoke to Francis in San Damiano, asking him to "repair his church" *(see p84)*.

⬆ Duomo (San Rufino)

Piazza San Rufino. **Tel** 075 816 016, 075 812 283. **Open** summer: 8am–1pm, 2–6pm daily; winter: 8am–1pm, 3–7pm daily (holy week, Aug & the day before public hols: 7am–7pm).

From Santa Chiara, a climb up stepped streets leads to the duomo, built on a Roman religious site in around 1029 by Archbishop Ugone, and then rebuilt in the 12th–13th centuries. The church was consecrated in 1253, the year construction was completed, by Pope Innocent IV.

Less well-known than the other basilicas of Assisi, the cathedral is worth a visit just for its splendid façade, a masterpiece of Umbrian Romanesque. It is divided into three horizontal sections. At ground level are three doors decorated with lions, with bas-relief lunettes; above, divided from the lower level by a band of sculpted corbels, are three rose windows with symbols of the Evangelists. At the top is a triangular tympanum with a Gothic arch. To one side, rising above the scene, is the bell tower, part of the 11th-century church and with double-mullioned windows.

The interior, laid out on a rectangular plan, dates from the 16th century. It still has the old baptismal font where both St Francis and St Clare were baptized, a wooden choir dating from the 16th century and the underground Franciscan oratory, where the saint would withdraw before preaching to the crowd. The Cappella del Sacramento, by Giacomo Giorgetti, is a Baroque composition on the

The town of Assisi, with its walls and fortifications, from Monte Subasio

theme of the Eucharist. Adjacent to the church is the Museo della Cattedrale (cathedral museum), which contains pieces from the original church, a series of frescoes from the Oratorio di San Rufinuccio and paintings from various churches in Assisi. To the left of the church are the ruins of a Roman theatre and, a little further north, those of an amphitheatre. In the church courtyard a plaque shows the site of the house where St Clare was born.

Piazza del Comune

From the cathedral, heading along Via di San Rufino, you reach the square that has always been the true heart of the city. It was created in its current form in the 13th century. The main focus of the piazza is the **Temple of Minerva**, built in the 1st century BC on a set of terraces that once marked the centre of the town. This beautifully preserved Roman temple has changed function at various times over the centuries: first a church, then a group of shops, then seat of the town hall until, in 1456, it finally became a church again, with the name of Santa Maria sopra Minerva.

On the left of the temple portico is the Palazzo del Capitano del Popolo, built in the 13th century and extensively restored in the 20th century. At the foot of the bell tower (Torre del Popolo), you can see the 14th-century measures for bricks, tiles and fabrics then in use in Assisi, set into the wall. On the opposite side of the piazza is the Palazzo dei Priori, begun in 1275 and completed in the late 15th century. On the right is the Arco della Volta Pinta, with 16th-century frescoes. The Fonte di Piazza, at the far end of the square, is an 18th-century fountain built on the foundations of a 13th-century water basin.

A brief descent through the Arco dei Priori leads to the 17th-century **Chiesa Nuova**, which was commissioned by Philip III of Spain to mark the spot where St Francis was said to have been born.

Temple of Minerva
Piazza del Comune. **Tel** 075 812 268. **Open** 7:15am–7pm Mon–Sat; 8:15am–7pm Sun & public hols. **Closed** 2–5:15pm Tue, Fri.

Chiesa Nuova
Piazzetta Chiesa Nuova. **Tel** 075 812 339. **Open** 6:30am–noon, 2:30–6pm (winter: 5pm).

Museo and Foro Romano
Via Portica 2. **Tel** 075 815 5077. **Open** Mar–Oct: 10am–1pm, 2–6pm daily; Nov–Feb: 10am–1pm, 2:30–5pm (Jun–Aug: till 7pm) daily.

On the corner of Piazza del Comune, beyond the Arco del Seminario – the ancient limit of the walled city in the Roman era – is a museum of Roman finds. From the museum, visitors can gain access to the ruins of what may have been the Roman forum, beneath the Piazza del Comune.

Via San Francesco
Heading towards the Basilica di San Francesco, you cover the whole length of Via del Seminario, which becomes Via San Francesco. Along the way you pass the Palazzo Giacobetti (17th century) and, opposite, the delightful **Oratorio dei Pellegrini** (15th century), once part of a

The Loggia dei Maestri Comacini, on Via San Francesco

pilgrim's hospice, followed by the arches of the Portico del Monte Frumentario, part of a 13th-century hospital. Next comes the Palazzo Vallemani, which is the temporary home of the **Pinacoteca Comunale**; the art gallery's most important work is probably the *Madonna in Maestà* (Giotto school), found near the entrance. A little further along is the Loggia dei Maestri Comacini, a 13th-century *palazzetto* which, according to tradition, was the seat of the Lombard rulers; it is adorned with 15th-century coats of arms. Nearby, the steep Vicolo di Sant'Andrea climbs up to the Piazza di Santa Margherita, from where there are classic views towards the Basilica di San Francesco. It is especially moving at sunset or at dawn.

Madonna in Maestà

Oratorio dei Pellegrini
Via San Francesco 13. **Tel** 075 812 267. **Open** 10am–noon, 4–6pm Tue–Sat.

Pinacoteca Comunale
Palazzo Vallemani, Via San Francesco 12. **Tel** 075 815 5234. **Open** Mar–Oct: 10am–1pm, 2:30–6pm (till 7pm Jun–Aug); Nov–Feb: 10:30am–1pm, 2–5pm.

The late Renaissance façade of the Chiesa Nuova

Assisi: Basilica di San Francesco

St Francis died on 4 October 1226. Just 18 months later Frate Elia, Vicar-General of the Franciscan Order, was charged by Pope Gregory IX with building a church dedicated to the saint. After the laying of the first stone, the Lower Church was the first part to take shape; the Upper Church was eventually built on top of it. The basilica was consecrated by Pope Innocent IV in 1253, though the chapel of Santa Caterina, the final stage in the basilica's construction, was not completed until 1367. Some of the greatest artists of the age, including Cimabue and Giotto, left their mark on the building. On 26 September 1997, a severe earthquake badly damaged the church: part of the vault collapsed and cracks appeared in the transept. Just two years later, however, the basilica reopened for visits and worship, the culmination of an exceptional feat of restoration.

★ **Quattro Vele**
The celebrated allegorical frescoes of the Quattro Vele (vault above the altar), in the Lower Church, represent *The Three Virtues of St Francis*. Long attributed to Giotto, they are now thought to be the work of one of his assistants. A detail of the *Allegory of Obedience* is shown here.

KEY

① **The Tomb of St Francis**, in the crypt, was discovered only in 1818. The exact location had never been revealed for fear that someone might want to seize such a precious relic. The remains of the saint were transferred here in 1230, before the basilica was finished.

② **The wooden choir**, situated in the apse and on the sides next to the crossing, is an example of Gothic Renaissance engraving and inlaid wood, the work of Domenico Indovini.

③ **The walls of the transept**, are decorated with an outstanding cycle of frescoes painted by Cimabue and his assistants. The Crucifixion in the left transept is superb.

④ **The façade**, is an example of Italian Gothic. It has a double rose window in Cosmatesque style and a double door.

⑤ **The Cappella di San Martino**, the first on the left in the Lower Church, was decorated by Simone Martini (1312–1320). His frescoes, depicting several saints and a cycle illustrating the *Life of St Martin*, are true masterpieces.

★ **Frescoes in the Crossing**
The left side of the crossing was decorated by Pietro Lorenzetti in 1515–20. This is one of two portraits of the *Madonna and Child*.

Frescoes in the Nave
The vault in the nave is decorated with frescoes by various masters, one of whom may have been the young Giotto. The vault in the first bay represents the Four Doctors of the Church working in their studies, each with an assistant. St Augustine is shown here.

Interior of the Upper Church
The bright, soaring, single-nave Upper Church is typical of Franciscan monastic architecture. It takes the forms of French Gothic, but simplifies them and adds local elements. It was intended to symbolize the asceticism and spirituality that characterized the life of St Francis.

Entrance to the Upper Church

Entrance to the Lower Church

★ Life of St Francis
The frescoes on the lower walls of the nave (1290s), long thought to be by Giotto and his assistants, are now attributed by most specialists to a superb unknown artist, often referred to as the Maestro di San Francesco.

Assisi: The Frescoes in the Basilica

It was not without controversy that Frate Elia erected such a grandiose building to hold the relics of a saint who had preached poverty. It appears that two buildings, one above the other, were envisaged from the very beginning, although the exact date of the commencement of work on the Upper Church is not known. The Lower Church, both smaller and simpler, was to function as the saint's burial place and to accommodate pilgrims, while the Upper Church was for regular worship. The speed with which the work was carried out evidently did not allow for much sculptural decoration, and the vast plain walls seemed designed for impressive cycles of frescoes, on which the greatest painters of the age could work. Together they created one of the finest and most loved monuments in the history of Western art.

Lower Church

Austere and rather gloomy, the Lower Church shows the influence of the Romanesque style. The solemnity is lightened by the wonderfully rich pictorial decoration, which is less famous than the decoration

Detail from the *Deposition*, Pietro Lorenzetti

in the Upper Church, but more representative of Italian art of the time, given the number and quality of the artists who worked here.

Main Frescoes in the Lower Church
Walls
Maestro di San Francesco.
Left: *Stories from the Life of St Francis*; Right: *Scenes from the Passion* (c.1260, much damaged, only half visible).
Quattro Vele (vault above the altar)
Maestro delle Vele.
Apotheosis of St Francis; *Allegory of Obedience*; *Allegory of Poverty*; *Allegory of Chastity* (c.1315–20).
Right Transept
Vaults:
Workshop of Giotto.
Infancy and Adolescence of Jesus (c.1315–20).
West and north walls:
Workshop of Giotto.
Posthumous Miracles of St Francis (c.1320).

East wall:
Cimabue. *Enthroned Madonna with Angels and St Francis* (c.1280); Giotto (?), *Crucifixion* (c.1320); Simone Martini, *Madonna with Child and two Magi Kings* (c.1321–6).
Cappella di San Nicola:
Simone Martini, Giotto.
Saints Francis, Louis of Toulouse, Elizabeth of Hungary, Clare and an Unknown Saint (c.1321–6).

Left Transept
Entirely frescoed by Pietro Lorenzetti and workshop (c.1315–20).
Barrel vault:
Entry into Jerusalem; The Last Supper; Washing of the Feet; Expulsion from the Temple; Ascent to Calvary; Flagellation; Crucifixion.
South wall:
Descent from the Cross; Deposition; Descent into Limbo; Resurrection.
East wall:
Crucifixion; Madonna and Child; St Francis and St John the Evangelist.
West wall:
Death of Judas; St Francis receives the stigmata.
Cappella di San Giovanni Battista:
Madonna with Child and Sts Francis and John the Baptist.
Cappella di San Martino di Tours (first on the left) Entirely frescoed by Simone Martini (c.1321–6). Figures of saints and cycle of frescoes depicting the *Life of St Martin.*

Upper Church

The Upper Church is as airy and light as the Lower Church is low and dark. Its pictorial decoration is divided substantially into two main blocks: the frescoes of the apse, transept and the crossing, by Cimabue and his school; and those of the nave and vaults, where the life of St Francis and episodes from the Old and New Testament are portrayed in one of the world's great masterpieces.

Madonna and Child, Pietro Lorenzetti, detail, Lower Church

◄ The interior of the Upper Church, Basilica di San Francesco, Assisi (pre-1997 earthquake)

Frescoes in the Apse and the Transepts
Cimabue and his school (1280).
Left Transept
Crucifixion; Scenes from the Apocalypse; Michael and the Angels.
Main Apse
Scenes from the Life of the Virgin Mary.
Right Transept
The Apostles.
Crossing
The Evangelists.

Detail, *Dream of the Throne*, from the Life of St Francis cycle

Frescoes in the Nave
Scenes from the Life of St Francis, either by Giotto or the Maestro di San Francesco; the upper register and vaults by Cimabue and others.

Detail from *Miracle of the Spring*, 14th scene, Giotto cycle

Life of St Francis

I	Francis honoured in the piazza
II	Gift of the Cloak
III	Dream of Arms
IV	Prayer in San Damiano
V	Renounces worldly goods
VI	Dream of Innocent I
VII	Approval of the Order
VIII	Apparition in Chariot of Fire
IX	Dream of the Throne
X	Expulsion of Demons from Arezzo
XI	Francis before the Sultan
XII	Francis in ecstasy
XIII	Celebration of Christmas
XIV	Miracle of the Spring
XV	Preaching to the birds
XVI	Death of the Knight
XVII	Prayer before Honorius III
XVIII	Apparition in Arles
XIX	Francis receives the stigmata
XX	Death of Francis
XXI	Apparition of the saint
XXII	Girolamo accepts the truth of the stigmata
XXIII	Poor Clares mourn the saint
XXIV	Canonization
XXV	Dream of Gregory IX
XXVI	Healing of the man from Ilerda
XXVII	Revival of the devout woman
XXVIII	Liberation of Pietro di Alife

Key to Frescoes in the Nave and Vaults

Old Testament
1 Creation of the World
2 Creation of Adam
3 Creation of Eve
4 Original sin
5 Expulsion from Paradise
6 The labours of Adam and Eve
7 Cain and Abel
8 Cain kills Abel
9 Noah builds the Ark
10 Boarding the Ark
11 Sacrifice of Isaac
12 Abraham and the three angels
13 Isaac blessing Jacob
14 Esau before Isaac
15 Joseph thrown into the well by his brothers
16 Joseph forgives his brothers

New Testament
17 Annunciation
18 Visitation
19 Nativity
20 Adoration of the Magi
21 Presentation at the Temple
22 Flight into Egypt
23 Christ among the Doctors
24 Baptism of Christ
25 Marriage at Cana
26 Resurrection of Lazarus
27 Capture of Christ
28 Flagellation
29 Ascent to Golgotha
30 Crucifixion
31 Lament over the dead Christ
32 Maries at the Sepulchre

Monastic Orders

Anyone visiting Umbria, and in particular Assisi, will be aware immediately of the many convents and monasteries belonging to different religious orders, direct descendants of the ministry of St Francis and St Clare. Monastic orders in Europe were born officially in the 6th century, with the drawing up of St Benedict's Rule. Reforms to the Benedictine Order instigated at Cluny in the 10th century gave a great boost to the monastic movement, as did the development of the Cistercian Order two centuries later. St Francis (1182–1226) broke new ground by reacting against the luxury and seclusion of old-fashioned monasticism, with its great abbeys, and instead invited his followers to live a life of poverty and renunciation, ministering to the urban poor. It was very hard to apply such a severe precept to a group, even of monks, which led to the the birth of other Franciscan orders. Three exist today.

A rosary hangs from the white cord tied around the waist.

Cape, detached from the habit, which covers the shoulders.

Cape covering the shoulders, chest and back.

A conventual is never bearded.

Stiff white collar

Black habit

The rosary is made up of 70 beads.

Brown habit

Habit has two vertical pockets at rib level.

Friars wear socks and shoes.

Friars wear leather sandals or wooden clogs.

The Friars Minor

Founded in 1223, the Order of Friars Minor numbers just under 20,000, mainly priests. The monks do not normally have a beard, which is reserved for lone missionaries.

Friars Minor Conventuals

After a lengthy controversy concerning the literal observance of the Rule of St Francis, in 1517 Pope Leo X decided to group together all the small orders that had been generated by Franciscanism. Following this reform, only two orders were recognized: the Friars Minor and the Conventuals. Around 4,500 belong to the latter Order, divided into 675 houses scattered throughout the world.

The cloister of the convent of San Damiano

Poor Clares, Franciscan Nuns and Capuchin Nuns

The origin of the Order of Poor Clares (Clarisse) dates back to when St Clare (Santa Chiara) took the veil, celebrated by St Francis in 1212 at Santa Maria degli Angeli *(see p84)*, when Clare was just a teenager. Having entered a traditional Benedictine convent, she left with a group of sisters and went to the church of San Damiano *(see p84)*, where she decided to follow in the footsteps of St Francis by establishing a female Franciscan Order. The Rule of the Poor Clares was drawn up in 1224 by Francis himself and was observed with rigour by St Clare. Over time, the severity of the original Rule was slightly relaxed. In the 15th century, the establishment of the Reformed Franciscan Order of nuns signalled a return to the earlier, stricter observance, and in 1525 a female branch of the Capuchin Order was founded. The three orders survive to this day.

Robe of St Francis Traditionally regarded as the first robe worn by St Francis, this item of clothing reflects the saint's own rules of poverty and is in keeping with the description that history provides of his renunciation of worldly goods.

The Capuchin always has a beard, once unkempt, but today less neglected.

Pointed hood

There are two pockets within the sleeves.

Brown habit

Capuchin Friars

Seeking a return to the rigour of the traditional Rule of St Francis, in 1525 Matteo da Bascio founded the first house of the Capuchins at Camerino. The Order spread throughout Italy as well as abroad, but its members suffered persecution because of the character of the Friars' rule, which was considered to be too rigid and extreme. Currently, around 11,000 belong to this Franciscan Order (including 70 bishops, 7,300 priests and 3,500 lay members).

Impressive façade of the church of San Pietro

🏛 San Pietro

Piazza San Pietro. **Tel** 075 812 311. **Open** Easter–Nov: 8am–7pm; Nov–Easter: 8am–6pm.

It is just a short walk from Basilica di San Francesco along Via Frate Elia to the church of San Pietro, which was founded, along with the adjacent monastery, by the Benedictines in the 10th century. The existing church dates from the same period as the Basilica of St Francis, and was consecrated in 1254.

The striking Romanesque-Gothic façade was originally decorated with a pediment, taken down in the 19th century. The interior, mainly Romanesque, contains no works of art of note. Its distinguishing features are its sober simplicity and the height of its nave.

🏛 Santa Maria Maggiore

Piazza del Vescovado. **Tel** 075 813 085. **Open** Easter–Nov: 8:30am–7pm, Nov–Easter: 8:30am–5pm.

Walking east from San Pietro, you eventually emerge into Piazza del Vescovado. This square was an important site in the Middle Ages, shown by the presence of the Palazzo Vescovile (Bishop's Palace) and the church of Santa Maria Maggiore, the city cathedral until 1020. The church was probably founded in the 10th century, but was rebuilt in Romanesque form around 1163. From the crypt, which is original, there is access to what is supposed to be the House of Propertius (Casa di Properzio) – "supposed", since the origins of the great Roman poet (c.50–16 BC) are anything but clear. In fact, at least three Umbrian cities – Assisi, Spello and Bevagna – have claimed to be the poet's birthplace.

🏰 Rocca Maggiore

Via della Rocca. **Tel** 328 384 0669. **Open** 10am–dusk daily. **Closed** 1 Jan, 25 Dec.

This well-preserved fortress stands at the northern edge of the city, reached by walking up Via di Porta Perlici from Piazza San Rufino. The panorama, overlooking the Valle del Tescio, the Valle Umbra and Assisi itself, with the façade of the duomo in the foreground, more than compensates for the effort of the climb.

The fortress was built in the 12th century and was used by Duke Corrado di Urslingen (who was tutor to the future Emperor Frederick II). It was destroyed and rebuilt more than once, including by Cardinal Albornoz in 1367, from which period most of what is now visible dates. Later additions include the polygonal tower (1458) and the round tower by the entrance (1553–8).

The striking fortress of the Rocca Maggiore

San Damiano, its formal simplicity suited to such a mystical place

⬆ Sanctuary of San Damiano

Via Padre Antonio Giorgi. **Tel** 075 812 273. **Open** summer: 10am–noon, 2–6pm (winter: 4:30pm); Vespers at 7pm (summer) and 5pm (winter).

From Porta Nuova, a walk of around 15 minutes leads to the Franciscan church of San Damiano, one of the most significant places in the life of St Francis. It was here that, in 1205, the saint said he heard the words: "Francis, go and repair my church which is falling down". According to the great chronicler of Francis' life, Tommaso da Celano, the words were spoken by the Crucifix which is now in Basilica di Santa Chiara (see p74). The building indicated by the crucifix was that of the church of San Damiano. Francis himself, together with a few faithful followers, undertook the restoration.

St Francis brought St Clare to San Damiano; she and her first followers congregated here, and founded the convent in which St Francis composed his *Canticle of the Creatures* (1225). Today, the convent is run by the Order of the Frati Minori Osservanti (Friars Minor).

Besides the spiritual value of the place, the sanctuary is worth a visit from both an architectural and artistic point of view, especially for the old convent rooms: the Oratorio di Santa Chiara, the cloister with frescoes by Eusebio da San Giorgio (1507) and the refectory. A good part of the 13th-century structure of the building can still be seen.

⬆ Santa Maria degli Angeli- Porziuncola

Santa Maria degli Angeli. **Tel** 075 805 11. **Open** summer: 6:15am–7:45pm (Jul–Sep): also 9–11pm); winter: 6:15am–12:30pm, 2–7:45pm; rosary and procession at 9:15pm Sat.

Another place that was dear to Francis is at the bottom of the hill (through Porta San Pietro). Built at the end of the 16th century, the church of Santa Maria degli Angeli (the seventh-largest church in the world) was, in fact, designed to accommodate the buildings of the 11th-century Porziuncola ("the little portion"), the chapel where St Francis lived and which was the centre of the early Franciscan Order. In 1569, Pope Pius IV laid the first stone of the vast Santa Maria, constructed to receive hordes of pilgrims. The project was given to Galeazzo Alessi, and work was concluded more than a century later with the building of the great cupola (1667) and one of the two bell towers. Inside the vast church, beneath the dome, is

The little oratory of the Porziuncola

the old oratory, known as the Cappella della Porziuncola; on the right is the Cappella del Transito, the old infirmary cell where the saint died on 4 October 1226; the door is original. This chapel contains a majolica statue of St Francis by Andrea della Robbia. Also of note is the Cappella del Roseto (chapel of the rose garden), with early 16th-century frescoes by Tiberio d'Assisi. The chapel takes its name from a legend, according to which St Francis rolled naked on the roses in the garden (to mortify his body), only to find that all the thorns immediately vanished.

In the convent there is a small museum, with a painted *Crucifix* by Giunta Pisano (mid-13th century) and a *St Francis* by an unknown artist who later passed into history as the Maestro di San Francesco.

Environs

About 5 km (3 miles) south of Assisi, on the road to Foligno, is the imposing **Santuario di Rivotorto**, built in 1854 in Neo-Gothic style on the site of a stone hut where the first community of Franciscan friars lived briefly, in 1209; St Francis wrote the first set of rules for his Order here. On the façade are the symbols of the Basilica di San Francesco. Also in Rivotorto is the peaceful British and Commonwealth "Assisi War Graves" cemetery.

⬆ Santuario di Rivotorto

Rivotorto di Assisi, 5 km (3 miles). **Tel** 075 806 5432. **Open** 6:45am–12:30pm, 2:30–7pm daily (from 7:30am Sun).

Crucifixion, 1561, fresco by Dono Doni in the duomo of San Rufino

❿ The Franciscan Path of Peace

There are many trails in the Umbrian hills, among them this one, established in 2000. It retraces the journey taken by St Francis in 1206. Along the way, the saint decided to abandon his lay life and discovered the force of his spiritual conversion. The route, which is reasonably easy to walk, links Assisi and Gubbio and not only follows the physical paths trodden by Francis, but also recaptures the future saint's spiritual journey.

Tips for Drivers

ℹ Piazza del Comune 10, Assisi, 075 812 534. Length: 40 km (25 miles). Time needed: 2 days. Stopping-off points: Assisi, Valfabbrica, Gubbio. Lodgings at Vallingegno abbey, 075 920 158.
Ⓦ ilsentierodifrancesco.it

⑥ Abbey of Vallingegno
Another notable spiritual stopping place is the abbey dedicated to San Verecondo, a Benedictine centre from the 11th century, still in good condition. The church, cloister and crypt can be visited.

⑦ Gubbio
Just before the town is the "Vittorina", the church dedicated to Santa Maria della Vittoria, where it is said that Francis tamed the wolf. In Gubbio, the trail ends at the church of San Francesco.

④ Pieve di Coccorano
This is one of many chapels that Francis must have encountered on his journey, giving him the chance to stop and pray. The countryside here is particularly beautiful and tranquil.

⑤ Church of Caprignone
Foremost among all the churches that Francis built, stone by stone, during his life, this simple church sums up the austerity of the Order and marks the start of the history of the Franciscan movement.

③ Abbey of Valfabbrica
This may well have been the place where Francis stayed before continuing to Gubbio. Only the little church of Santa Maria remains today, with frescoes of the Umbrian school.

② Pieve San Nicolò
After a hilly journey from Assisi, you reach this village, which marks the divide between Assisi and Valfabbrica. Both towns can be seen from here, and, when the weather is good, you can even see as far as Gubbio.

① Assisi
The trail starts from Porta San Giacomo, probably the gate through which Francis passed when he left Assisi. It is near the Basilica di San Francesco, where the body of the saint now lies.

Umbertide

⑦

Ponte d'Assisi •

• **Castiglione**

• **Santa Maria di Colonnata**
S298

⑥

• **Mengara**

Chiascio

⑤
S219

•
Biscina

④
S318

③
S318

• **Pianello**

②

• **Rocca Sant'Angelo**

Palazzo •

Perugia
S147
①
Spello

Key

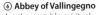

▬▬ Tour route
▬▬ Other roads

0 kilometres   3

0 miles   3

Vineyards belonging to the Lungarotti family, near Torgiano

⓫ Torgiano

Perugia. **Road Map** C4. 🏔 6,000.
🚈 Perugia and Assisi stations, 5 km
(3 miles) and 8 km (5 miles), Foligno–
Terontola line. 🚌 ℹ️ Pro Loco, Corso
Vittorio Emanuele 33, 075 985 297.

The small town of Torgiano,
15 km (9 miles) south of
Perugia (just east of the main
road 3bis), occupies a lovely
position at the confluence of
the Tiber and Chiascio rivers.
Inhabited since the Roman
era, it was rebuilt during the
Middle Ages as a fortified site
to guard over the territory of
Perugia – as the Torre Baglioni
(probably 13th century) still
bears witness.

Torgiano is not an especially
remarkable town in itself, and
yet it is famous for the now
historic production of wine,
acknowledged in the town's
coat of arms and recorded in
the excellent **Museo del Vino
and Osteria**. Housed in the
17th-century Palazzo Baglioni,
this is a private museum owned
by the Lungarotti family,
probably the best-known wine
producers in Umbria; the
Rubesco Riserva di Torgiano is
one of Italy's best red wines.

The 19 rooms illustrate the
history of oenology and vine-
growing since antiquity: on
display, with good notes and
explanations (including in
English), are the tools used for
the production of wine over
the centuries, as well as old
books and printed material
relating to wine. There is also a
valuable collection of majolica

pieces, among them a plate
by Maestro Giorgio da Gubbio
(1528) and a tondo with
Bacchus which is attributed
to Girolamo della Robbia.

Next door to the
museum is the Osteria
del Museo, where
it is possible to
taste and buy wines
from the **Cantine
Giorgio Lungarotti**.

In an additional
demonstration of the
high esteem in which
local agricultural
products are held, the
Lungarotti Foundation
has also added a **Museo
dell'Olivo e dell'Olio**,
where displays relating
to olives and oil are
housed in attractively
restored medieval dwellings.
High-quality olive oils and
balsamic vinegar produced on
the estate are offered for sale in
the winery shop.

🏛 **Museo del Vino
and Osteria**
Corso Vittorio Emanuele 31–33.
Tel 075 988 0200. **Open** Apr–Jun:
10am–1pm, 3–6pm Tue–Sun; July–
Sep: 10am–6pm daily; Oct–Mar:
10am–1pm, 3–5pm Tue–Sun.
Closed 25 Dec. 🅿️ 🌐 lungarotti.it

🍷 **Cantine Giorgio Lungarotti**
Tel 075 988 661 (call ahead).

🏛 **Museo dell'Olivo e dell'Olio**
Via Garibaldi 10. **Tel** 075 988
0200. **Open** Apr–Jun: 10am–1pm,
3–6pm Tue–Sun; July–Sep:
10am–6pm daily; Oct–Mar:
10am–1pm, 3–5pm Tue–Sun.
Closed 25 Dec. 🅿️ ♿

⓬ Bettona

Perugia. **Road Map** C4. 🏔 3,700.
🚈 Perugia and Assisi stations, 7 km
(4 miles) and 4 km (2 miles), Foligno–
Terontola line. 🚌 ℹ️ Pro Loco, Corso
Marconi, 075 997 5643.

It is worth taking the time to
travel the 6 km (4 miles) along
the Assisi road from Torgiano,
in order to visit the village of
Bettona. Apart from offering
lovely views over the
surrounding countryside,
Bettona is unusual historically:
it is among the extremely
rare centres of culture of
Etruscan origin found to the
east of the River Tiber.
Evidence of Etruscan
beginnings is clear
from the huge blocks of stone
set into the medieval walls.

Significant sections of the
walls remain, dating from
the 4th century BC and
typically Etruscan in
design. The best
example is the 40-m
(131-ft) section at the
northwestern corner;
the other sections are of
medieval origin, but rest
on an Etruscan base. The
entire circuit of the outer
walls can be explored
on foot. Bettona has
largely kept its
medieval feel. It is
home to works of art
that some have
attributed to the school of
Perugino, while others believe
they are the work of the
master himself. The first is
a processional banner with
a *Madonna and Child and
St Anne*. Until recently, it was

*St Anthony, by
Perugino*

Bettona's village wall, with Etruscan and
medieval stonework

kept with other important works in the church of Santa Maria Maggiore, erected in the 13th century but later rebuilt. Today, the work is on display in the **Pinacoteca Comunale**, a good art collection housed in the Palazzo del Podestà, on Piazza Cavour.

The gallery also has a *St Anthony of Padua* by Perugino, an *Adoration of the Shepherds* by Dono Doni (a masterpiece from 1543, once kept in the church of San Crispolto), and other works of importance by Jacopo Siculo, Niccolò Alunno, Tiberio d'Assisi and Fiorenzo di Lorenzo.

🏛 Pinacoteca Comunale

Palazzo del Podestà, Piazza Cavour 3. **Tel** 075 987 347. **Open** Apr–Sep: 10:30am–1pm, 3:30–6:30pm Tue–Sun; Oct–Mar: 10:30am–1pm, 3:30–6pm Tue–Sun. **Closed** 1 Jan, 25 Dec. 🎫 call 199 151 123.

A work by Niccolò Alunno, in the Pinacoteca in Bettona

⑬ Deruta

Perugia. **Road Map** C4. 🗺 9,000. 🚌 𝑖 Pro Loco, Piazza dei Consoli 4, 075 971 15 59.

Heading out of Torgiano along road 3bis, you soon reach Deruta, just 6 km (4 miles) south. On a knoll overlooking the Tiber valley, Deruta has been inhabited since Neolithic times, and still bears traces of its history in part of the walls and in the three arches that give access to the old centre. The town's name may derive from the fact that it has been destroyed ("*distrutta*") several times.

The heart of Deruta is Piazza dei Consoli where, as in most medieval settlements, all the

chief religious and civic monuments stand. Palazzo dei Consoli, housing the town hall and also the excellent Pinacoteca (art gallery), is here, as well as the Romanesque-Gothic church of San Francesco.

Residing in the former monastery of San Francesco, next door to the church, is the **Museo Regionale della Ceramica**, which highlights the importance of ceramics in Deruta. The production of jars, plates and other everyday items started in the Middle Ages and is documented in perhaps the most important museum of its kind in the region. On the ground floor, Room 5 is of most interest, with pieces of ancient pottery; on the first floor are fragments from the floor in the church of San Francesco. On the second floor are more valuable pieces, among them a series of Renaissance plates, including one depicting the

myth of Pyramus and Thisbe, from the late 16th century.

The production of ceramics is still a thriving industry in the town, and there are many workshops making and selling majolica pieces. Pottery is also the main attraction at the church of the **Madonna dei Bagni** (1657), 2 km (1 mile) south of Deruta. Its walls are covered in old ex votos made of Deruta pottery.

🏛 Museo Regionale della Ceramica

Largo San Francesco. **Tel** 075 971 10 00. **Open** Apr–Jun: 10:30am–1pm, 3–6pm Wed–Mon; Jul–Sep: 10am–1pm, 3–6pm Wed–Mon; Oct–Mar: 10:30am–1pm, 2:30–6:30pm Wed–Mon. **Closed** 1 Jan, 25 Dec, Jan–Aug: Mon & Tue; Sep & Oct: Mon. ♿

⛪ Madonna dei Bagni

SS E45, exit Casalina. **Tel** 075 973 455. **Open** 8am–noon, 2:30–6:30pm daily **Closed** during Mass. ♿

The fertile Umbrian countryside near Deruta

⑭ Perugia

Now with over 160,000 inhabitants, Perugia has always been the largest city in Umbria. The historic centre of the city has a medieval appearance but is based on an Etruscan layout. The old city occupies a strategic position on a hill dominating the Tiber valley, while the modern city, with flourishing clothing and food industries, developed down below. The Etruscans settled *Perusia* in the 5th century BC or earlier, and it was conquered by the Romans in 309 BC. Perugia saw its greatest splendour in the 13th and 14th centuries, after which civil strife undermined the city's stability; it came under the jurisdiction of the papacy in 1531. Modern Perugia has a distinctly young, cosmopolitan and artistic population and outlook that sets it apart from other cities in the region. It has a thriving Università per Stranieri (University for Foreigners), hosts Italy's top jazz festival, Umbria Jazz *(see p37)* and an annual chocolate festival, Eurochocolate.

Porta Marzia, set into the eastern bastion of the Rocca

Exploring Perugia

Visitors arriving by car are advised to leave their vehicle in the underground car park at Piazzale Partigiani, and from here to take the escalators or microtrain, which take about ten minutes to reach the historic centre, passing by the ruins of the Rocca Paolina and emerging in Piazza Italia.

🏛 Rocca Paolina and Porta Marzia

Built in 1543 and virtually destroyed in

Embossed bronze plate

1860, this fortress is a symbol of papal domination over Perugia. It was built on the orders of Pope Paul III Farnese, who sacked the city in 1540 and annexed it to the Church. Construction of the fortress was entrusted to Antonio da Sangallo, the great exponent of military architecture of the age. To make way for the Rocca, many other buildings were razed. This only increased the hatred of the people of Perugia towards the edifice, which was destroyed as soon as the city gained independence from the pope in the mid-1800s. The gap created was filled with Piazza Italia.

Parts of the fortress survive, including the Porta Marzia, an astonishing Etruscan archway which Sangallo liked so much that he incorporated it into the wall of his own building. Beneath the archway is the entrance to the bizarre Via Bagliomi Sotterranea, a medieval street once buried beneath the Rocca Paolina.

🏛 Museo Archeologico Nazionale dell'Umbria

Piazza G Bruno. **Tel** 075 572 7141. **Open** 8:30am–7:30pm Tue–Sun, 10am–7:30pm Mon (ticket office closes 6:30pm). **Closed** 1 Jan, 1 May, 25 Dec. 🈂 ♿ ♿ partial.

Along Corso Cavour is the Church of San Domenico and its attached monastery, now home to the Museo Archeologico. The collection underwent a major renovation and there is now much more to see than the original Etruscan and Roman finds. The Carri Etruschi di Castel San Marino is a particularly fine exhibit of 6th century BC bronze chariots. Another must-see is the Cippus Perusinus, an Etruscan boundary stone which bears one of the longest inscriptions in Etruscan ever found.

Perugia Town Centre

① Rocca Paolina & Porta Marzia
② Museo Archeologico Nazionale dell'Umbria
③ San Domenico

⛪ San Domenico

Piazza G Bruno. **Tel** 075 572 4136.
Open 7am–noon, 4–7pm daily. 🅿️
♿ 📷 Sat, Sun am; 075 573 1635.

This huge church was built in the 14th century, to a design reminiscent of the Florentine churches of Santa Croce and

Detail from the polyptych, San Pietro

Santa Maria Novella. It was rebuilt in the Baroque style in the 17th century, but was never finished. Inside, note in particular the Cappella del Rosario, with statues by Agostino di Duccio (second half of the 15th century), and also the wonderful stained-glass window (1411), the second largest in Italy after the one in Milan cathedral.

VISITORS' CHECKLIST

Practical Information
Road Map C3. 🏠 168,000. ℹ️
Piazza Matteotti 18, 075 573 6458.
🆆 turismo.comune.perugia.it

Transport
🆂 Cortona–Foligno & Rome–Perugia lines, 892021; FCU line, 075 575 401.
🚌 APM, 075 9637 637.

there were underground passages. These rooms were used for burial first by the Etruscans and then by the Romans, before being converted into a building dating from the Early Christian era (6th century AD).

San Pietro is strikingly original in its sumptuous decoration, which is more reminiscent of the Venetian than the local tradition. There are also numerous works of art by several notable artists, including Perugino, Guercino, Guido Reni and Sassoferrato.

An impressive amount of the original Romanesque church survives, including the partially frescoed façade. The exuberant decoration inside is late Renaissance, and includes cycles of large paintings reminiscent of those done by Tintoretto. There is also a painted coffered ceiling and wonderful wooden choir stalls, the work of various artists in the 16th century. The vault is frescoed with *Stories from the Old Testament*. In the sacristy are five small canvases by Perugino depicting the saints. Visitors should ask the sacristan for permission to view the artworks.

⛪ San Pietro

Borgo XX Giugno. **Tel** 075 337 53.
Open 8am–noon Mon–Fri (also 3:30–6pm Tue & Thu).

Further along Via Cavour, beyond Porta San Pietro (14th–15th centuries, built with some help from Agostino di Duccio), is one of the oldest religious buildings in Perugia, the Benedictine church of San Pietro. The church was founded in the 10th century, but there is some evidence to suggest that, in this slightly elevated site,

④ *Palazzo dei Priori pp90–91*
⑤ *Galleria Nazionale dell'Umbria pp92–3*
⑥ Duomo
⑦ Etruscan Well
⑧ Palazzo del Capitano del Popolo

⑨ San Severo
⑩ Arch of Augustus
⑪ Oratorio di San Bernardino
⑫ San Michele Arcangelo
   (Sant'Angelo)

The 16th-century entrance to the church of San Pietro

For keys to symbols *see back flap*

Perugia: Palazzo dei Priori

Piazza IV Novembre is home to two of the most important monuments in Perugia, the Palazzo dei Priori and the Fontana Maggiore. The imposing palazzo, topped by crenellations, was built to hold the town council's administrative offices, and was constructed in stages between 1293 and 1443, during an era of great splendour in the city. Though sombre outside, this is one of the most impressive medieval buildings in Italy, with truly gorgeous interiors. The palazzo is, in fact, composed of several buildings which face onto either Corso Vannucci or the piazza. These house four separate visitors' attractions, including the splendid Galleria Nazionale dell'Umbria *(see pp92–3)*.

★ Collegio del Cambio
In the Sala dell'Udienza of the Collegio del Cambio (1452–7), where money changers operated, there is a cycle of frescoes by Perugino, painted from 1496 to 1500. The iconography brings together religious themes and figures with secular ones, a hallmark of Renaissance Humanism.

KEY

① **The Arco dei Priori**, marks the start of Via dei Priori, which, it is said, flowed with rivers of blood as a result of civil strife during the Middle Ages.

② **Il Collegio della Mercanzia**, is a room on the ground floor of the palazzo which was placed at the disposal of the Merchants' Guild in 1390, for meetings. The ceiling and walls are lined with inlaid wood and date from the middle of the 15th century.

③ **The Guild of Money Changers**, acquired the right to establish its headquarters in the Palazzo dei Priori between 1452 and 1457.

④ **Belfry**

⑤ **A stone griffin**, (a copy of the 1274 original), high above the entrance, is the symbol of Perugia.

⑥ **The fan-shaped flight of steps**, in Piazza IV Novembre leads up to the Sala dei Notari.

★ Portale delle Arti
Framed by rounded arches, the doorway dates from 1346 and is adorned with sculptures and reliefs representing vices and virtues, as well as symbolic animals.

★ Sala dei Notari
The lawyers' meeting hall, with its magnificent vaulting, is one of the oldest parts of the palazzo, dating from the late 1290s. The rich decoration includes frescoes by local artists, dating from the same period.

VISITORS' CHECKLIST

Practical Information

Corso Vannucci 19. Sala dei Notari: **Tel** 075 573 6458. **Open** 9am–1pm, 3–7pm Tue–Sun. Collegio della Mercanzia: **Tel** 075 573 0366. **Open** Mar–Oct: 9am–1pm, 2:30–5:30pm Tue–Sat, 9am–1pm Sun & pub hols; Nov–Feb: 8am–2pm Tue, Thu & Fri, 8am–4:30pm Wed & Sat, 9am–1pm Sun & pub hols. ♿ combined ticket with Collegio del Cambio. ♿ Collegio del Cambio: **Tel** 075 572 8599. **Open** 9am–12:30pm, 2:30–5:30pm Mon–Sat, 9am–1pm Sun & pub hols. ♿ combined ticket with Collegio della Mercanzia. ♿ **Closed** all sites: 1 Jan, 25 Dec (Collegio del Cambio also Mon pm Nov–31 Mar).

Fontana Maggiore
This is a suberb piece of work, featuring many exquisite bas-reliefs and sculptures by Nicola and Giovanni Pisano.

The Fontana Maggiore

Built from 1275 to 1278, and recently restored, this fountain was designed by a monk called Fra Bevignate, and decorated by Nicola Pisano and his son, Giovanni. It is both a magnificent architectural creation (one of Italy's top Romanesque monuments) and a complex feat of hydraulic engineering. It was thanks to the engineer Boninsegna da Venezia that waters from a new aqueduct from Monte Pacciano converged here.

The fountain is built on three levels: two polygonal basins in marble, one above the other, with 25 and 24 sides respectively, and a third basin in bronze. The series of bas-reliefs is exceptional: on the lower basin are three consecutive cycles depicting episodes from the Old Testament, the Liberal Arts and the Labours of the Months. On the upper basin are 24 sculptures representing biblical figures (David, Moses, Solomon, Salome), saints, mythological figures or allegories from the history of the city, as well as the Perugian *condottiere* Ermanno di Sassoferrato, Capitano del Popolo in 1278.

Stylistically, all kinds of influences converge in the reliefs (including classical, Byzantine and medieval), making it difficult to attribute individual panels to one or other of the two artists.

Lower Basin

1 Temptation / Expulsion from Paradise
2 Samson and the Lion/Samson and Delilah
3 Lion / Puppy
4 David / Goliath
5 Romulus / Remus
6 She-wolf / Mother of Romulus and Remus
7 Wolf and Crane / Wolf and Lamb
8 January / Woman
9 February / Man
10 March / Man
11 April / Woman
12 May / Woman
13 June / Man
14 July / Man
15 August / Woman
16 September / Woman
17 October / Man
18 November / Man
19 December / Man
20 Lion / Griffin
21 Grammar / Dialectics
22 Rhetoric / Arithmetic
23 Geometry / Music
24 Astronomy / Philosophy
25 Eagle / Eagle

Upper Basin

26 Melchizedek
27 Ermanno di Sassoferrato
28 Victory
29 St Peter
30 Roman Church
31 Rome
32 Theology
33 St Paul
34 Cleric of St Laurence
35 St Laurence
36 Chiusi
37 Perugia
38 Lake Trasimeno
39 Sant'Ercolano
40 The Traitor Cleric
41 St Benedict
42 John the Baptist
43 Solomon
44 David
45 Salome
46 Moses
47 Matteo da Correggio
48 Archangel Michael
49 Euliste (founder of Perugia)

Perugia: Galleria Nazionale dell'Umbria

This is the most important museum, not only in Perugia but in Umbria as a whole, featuring works of art dating from the 13th to 19th centuries. Created partly out of Napoleon's seizure of works of art held by religious orders, the gallery was established in 1863. It was moved to the Palazzo dei Priori in 1879 and has been state-owned since 1918. A major renovation project has increased the number of rooms to 40, spread over two floors, mostly grouped to cover various eras, including the 15th-century Cappella dei Priori, which features some splendid Perugian scenes. While the emphasis is clearly on Umbrian art, Sienese masters are nevertheless dominant in the early rooms. Artsiders, a new project, will see new talent placed alongside old masters.

Donna alla Fonte (1278–81)
In Room 1 there are five statues which were originally part of a fountain, including the *Donna alla Fonte*, by Tuscan Arnolfo di Cambio (1240–1302). There are also two bronzes of a griffin and a lion.

★ **St Anthony Polyptych**
(1459–68)
In this work by Piero della Francesca, on show in Room 11, innovative use of perspective blends with a structure and colours that are still medieval.

Room 6 is dedicated to the International Gothic style, of which Gentile da Fabriano (1370–1427) was one of the major Italian exponents. His *Madonna col Bambino e Angeli* is displayed here.

3rd Floor

16
17
18
19
20
21
1a
1
15
8
4
2
14
9
6
3
13
11
10
7
36
12
26
25
24
23
22
34
27
33
32
31
28
30
29

★ **San Domenico of Fiesole Altarpiece** (1437)
This work by Fra Angelico (1395–1455) is one of the major Renaissance masterpieces in the museum. Also known as the *Guidalotti Polyptych*, it is displayed in Room 8.

2nd Floor

VISITORS' CHECKLIST

Practical Information
Palazzo dei Priori. **Tel** 075 572 1009.
Open May–Oct: 8:30am–7:30pm
daily (Nov–Apr: Tue–Sun, last adm
6:30pm). **Closed** Oct–May: Mon,
1 Jan, 1 May, 25 Dec. 🐾 🖸 🖼
🔲 gallerianazionaleumbria.it

Key

⬜ 6th and 7th centuries
⬜ 8th century
⬜ 13th and 14th centuries
⬜ Late Gothic period
⬜ Early Renaissance
⬜ 15th century
⬜ Treasury and decorative arts
⬜ Cappella dei Priori
⬜ Renaissance masterpieces
⬜ Perugian and Umbrian art
⬜ Luigi Caratolli collection

To Rooms
22–40

Entrance and
ticket office

39   40

38

The duomo's Gothic doorway, the unfinished pulpit and papal statue

🏛 Duomo

Piazza Danti. **Tel** 075 572 3832.
Open 7:30am–12:30pm, 3:30–7pm
Mon–Sat; 8am–12:45pm, 4–7pm
Sun. ♿

The duomo, dedicated to San
Lorenzo, was built on the site of
a 10th-century basilica. The first
stone of the new building was
laid in 1345, but the Black Death
(1348) delayed progress for
many years, with work starting
again properly only in 1437.
Even then, the façade
was left unfinished.

The façade, which
gives onto Piazza
Danti, is undoubtedly
of much less interest
than the left-hand side
of the duomo, which
overlooks Piazza IV
Novembre. This is
covered in distinctive
pink and white
marble, and features
an impressive
monumental Gothic doorway,
designed by Galeazzo Alessi in
1568. In a niche above the doorway is a cross, beneath which the
Perugians symbolically laid down
the keys to the city following
their defeat by Pope Paul III
Farnese in the Salt War of 1540.
In contrast, a statue of Pope
Julius III, sculpted by Vincenzo
Danti in 1555, to the left of the
doorway, was commissioned
by the people of Perugia to
celebrate the pope who had
restored some communal liberty
to the city. On the right is an

**Detail from the
cathedral**

unfinished, 15th-century pulpit,
from which St Bernardino of
Siena preached to vast crowds
of Perugians in the 1420s. The
saint was so popular with
Perugians that they built a
church in his honour (see pp94–5).

Also on the side of the duomo
that overlooks the piazza is a
loggia with an arched portico,
built for Braccio Fortebraccio,
the celebrated *condottiere* from
Montone, in 1423.

The interior is bare and
solemn, unusual in
Italy, being more
reminiscent of the
great churches of
northern Europe.
Inside is the Virgin's
"wedding ring",
housed in the
Cappella del Sant'
Anello and said to
change colour
according to who wears
it. On the left, just past
the entrance, is the Cappella di
San Bernardino da Siena, home
to one of the two major works of
art in the building, a *Descent from
the Cross* by Federico Barocci,
dated 1567–9. The other is a
masterpiece by Luca Signorelli,
Enthroned Madonna with Saints,
which was painted in 1484 and
has been beautifully restored to
show off its original brilliance.

Another restored feature
worth seeing is the choir,
featuring inlaid wooden stalls:
the work of Domenico del Tasso
and Giuliano da Maiano.

Room 15 displays this *Adoration
of the Magi* by Perugino (1450–
1523). There are also splendid
paintings from the Umbrian
school. More works by Perugino
can be found in Rooms 22–24,
including the *Madonna
della Consolazione*.

Post-Modern Perugia

The quarter of Fontivegge is in the new part of Perugia, southwest of the historic centre, near the railway station. It stands out from the other quarters of the modern city because it was designed as a completely new district between 1982 and 1989 by the architect Aldo Rossi and his colleagues. It is one of the most successful examples of post-modern architecture in Italy, featuring buildings that are both futuristic and full of classical references (see in particular the Palazzo della Regione, in Piazza Nuova), and also include: elements from the past; a 17th-century fountain and a chimney from the old Perugia factory have both been incorporated into the new architectural context.

The Fontivegge quarter

🏛 Etruscan Well

Piazza Danti 18. **Tel** 075 573 3669. **Open** 10am–1:30pm, 2:30–6pm (Nov–Mar: 11am–1:30pm, 2:30–5pm). **Closed** Mon (except in Apr & Aug), 1 Jan, 25 Dec.

The Etruscan Well (Pozzo Etrusco) in the basement of Palazzo Bourbon-Sorbello, next to the cathedral façade in Piazza Danti, is an astonishing feat of engineering: it was capable of providing a constant supply of water to the entire city. The well (the bottom of which is accessible) is partially covered in vast blocks of travertine, from which the original cover was also made. You can still see the furrows left by the ropes that the Etruscans used to pull the buckets of water to the surface.

Behind Piazza Danti is the district of Rione di Porta Sole, where the Rocca del Sole fortress was built in 1372. It was the largest fortification of its time, but was destroyed shortly after its completion.

🏛 Piazza Matteotti

This long square, which runs parallel to Corso Vannucci, is home to two notable 15th-century buildings. The first is Palazzo del Capitano del Popolo (1472–82), designed by the Lombard architects Gasparino di Antonio and Leone di Matteo, and the seat of the judiciary in the era of the communes.

Justice, detail

Its traditional medieval town-hall design has been embellished with Renaissance elements. The palazzo was originally built on three floors, but the third was demolished following the earthquake of 1741. Behind the porticoes alongside the palazzo is a 1930s covered market, from where you can see the piazza foundations.

The other building of note is Palazzo dell'Università Vecchia, mostly from the same era as the Palazzo del Capitano del Popolo (the same Gasparino di Antonio collaborated in its construction); the building was made the seat of the university by Pope Sixtus IV in 1483.

🏛 San Severo

Piazza Raffaello. **Tel** 075 573 3864. **Open** 10am–1:30pm, 2:30–6pm (Nov– Mar: 11am–1:30pm, 2:30–5pm). **Closed** Mon (except in Apr & Aug), 1 Jan, 25 Dec.

Following the narrow streets up through the Porta Sole quarter, you reach the church of San Severo, famous as the home of one of Raphael's earliest frescoes (1507–8), of the *Holy Trinity and Saints*. Perugino finished the work in 1521, adding the saints lower down on the same wall. Also look out for the 16th-century terracotta group of a Madonna and Child by an unknown Tuscan sculptor. The church is of ancient origin: it certainly existed

in the 11th century, and the site was probably used for sacred buildings before that. Its current appearance dates from the mid-18th century.

🏛 Arch of Augustus

Piazza Fortebraccio.

A scenic descent signals the end of the Porta Sole quarter, marked by the splendid 3rd-century BC Arch of Augustus (Arco di Augusto). This civic gate is also known as the Etruscan Arch, since it was, in fact, of Etruscan origin, and was later modified by the Romans. The still-legible inscription, "Augusta Perusia", was placed here by Octavius Caesar (later Emperor Augustus); having destroyed and then rebuilt the city, he renamed it after himself.

Façade of the Oratorio di San Bernardino

🏛 Oratorio di San Bernardino

Piazza San Francesco al Prato. **Tel** 075 573 3957. **Open** 8:30am–12:30pm, 3:30–5:30pm daily.

Passing under the Arco dei Priori, part of the palazzo of the same name *(see pp90–91)*, and heading down Via dei Priori, you cross what was once a main road through medieval Perugia. Beyond the city walls, the street widens into a piazza with the church of San Francesco al Prato, built in the mid-13th century on a particularly subsidence-prone piece of ground; it is now partially ruined. To the left of the church is the small and elegant Oratorio di San Bernardino (1452), whose fine multicoloured bas-reliefs on the façade make it a masterpiece of the Umbrian Renaissance. The sculptures, by Agostino di Duccio, are remarkable for the realism of the undulating lines and of the drapery.

Inside, in the first chapel on the left, are a 15th-century gonfalon (banner) showing the Madonna sheltering Perugia from the plague, by Benedetto Bonfigli, and the tomb of Braccio Fortebraccio da Montone. The altar was made from an ancient Early Christian sarcophagus.

Borgo Sant'Angelo

Corso Garibaldi, running north from Piazza Fortebraccio, is the principal medieval street, along which the area of Borgo Sant'Angelo developed. Now the seat of Perugia's university, this district grew up around an Augustinian monastery and has the city's most important monastic buildings, including

The Early Christian church of Sant'Angelo

the monastery of San Benedetto, the former hospital of the Collegio della Mercanzia, the convent of Santa Caterina and the monastery of Beata Colomba. It is in this last monastery that, according to popular tradition, St Francis met St Dominic in 1220.

At the end of the road, in the shelter of the walls and in a pretty setting, is the circular church of **San Michele**

Arcangelo (Sant'Angelo), whose origins date back to the late 5th century. Thanks to excellent restoration work, which included the removal of Baroque additions, major parts of the original church are now visible, along with a 14th-century Gothic doorway. The interior is rich with frescoes, and also 14th century. This is one of the oldest proto-Christian churches in Italy.

San Michele Arcangelo
Via Sant'Angelo, Corso Garibaldi. **Tel** 075 572 2624. **Open** 9am–5pm daily.

Environs
Around 7 km (4 miles) southeast of the city, along road 75bis, is one of the most interesting burial sites among many in the area: the Ipogeo dei Volumni. Built into the side of a hill, it consists of a great tomb chamber where, in the 2nd century BC, the nobles of the Etruscan Velimna family were buried. Their Latin name of Volumni gives its name to their mausoleum.

Inside the burial chamber of the Ipogeo dei Volumni

Umbria Jazz

A festival stage just before a concert

First held in 1973, Umbria Jazz is – the experts say – Europe's top jazz festival. After the first concerts, held in different towns throughout the region, the event went into crisis and was suspended. The festival was then transferred to Perugia, where it now takes place every July, and enjoys a fame and success second only to the famous Montreal festival. Concerts take place in different venues: from fields and open-air sites (where events are generally free) to the Morlacchi and Pavone theatres, for which audiences buy tickets. Every evening, stretched out on the grass, thousands of young people listen to music for free: a flashback to a time when Umbria Jazz was briefly the setting for mass youth gatherings. Historic open-air venues include the Giardini del Frontone, used since 1984 for the jazz festival's most important evening concerts. The gardens have hosted some of the most historic events, from Stan Getz to the get-together between John Scofield and Pat Metheny, from Bobby McFerrin to Phil Woods and Dizzy Gillespie hugging each other in the rain. As well as the main festival there are other events, including a jazz festival at Orvieto (Umbria Jazz Winter), and a gospel and soul festival (at Terni, at Easter) (www.umbriajazz.it).

Since 1937, another annual event has been staged in Perugia: the Sagra Musicale Umbra, a festival of sacred music, draws artists from all over the world in September.

⓯ Lake Trasimeno

The fourth-largest lake in Italy, Lake Trasimeno covers an area of 126 sq km (48 sq miles). The perimeter is almost 60 km (37 miles) long, and the lake lies at the fortified heart of medieval Umbria. No matter where you gaze among the low hills that surround the lake, you will inevitably catch sight of a castle, a tower or a fortified village. In fact, Lake Trasimeno has been the scene of battles since antiquity, and it was on these shores that Hannibal defeated the Romans on 21 June 217 BC. Although the water levels rise and fall, and the lake periodically floods the surrounding land, the area has always been inhabited. Over the centuries villages grew up on the shores of the lake, and the islands became home to monasteries and convents, later active fishing communities.

★ Isola Maggiore
Briefly a refuge for St Francis, this island is inhabited by fishermen who still stretch out their nets to dry between the churches of Sant'Angelo and San Salvatore.

Tuoro sul Trasimeno
Near the town are the battle sites where the Carthaginians fought the Romans. A historical-archaeological trail of the battle has been created, with maps and information points along the route. There is a modern sculpture park, the Campo del Sole, at Lido di Tuoro.

Vernazz

Terontola   Tuoro

Borghetto
(2)
Ferretto

Bosco del Ferretto

• Piana

Castiglione del Lago

• Pucciarelli

• Panicarola

Key

---- Ferry route

0 kilometres   5

0 miles   5

Castiglione del Lago
This is the main town on the shores of Lake Trasimeno, a departure point for ferries (*see p98*).

Passignano sul Trasimeno
This town of Etruscan origin is built on a chalk promontory. The most important monument in the town is the church of San Cristoforo, with 15th-century frescoes.

★ Isola Polvese
This is the largest island on the lake. The Province of Perugia has created an oasis for wildlife here, among gardens and parks. The ruins of the monastery of San Secondo and a 15th-century castle can also be seen.

Passignano sul Trasimeno

Torricella

Magione ④

Monte del Lago

San Feliciano ⑤

San Savino

Sant'Arcangelo ⑥

Monte Buono

⑦

KEY

① **The southern shores**, are characterized, more so than the others, by marshy terrain, fringed with reedbeds.

② **Borghetto** is a small village among olive groves, with a 16th-century parish church, San Martino.

③ **Isola Minore** is private and the smallest of the three islands.

④ **Magione** is a town in the hills behind the most populated stretch of shore, and moderately developed in terms of tourism. There is a castle here, the Castello dei Cavalieri di Malta, and, at nearby San Feliciano, a Museo della Pesca (Museum of Fishing).

⑤ **La Valle** is the name given to this stretch of lake, where there are vast reedbeds and an area of protected fish-breeding grounds.

⑥ **The Badia di Sant'Arcangelo**, in a lovely setting by the lake, is a castle of medieval origin with a Romanesque church.

⑦ **The Castello di Montalera** is one of many fortified sites along the lakeshore. It was at one time the property of the Baglioni family.

The Battle of Lake Trasimeno

After defeating the Romans at the battles of Ticino and Trebbia, Hannibal was informed that his adversaries, led by Caius Flaminius, were directing part of the Roman army towards Lake Trasimeno. The Carthaginian leader distributed his men around the surrounding hills and then, on 21 June 217 BC, aided by foggy weather, he gave the order to attack the enemy forces. Trapped between the lake and the hills, the Roman soldiers suffered a crushing defeat: Hannibal lost 1,500 men, compared with the Romans' 15,000.

Portrait of Hannibal

For keys to symbols *see back flap*

Lake Trasimeno as seen from Castiglione

⑯ Castiglione del Lago

Perugia. **Road Map** B3. 🚹 15,000.
🚊 Florence–Rome line. 🚌
🛈 Piazza Mazzini 10, 075 867 1182.
🎉 Festa degli Aquiloni, Apr.

The town of Castiglione del Lago occupies a promontory which dominates the western shore of Lake Trasimeno, and which, during floods, used to be cut off from the surrounding area, in effect becoming an island.

The area was fortified by both the Etruscans and the Romans because of its strategic position. Fought over by Perugia and by the Tuscans, the site was often destroyed and rebuilt. It was following the reconstruction ordered by Frederick II Hohenstaufen in the 13th century that the place acquired the name Castello del Leone, from which its current name derives.

In the 16th century, the village was given by the papacy to the della Corgna family, who built the town's most important building, the **Palazzo della Corgna**. It may have been designed by Galeazzo Alessi and the frescoes were done by Pomarancio.

Linked to the palazzo by a covered walkway, backing onto the lake and with a fine view, is the **Rocca del Leone**, an interesting example of medieval military architecture. In the 16th century it was considered to be one of the most impregnable fortresses in Italy. From the palazzo,

the street leads towards the real heart of the town, which is centred around Piazza Mazzini. Here, the church of **Santa Maria Maddalena** is worth a visit: the building is Neo-Classical, built by Giovanni Caproni from 1836, but houses a 16th-century altarpiece (*Madonna and Child, St Anthony Abbot and St Mary Magdalene*). This was formerly identified as a youthful work by Raphael, but is now known to be by Eusebio da San Giorgio, one of Perugino's circle.

🏛 Palazzo della Corgna and Rocca del Leone
Piazza Gramsci. **Tel** 075 951 099.
Open Mar: 10am–6pm; Apr–Sep: 9:30am–7pm; Oct: 9:30am–6:30pm; Nov–Mar: 9:30am–5pm Fri–Mon & hols (Christmas period daily). **Closed** 1 Jan, 25 Dec. 🅿 🆆 **palazzodellacorgna.it**

🏛 Santa Maria Maddalena
Via Vittorio Emanuele.
Tel 075 951 159.

⑰ Città della Pieve

Perugia. **Road Map** A4. 🚹 7,000.
🚊 Chiusi–Chianciano, 10 km (6 miles), Florence–Rome line. 🚌 🛈 Piazza Matteotti, 0578 298 520. 🎉 Palio dei Terzieri, Aug. 🆆 **cittadellapieve.org**

The fame of Città della Pieve, on the Tuscan border, is due primarily to the fact that it was the birthplace of the great Renaissance painter Pietro Vannucci. Known as Perugino (1450–1523) and famous in his own right, he also taught the young Raphael. Città della Pieve is worth a visit above all because it houses several major works by this artist.

Adoration of the Magi, Perugino, detail

An Etruscan colony of Chiusi (in nearby Tuscany), and later Roman, Città della Pieve suffered frequently from barbarian invasions. It finally developed as a fortified town in about 1000, around the church of Santi Gervasio e Protasio. The distinctive red coloration is due to the use of bricks – there was no stone available locally.

Fresco by Pomarancio, Palazzo della Corgna

Città della Pieve is known for its very narrow streets, including what some claim to be the narrowest in Italy, Vicolo Baciadonne, which is just 80 cm (31 in) wide. The central Piazza del Plebiscito is home to Palazzo della Corgna (with 16th-century frescoes by Pomarancio), the Biblioteca Comunale (library) and, most importantly, the cathedral of Santi Gervasio e Protasio. This was rebuilt on the site of the original parish church, perhaps in the 8th century, and then remodelled and restored at intervals between the 12th and 17th centuries. Inside, among various precious works of art (by Domenico Alfani, Giannicola di Paolo and Pomarancio), there are two paintings by Perugino – a *Baptism of Christ* and a *Madonna and Child and Saints Peter, Paul, Gervasio and Protasio*.

In the church of Santa Maria dei Servi (included in the ticket for Palazzo della Corgna), just south of the centre, there were once some spendid frescoes by Perugino; only a Deposition survives, dating from 1517. Visitors will find a far more beautiful fresco by Perugino in the church of Santa Maria dei Bianchi, in Corso Vannucci, just off Piazza del Plebiscito. This depicts the *Adoration of the Magi* (1504), and is perhaps the best of all the works by Perugino found in his native city; the scene includes the view from Città della Pieve towards Lake Trasimeno, as well as a party of elegant Renaissance figures.

⑱ Southern Lake Trasimeno

In the mountains that rise to the south of Lake Trasimeno lies a series of villages where art and history have always played an important role. The painter Pietro Vannucci, better known as Perugino, was born and worked here. This tour partly retraces the steps of the great artist and partly seeks out small medieval hill towns, among the great treasures of Umbria.

Tips for Drivers

ℹ️ Piazza Mazzini 10, Castiglione del Lago, 075 965 2484. Length of tour: 55 km (34 miles). Time needed: 1 day. Stopping-off points: in villages along the route.

② Panicale
This fortified town is perched on a rocky spur. Perugino's *Martyrdom of St Sebastian* (1505) can be seen in the church of San Sebastiano.

③ Tavernelle
Just north of this village is the Santuario della Madonna di Mongiovino, a 16th-century church with frescoes from the same period.

① Paciano
Encircled by walls and in a lovely hilly setting of woods and olive groves, this is one of the best-preserved of the medieval villages in the area.

Magione

S75b

Lake Trasimeno

S599

Perugia

S220

S71

S220

Città della Pieve

S220

S71

Orvieto

Nestore

⑤ Corciano
Almost intact 13th-century walls, protected by tall towers and a castle, extend for a kilometre around this pretty village. Corciano has both Etruscan and Roman origins, as do other villages on this tour.

④ Fontignano
This medieval village, built on a hillside, was where Perugino died in 1523. He left his last work of art here: a *Madonna and Child* in the church of the Annunziata.

Key

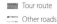 Tour route

‑‑‑ Other roads

| 0 kilometres | 5 |
| 0 miles | 5 |

SOUTHERN UMBRIA

The countryside of Southern Umbria is very hilly, rising to the peaks of the Monti Sibillini towards the eastern fringes. Rocks and water are constant features of the landscape, as at the spectacular Cascata delle Marmore and the springs of Clitunno. Most of the towns are medieval in appearance, but were once part of the Etruscan world. Even the language spoken has affinities with Tuscan.

In the past, this part of the region was dominated by the Duchy of Spoleto, whose lands were regarded by geographers as the real heart of Umbria until the 16th century. Also culturally and politically part of this territory were Todi, of ancient Italic and Etruscan origin, and the Roman town of Narni, while Orvieto was viewed as an independent commune.

Despite the vicissitudes of history, here, as in the rest of Umbria, the sense of local identity derived from a long-standing communal spirit is strong and heartfelt. Every town has its own artistic and historical treasures, and each cherishes and takes pride in its own ancient past, manifested in numerous feast days and secular festivals. Hills, and especially water, feature large in the natural landscape of southern Umbria. The River Tiber forms the Lago di Corbara, while the River Nera flows along the edge of the splendid valley known as the Valnerina. In the west, pale tufa soil

and the high ridges of Orvieto signal the land of the Etruscans. The wilder peaks of the Apennines, on the other hand, occupy the southeastern corner of the region. Here, Cascia, Piediluco and Norcia are the last towns before the steep rise towards the windswept plateaus of Castelluccio, just a stone's throw from Le Marche and Lazio.

The cultural and gastronomic traditions of this corner of Italy are still quite individual, successfully uniting flavours and ideas from different areas. Norcia, in the Valnerina, is a byword for good food all over Italy.

Between August 2016 and January 2017, three strong earthquakes devastated Central Italy. In particular, the earthquake of October 2016 heavily damaged and sometimes destroyed most of the churches in Norcia. It may take years for reconstruction to be completed, but the affected towns have not lost their mystical splendour. Visitors may find many churches in the area closed while structural tests are conducted.

Detail of the *Coronation of the Virgin*, by Filippo Lippi (1467), apse of Spoleto cathedral

◀ Charming alleys in the hillside town of Spello

Exploring Southern Umbria

Orvieto, Todi, Terni, Spoleto: a string of historical towns unravels from east to west in Southern Umbria. In between is fertile countryside, dotted with farmhouses and cultivated fields, and important stretches of river, including the lower course of the River Tiber and the River Nera. There are also thermal springs and archaeological areas, as well as nature reserves, chief of which is the spectacular national park of the Monti Sibillini, superb territory for walking, mountain-biking and hang-gliding.

Entrance to the duomo at Piazza del Popolo, Todi

Getting Around

The Autostrada del Sole (A1) motorway skirts the western side of Southern Umbria, with exits at Orvieto and at Orte, from where Superstrada 204 runs east towards Terni. The other two principal artery routes are, as for Northern Umbria, state roads 3 and 3bis, which serve Spoleto and Todi respectively and divide the region from north to south. The main railway line connects Rome to Ancona, passing through various Umbrian towns en route. There is also a private line linking Perugia and Terni. Most smaller villages are linked by road.

Sights at a Glance

Classic agricultural landscape near Orvieto

The medieval village of Campello Alto, near Fonti di Clitunno

Key

━━ Motorway
━━ Major road
━━ Secondary road
┄┄ Minor road
━━ Scenic route
╍╍ Main railway
── Minor railway
── Regional border
△ Summit

For keys to symbols *see back flap*

❶ Spello

Spello lies on a hillside in the shadow of Monte Subasio and is built, like nearby Assisi, out of pink stone. A settlement founded here by the Umbri grew in size under the Romans, while the town walls were built in the Augustan era. Later, the town was sacked by the Lombards, who made it part of the Duchy of Spoleto before it was crushed again by Frederick II. In 1389, Spello was given to the Baglioni family as a feudal estate. They ruled until the mid-16th century, after which Spello followed the fortunes of the rest of the region. The reminders of the town's past make it a fascinating place today. Spello felt the earthquake of 2016 and experienced some small damage. Some churches may be closed for structural tests as a result.

Dispute in the Temple, detail

Porta Consolare, one of the Roman gateways to the town

Exploring Spello

From Piazza Kennedy, access to the walled town is through Porta Consolare, a well-preserved Roman gateway. Heading north into the centre, Piazza della Repubblica marks the real centre of Spello.

🏛 Santa Maria Maggiore
Piazza Matteotti.
Completed in 1285, this church is the most important monument

in Spello. Its façade was reconstructed, using the original materials, in the 17th century.

The single-nave church owes its fame to the Cappella Baglioni, where there is a series of frescoes by Pinturicchio, perhaps the finest ever done by the artist. Painted from 1500–1501, the frescoes depict the *Four Sibyls* (on the vault) and *Scenes from the Life of Christ* (on the walls). The most important frescoes are an *Annunciation* (under which hangs a self-portrait of Pinturicchio), an *Adoration of the Magi* and a *Dispute in the Temple*. The floor of the chapel was made of majolica tiles from Deruta. More Pinturicchio frescoes can be found in the Cappella del Sacramento, reached from the left transept. In the right transept is the Cappella del Sepolcro, which at one time housed the town art gallery. Also of interest are a pulpit in sandstone and a tabernacle on the high altar. The church canopy suffered some damage after the earthquake of 2016.

🏛 Pinacoteca Civica
Piazza Matteotti 10. **Tel** 0742 301 497. **Open** Apr–Sep: 10:30am–1pm, 3–8pm Tue–Sun; Oct–Mar:10:30am–12:30pm, 3–5pm Fri–Sun.

Since 1994 the civic art gallery has been housed in the Palazzo dei Canonici (15th century), to the right of Santa Maria Maggiore. Among the varied works in the collection, one highlight is a splendid *Wooden Madonna* dating from around 1240, brightly coloured and yet serene and stately. Also of note are several polyptychs of the 14th and 15th centuries and other significant works of the local school.

🏛 Sant'Andrea
Via Cavour.
Near the Pinacoteca, the church of Sant'Andrea (13th century) has a rather gloomy interior; and yet in the right transept is a superb fresco by Pinturicchio of the *Madonna and Child with Saints*. In the left transept, look out for the mummified body of Andrea Caccioli, one of the first followers of St Francis.

🏛 Piazza della Repubblica
In this not particularly notable square at the end of Via Cavour is the 13th-century Palazzo Comunale (now restored), which contains the Library and the Town Archive.

Heading north along Via Garibaldi, you pass Palazzo Cruciani, seat of the town council, and then the 12th-century church of San Lorenzo, an architectural hotchpotch. Of interest inside is the carved wooden pulpit, the work of Francesco Costantini (1600).

🏛 Porta Venere
Via Torri di Properzio.
A short detour west from Piazza della Repubblica takes you to Porta Venere, a Roman gateway flanked by two imposing 12-sided towers dating from the Middle Ages. The gate, heavily restored over the centuries, dates from the Augustan era:

The town of Spello, on a hillside above the Valle Umbra

Roman Porta Venere, with its two characteristic 12-sided towers

the structure that you see today originally had a double curtain giving way to an internal courtyard. The gate offers good views over the surrounding countryside.

🏛 Porta dell'Arce
Via Arco Romano.
One of the oldest entrances to the town, this gate is an example of how Roman buildings were integrated into the medieval fortifications. Nearby is the terrace of the Belvedere, from which the Topino valley, as well as the outline of Assisi's Santa Maria degli Angeli, can be admired.

🏛 San Claudio
Via Fontevecchia.
From the Belvedere, you can descend to the plain via the narrow Via dei Cappuccini and then the long Via Fontevecchia. Here, you'll find the delightful church of San Claudio, dating from the 12th century. Perhaps Spello's most interesting church architecturally, it has retained intact its Romanesque decoration and layout. The simple façade is topped by the original belfry.

The Romanesque façade of San Claudio

🏛 Roman Ruins
Via Centrale Umbra.
The Roman city was built at a lower level than the medieval town, which was constructed more defensively on the hill. The amphitheatre, near the church of San Claudio on the main road to Foligno, dates from the 1st century AD, but little survives.

A kilometre from Spello towards Perugia is Villa Fidelia, once at the centre of the Roman city, and where an epigraph, known as the "Rescritto di Costantino" (rescript of Constantine), was found in 1733. According to this ordinance, the great emperor, in the years between 324 and 337 AD, authorized the Umbrians to hold their celebrations at Spello and not in Orvieto.

Spello Town Centre

① Santa Maria Maggiore
② Pinacoteca Civica
③ Sant'Andrea
④ Piazza della Repubblica
⑤ Porta Venere
⑥ Porta dell'Arce
⑦ San Claudio
⑧ Roman Ruins

Foligno's Piazza della Repubblica with the cathedral's south façade

❷ Foligno

Perugia. **Road Map** D4. 🔼 56,000.
🚇 Rome–Ancona line. 🚌 ℹ Corso
Cavour 126, 0742 354 459. 🎪 Giostra
della Quintana, 2nd Sun in Sep.

The town of Foligno, of Roman
origin, lies in the plain of the
River Topino, which skirts its
northern edge. One of the few
Umbrian towns
to be built on flat
land, Foligno
was sited at the
crossroads of
two commercial
roads of great
importance: the
Via Flaminia and
the road from
Perugia to Assisi.

A 15th-century fresco in Foligno's
Palazzo Trinci

The principal manufacturing
and commercial centre in
the region, with the exception
perhaps of Perugia, Foligno is
a lively, dynamic city. Because
of its location, the city has been
able to sprawl out onto the
plain, helped by the destruction
of the 14th-century walls after
the unification of Italy. While the
original oval layout can still be
discerned, the historic centre
features a mix of old and
modern architecture.

The railway station, east of
the centre, is both a good point
of reference and a good place
from which to start a tour. From
here, passing by streets where
walls once stood, you rapidly
reach the historic centre along
Via Ottaviani and Via Umberto I.
Halfway along Via Umberto I is
Via Piermarini, named after the
famous Foligno architect who

designed La Scala opera house
in Milan. Opposite is the entrance
to Via dei Monasteri, where you'll
find the monastery of Sant'Anna.
While still in possession of
several precious works of art,
the monastery is most famous
as the former home (until
1798) of Raphael's celebrated
Madonna di Foligno, removed
by Napoleon's
men and now
on display in the
Vatican museum
in Rome.

Back on Via
Umberto I, at the
corner with Via
Garibaldi, is the
little brick church
of the Nunziatella
(late 15th century), of interest to
visitors because of two works by
Perugino. Above the right-hand
altar is a *Baptism of Jesus* and, in
the lunette, a *God the Father*.
Both works date from 1507.

From here it is just a short
distance to the central Piazza
della Repubblica, the heart of
the city and home to the main
centres of religious and civic
power, as was traditional in the
Middle Ages. These include the
duomo, built and modified
between 1133 and 1512 and
restored to its original Romanesque form in the early 20th
century. The cathedral is
unusual for having two façades.
The main façade faces the
small Piazza del Duomo. The
building's better side, however,
is the south front, with its
richly decorated lateral façade
adorned with a splendid

doorway (1201), which looks
onto Piazza della Repubblica.

Opposite is the Palazzo
Comunale, with a Neo-Classical
façade. Originally built in the
13th century, the palace was
rebuilt several times and altered
completely following the
earthquake of 1832. The only
historic element to be kept was
the battlemented tower, which,
however, succumbed to the
earthquake of 1997.

The palace is linked to
Palazzo Orfini, which is famous
because it was probably the
home of the printing house of
Orfini. This was among the
earliest of all Italian printing
houses (1470), and the first to
publish a work in Italian, Dante's
Divine Comedy (1472).

On the northwestern side
of Piazza della Repubblica is
another important building,
Palazzo Trinci, home of the
Pinacoteca Comunale and the
Museo Archeologico. Among
many works of art in the gallery
are pictures by three notable
painters born in Foligno:
Ottaviano Nelli, Niccolò Alunno
and Pier Antonio Mezzastris.

Via Gramsci, which leads west
off the piazza, contains several
palaces dating from the 16th to
18th centuries, some constructed
over older medieval buildings.
Of these, the Renaissance
Palazzo Deli (Via Gramsci 6) is
the most beautiful. It features a
medieval tower that was once
part of Palazzo Trinci.

Nativity, Niccolò Alunno, church of
San Niccolò

Well from 1340 in the Romanesque cloister of the abbey of Sassovivo

In Piazza San Domenico, at the end of Via Gramsci, is the Romanesque church of Santa Maria Infraportas, whose exterior portico dates from the 11th or 12th century. Inside is the Cappella dell'Assunta (12th century), which has Byzantine-like frescoes that are of interest even though they are in a rather bad state. Another fine work in the church is a *St Jerome and Two Angels* by Mezzastris.

The church of San Niccolò, nearby on Via della Scuola di Arti e Mestieri, was rebuilt in the 14th century by Olivetan monks, remodelled in the following century and then completely rebuilt again in the 18th century. Inside are several works by Niccolò Alunno, among them the *Polyptych of the Nativity*, one of his best-known works. The School of Arts and Crafts, after which the street is named, was based in the monastery alongside.

In Piazza XX Settembre, reached from San Niccolò along Via Mezzalancia, is one of the most beautiful private palazzi built in the 17th century, Palazzo Monaldi-Bernabò, now a school.

🏛 **Museo di Palazzo Trinci**
Piazza della Repubblica. **Tel** 0742 330 585 or 0742 330 584. **Open** 10am– 1pm, 3–7pm Tue– Sun. **Closed** 1 Jan, 25 Dec. 🐾 ♿

Environs
Heading east out of Foligno along the main road no. 77, then taking a fork to the right after about 2 km (1 mile), drivers will come to a scenic road that leads up to the Abbazia di Sassovivo surrounded by a dense forest of holm oaks. Founded in around 1000, the Benedictine abbey was an important political and cultural centre at least until the 15th century. The abbey church is of much less interest than the 13th- century Romanesque cloister, which is the finest of its kind in the region. It features 128 variegated double or spiral columns supporting 58 round arches, decorated with coloured marbles and two bands of mosaics. There is a 13th-century fresco, too. Also of note is the Loggia del Paradiso in the monastery.

The façade of Santa Maria Infraportas

❸ Altopiano di Colfiorito

Perugia. **Road Map** E4. 🚍 Foligno, 24 km (15 miles), Rome–Ancona line. 🚌 ℹ Corso Cavour 126, Foligno, 0742 354 459.

Heading east from Foligno along main road no. 77, shortly before the border of Le Marche you reach the Altopiano of Colfiorito. This upland plain, which reaches over 700 m (2,300 ft) above sea level, consists of seven broad basins, once part of a lake which was drained in the 15th century. Of the original natural formation, a marsh called the Palude di Colfiorito remains. The 100-ha (250-acre) wetland is of great interest for its aquatic vegetation and associated wildlife.

Various calcareous plains alternate with steep slopes, in a fascinating undulating landscape. Silhouetted around the fringes are the Apennine peaks of Monte Pennino, Monte Acuto, Monte Le Scalette, Monte Profoglio and Col Falcone.

This upland plain and the surrounding area now form part of the Parco Regionale di Colfiorito, a protected area that was set up to preserve this unique region. Now that the park is well established, visitors can explore the Altopiano using a series of signposted routes. There are also traces of ancient human habitation, the most obvious of which are the so- called *castellieri*, pre-Roman villages. The most visited is that of Monte Orve. The park also houses Museo Naturalistico, which was set up for the observation of main species of flora and fauna here.

The slopes of Monte Pennino and the marsh of Colfiorito

Piazza Silvestri, in the heart of Bevagna

❹ Bevagna

Perugia. **Road Map** D4. 🚍 5,100. 🚆 Foligno, 9 km (6 miles), Rome–Ancona line. 🚌 ℹ️ Pro Loco, Piazza Filippo Silvestri, 1, 0742 361 667. 🎭 Mercato delle Gaite, Jun. 🌐 **prolocobevagna.it**

Situated at the western margins of the Valle Umbra, Bevagna has long been at the centre of a busy road network, Inhabited probably since the 7th century BC, ancient *Mevania* experienced its most affluent period under the Romans, thanks largely to its position on the Via Flaminia. Many illustrious citizens of ancient Rome built their country houses here. Following a period of decline during the Lombard era, when this branch of the Via Flaminia lost importance, the town experienced a revival in the 12th century, and this was when Bevagna acquired its current appearance. Town walls, incorporating part of the

Roman walls, were built, with a main square at the centre. Not only are the walls still a feature, but remarkably little has been built outside them since the Middle Ages.

Porta Foligno is the main entrance into the town, from where Corso Matteotti leads to the heart of the city, Piazza Silvestri. Around this clearly medieval piazza stand the Gothic Palazzo dei Consoli and three churches: San Silvestro, San Michele Arcangelo and Santi Domenico e Giacomo.

Corso Matteotti follows the route of the cardo – one of the main streets through the Roman settlement. In the northern part, where the Forum stood, various traces of the Roman era have been restored and some still survive, among them the ruins of a temple (incorporated into the church of the Madonna della Neve), a theatre and baths. In the same district, off Piazza Garibaldi, is the 13th-century church of San Francesco. Inside are frescoes by an artist known as Fantino. This painter was born in Bevagna at the end of the 16th century and left works of art in many local towns. The church also contains a stone which is said to have been mounted by St Francis when he preached to the birds (*see pp28–9*), an event which happened nearby.

Also worth a visit is the **Museo Civico**, which has many Roman and pre-Roman finds, as well as

Artemis, Museo Civico

the fine *Ciccoli Altarpiece* (1565–70) by Dono Doni. There is also a section devoted to the local 16th- and 17th-century artists.

🏛️ Museo Civico
Corso Matteotti 70. **Tel** 0742 360 081. **Open** Apr–Sep: 10:30am–1pm, 3–6pm Fri–Sun; Oct–Mar: 10:30am–1pm, 2:30–5:30pm. **Closed** 1 Jan, 25 Dec. 📷

Ciccoli Altarpiece, 1565–70, by Dono Doni, Museo Civico

❺ Montefalco

Perugia. **Road Map** D4. 🚍 5,592. 🚆 Foligno, 12 km (7 miles), Rome–Ancona line. 🚌 ℹ️ Pro Loco, Piazza del Comune, 0742 616 127. 🎭 Agosto Montefalchese, Aug.

Perched high on a hill dominating the valleys of the rivers Topino and Clitunno, Montefalco offers superb views over central Umbria, and has been nicknamed "the balcony of Umbria". It is also famous for its Sagrantino wine.

The small medieval comune, known as Coccorone, was badly damaged in 1249 in the course of bitter battles fought between the pope and Emperor Frederick II. When the latter rebuilt the town, he decided to call it Montefalco, in honour of his imperial eagle insignia. The town's artistic high point came in the 14th century, followed by decline once Montefalco came under papal jurisdiction.

Montefalco retains some elements of Roman origin, but

Historic Bevagna, at the fringes of the Valle Umbra

the atmosphere is, above all, medieval, focused on the circular Piazza del Comune. This feudal nucleus is enclosed within a circle of medieval walls with five gates, from which five main streets lead, in the shape of a star, to the central piazza.

The main access to the town is via the 14th-century Porta Sant'Agostino, which has a tower on top. From here, Via Umberto I and then Corso Mameli lead up to the main square. Along the way is the church of Sant' Agostino (late 13th century), whose façade is adorned with slender columns and a rose window. Inside the church are a number of interesting frescoes, among them one attributed to Ambrogio Lorenzetti. You also pass palazzos Tempestini, Langeli and Moriconi.

Laid out during the 14th century, the central Piazza del Comune is home to the Palazzo Comunale, heavily reworked in the 19th century, the former church of San Filippo Neri (now a theatre) and the Oratorio di Santa Maria, which was used as a public meeting place during the Renaissance.

Just north of Piazza del Comune, along Via Ringhiera Umbra, is the most important monument in the town, and indeed one of the most famous in the entire region – the former church of **San Francesco**. The attached monastery houses the **Museo Comunale**. The highlight of a visit to the deconsecrated

Scenes from the Life of St Clare, detail, church of Santa Chiara

14th-century church are the frescoes painted by Benozzo Gozzoli (1420–97), a pupil of Fra Angelico and famous above all for his exquisite frescoes in the Palazzo Medici in Florence. Gozzoli's frescoes in San Francesco are found in the Cappella di San Girolamo and, more importantly, in the central apse, where the magnificent and colourful *Life of St Francis* (1452) is the most important pictorial cycle dedicated to the saint after the one in the Basilica di San Francesco in Assisi.

The church-cum-museum also contains works of art salvaged from other local churches, as well as other objects: note, in particular, a *Crucifix* by the Maestro Espressionista di Santa Chiara (late 13th–early 14th centuries), a *Madonna and Child* from the workshop of Melozzo da Forlì (late 15th century), a *Nativity* painted by Perugino (1503) and, among the sculptures, a *Coronation of the Virgin* from the workshop of Andrea della Robbia (16th century).

From Piazza del Comune, a flight of steps leads southwards down to the medieval church of San Bartolomeo, and to the town gate of the same name. Beyond is Viale Federico II (named in honour of the emperor who stayed in the town in 1240 during his battles against the pope), which leads on to the quarter called Borgo

Crucifix, Museo Comunale

di San Leonardo. Walking westwards, outside the old walls, you reach the convent and church of Santa Chiara. These are dedicated not to the famous Clare of Assisi, but to Chiara di Damiano of Montefalco (1268–1308), who had the complex built here in the 13th and 14th centuries, on the site of the older Cappella di Santa Croce. The chapel (opened on request by the nuns who still live in the convent) is now the apse of the church. It is completely covered in 14th-century frescoes by Umbrian artists, narrating the lives of the saints Chiara, Caterina (Catherine) and Biagio (Blaise), and of the Virgin. On the wall of the altar a *Calvary* includes more than 45 figures.

A short distance south, along Via Giuseppe Verdi, is the Renaissance church of Santa Illuminata, which was built from 1491 on the site where Santa Chiara and her sister were locked up by their father.

The Franciscan convent of San Fortunato, about 1 km (half a mile) south of the town, has frescoes by Benozzo Gozzoli (1449) in the church.

🏠 **San Francesco and Museo Comunale**
Via Ringhiera Umbra. **Tel** 0742 379 598. **Open** Apr, May, Sep & Oct: 10:30am–6pm daily; Jun–Aug: 10:30am–7pm daily; Nov & Dec: 10:30am–1pm, 2:30–5pm Wed–Sun. **Closed** 1 Jan, 25 Dec. 🖼️ ♿

Porta Sant'Agostino (or dello Stradone), gateway to Montefalco

❻ Trevi

Perugia. **Road Map** D5. 🚊 8,500.
🚉 Rome–Ancona line, FCU Perugia–
Terni line. 🚌 ℹ️ Piazza Mazzini 5,
0742 332 269. 🌐 **treviturismo.it**

The historic centre of Trevi
"unwinds" in a stunning spiral
fashion around a steep conical
hill, Monte Serano, which
dominates the plain of Spoleto.
Flooding from the nearby River
Clitunno used to be a constant
threat and forced the inhabitants
of Roman Trevi to move to higher
ground. Once this threat was
averted, however, the modern
city – the so-called Borgo Trevi –
was free to develop down on
the plain, among the fields and
olive groves.

Trevi converted early to
Christianity; according to legend,
this was because of the presence
of the martyr Emiliano. In the
4th century, after a brief period
of liberty, the town became part
of the papal states and remained
so until the unification of Italy.

The central Piazza Mazzini is
home to the Palazzo Comunale,
built in the 14th century but
with important later additions,
such as the 15th-century portico.
From here, Via San Francesco
passes the monumental Palazzo
Valenti en route to the huge
church of San Francesco.

This church, together with the
adjacent Raccolta d'Arte di San
Francesco, is the principal artistic
attraction in the town. The
church itself, which dates from
the 13th century, contains
interesting works, including a
fine organ from 1209. However,

Coronation of the Virgin (1522), detail

Trevi's most important works
of art are on display in the
Raccolta, which has been
housed in the church monastery since 1997. The finest work
is the *Coronation of the Virgin*
(1522), by Giovanni di Pietro,
known as Spagna, which was
commissioned by the friars of
the church of San Martino *(see
below)*; the predella includes
two scenes from the lives of
the saints: *St Martin gives
away his Cloak* and
*The Stigmata of
St Francis*. The art
collection also
includes paintings
from the Umbrian school
from the 14th century,
among the most
complete anywhere;
in particular, do not
miss the *Life of
Christ* by Giovanni di
Corraduccio (first half of
the 14th century). The cathedral
of Sant'Emiliano stands at the
summit of the hill. It was
extensively restored in the

20th century, but still has
the three original apses
(12th century), which are
among the best examples
of Romanesque in the
region. Next door is the
Palazzo Lucarini, which
houses the **Palazzo
Lucarini Contemporary**,
with a small permanent
collection of contemporary
art by Italian and foreign
artists, as well as changing
exhibitions.

A ten-minute walk along
pedestrian Viale Ciuffelli
takes you to the 14th-century
parish church of San Martino,
built in a scenic position on
the northeastern edge of town.
Inside the church are works
by Tiberio d'Assisi and Fantino,
among the most famous artists
of the Umbrian school. It is
also worth visiting the Santuario
della Madonna delle
Lacrime, just south of
the centre (not far from the
train station), where there is
a lovely *Epiphany*
by Perugino
(1512), as well as
an important cycle
of frescoes by Lo
Spagna, in the chapel of
San Francesco.

Painted cross (15th century),
Raccolta di San Francesco

🏛️ **Raccolta D'Arte
di San Francesco**
Largo Don Bosco 14.
Tel 0742 381 628. **Open** Apr–Sep:
10:30am–1pm, 2:30–6pm Tue–Sun (till
7pm Aug); Oct–Mar: 10:30am–1pm,
2:30–5pm Fri–Sun.

🏛️ **Palazzo Lucarini Contemporary**
Via Lucarini 1.
Tel 0742 381 021. **Open** 3:30–6:30pm
Thu–Sun. 🌐 **palazzolucarini.it**

Environs

Around 5 km (3 miles) north of
Trevi rises the 14th-century
church of Santa Maria a
Pietrarossa. Its name derives from
the red stone *(pietra rossa)* in the
presbytery, to which miraculous
powers were attributed. The
church has an extensive portico,
beneath which is a vast cycle of
votive frescoes dating from the
15th century. A few metres from
the church is the San Giovanni
spring, whose water is said to
be therapeutic.

Interior of the church of San Martino

The pool formed by the Fonti del Clitunno springs, framed by weeping willows and poplars

❼ Fonti del Clitunno

Perugia. **Road Map** D5. **FS** Campello sul Clitunno, Rome–Ancona line, Trevi, 10 km (6 miles), FCU Perugia–Terni line. 🚌

These famous springs emerge alongside the Via Flaminia, at Vene, and have been known since antiquity. The cool, limpid waters of this series of karst springs create a large pool with small islands, as well as a river of the same name.

On a literary level, the historic reputation of the springs derives from the oracular skills attributed to the god of the River Clitunno (Clitumnus, the messenger god). The oracle was often cited by poets, from Virgil to Byron. This does not mean that drinking the water makes you a good orator. The water's main effect, some say, is to remove the urge to imbibe alcohol.

The Roman Tempietto

The site owes its fortune to the fertility of the soil and the sheer abundance of water, which rises in such quantity that at one time the river was navigable. The Romans exploited the site and created a holiday area here, using the springs to create public baths.

Numerous buildings and villas were constructed along the river banks, although today they have almost totally disappeared. Votive buildings include the **Tempietto**, which many experts believe was built in the 4th–5th centuries, while others believe 7th–8th centuries, using the materials from an earlier Christian building. About 1 km (half a mile) north of the Fonti, the temple has a crypt and a room for worship. The latter is decorated with 7th-century frescoes, thought to be the oldest paintings with sacred

subjects in Umbria. In 2011, Spoleto's Tempietto del Clitunno was listed as a UNESCO World Heritage site.

🏛 Fonti del Clitunno
Tel 0743 521 141. **Open** Mar & Apr: 9am–1pm, 2–6:30pm daily; May–Sep: 8:30am–dusk daily; Oct: 9am–1pm, 2–6pm daily; Nov–Feb: 10am–1pm, 2–4:30pm daily. **Closed** 25 Dec. 🚫

🏛 Tempietto
Tel 0743 275 085. **Open** summer: 2:15–7:45pm Tue–Sat; winter: 12:15–5:45pm Tue–Sat **Closed** Mon. 🚫

Environs
Just south of the springs is Campello sul Clitunno, whose church of the Madonna della Bianca has fine 16th-century frescoes. Follow the steep road up from the village to Castello di Pissignano, where Barbarossa once stayed.

A trapezoid tower, part of the Castello di Pissignano

Umbrian Olive Oil

Olive oil made in Umbria can bear the label "denominazione di origine controllata" (denomination of controlled origin) if it conforms to the high quality standards set for the product. Umbria has been divided into five producing districts, each with differing quality criteria. The strictest rules are applied in the district centred around Trevi, one of the most important olive-growing areas.

❽ Parco Nazionale dei Monti Sibillini

Established as a national park in August 1993, the mountainous Sibillini park extends over 70,000 ha (173,000 acres). The park is divided between Umbria and Le Marche and offers a bewitching combination of nature and history. There are numerous abbeys and medieval hill towns as well as rich natural diversity. Trails cover the entire park and are suitable for both walkers and mountain bikers. The windy upland plains are popular for hang-gliding, and in winter the mountains attract skiers. Among the refuges higher up are Rifugio Città di Ascoli (Passo di Forca Canapine) and Capanna Ghezzi (above the plains of Castelluccio). Some of the trails were damaged in the 2016 earthquakes, but most are still in good shape.

Abbazia di Sant'Eutizio
The buildings of this abbey date from the late 12th century, but the area drew hermits from the 6th century onwards, and was important politically and culturally during the early Middle Ages.

Key

▨▨ Park road

▨▨ Scenic route

~~~ River

△ Peak

– – Regional border

0 kilometres ___3___

0 miles ___3___

Marcite di Norcia
These irrigated meadows benefit from the water that flows from karstic springs.

Wildlife in the Monti Sibillini

The park is an ideal habitat for many species. In terms of mammals, the wolf and wildcat are present in small numbers, but there are healthy populations of roe deer, marten and especially wild boar (to the degree that they are becoming a problem). Lynx have been seen, but doubt has been cast on sightings of the Marsican bear. The birdlife in the mountains is very varied. Foremost is the golden eagle, an elegant predator which is easily spotted in the area. Some rarer species such as the peregrine falcon and the goshawk are also present. Alpine choughs and wall creepers are common.

Golden eagle

**Map labels:**
Pievebovigliana
Lago di Fiastra
Fiastra
Acqua
Ussita
S209
Spoleto
Monte Moricone 1,429 m/4,687 ft
Nera
Castelsantangelo sul Nera
Preci
Monte Patino 1,884 m/6,180 ft
Norcia
Monte Ventoso 1,719 m/5,638 ft
Fiastra

Park Flora
Rare species of plants can be observed in flower on the northern slopes, including alpine orchids and daisies like these.

Lago di Pilato
According to legend, Pontius Pilate was buried in this lake after the buffaloes pulling his hearse refused to go any further, though another story says that a remorseful Pilate drowned himself here. The lake turns blood-red owing to a rare red-coloured algae that grows here.

Monte Vettore
At 2,476 m (8,121 ft), this is the highest peak in the park and one of the major mountains in the Apennine chain. From the summit there are fine views over the entire massif: the dark waters of Lago di Pilato dominate the scene below.

KEY

① **Visso**, now the park headquarters, was said to have been founded 907 years before Rome. From the Middle Ages to the 18th century, its territory was divided into five districts called "*guaite*" (guards). Castles and look-out towers are visible.

② **Monte Sibilla** is the peak that gave its name to the park. There is a grotto here: according to legend this was the home of the mythical Sibyl (*sibilla*), capable of predicting the future.

Plains of Castelluccio
There are three high plains at over 1,300 m (4,264 ft) on the western slopes of the park above the isolated village of Castelluccio (famous for its lentils). In spring, the ground here is carpeted in a breathtaking abundance of flowers, known as the *fioritura*.

Map labels: apaiombo, Bolognola, Monte Amandola 1,706 m/5,600 ft, Amandoia, 578, Ambro, Montefortino, Monte Priora 2,332 m/7,650 ft, Tenna, Gola dell'Infernaccio, ②, Monte Vallelunga 2,221 m/7,285 ft, Montemonaco, Foce, stelluccio, Monte Vettore 2,476 m/8,121 ft, Montegallo, Piano Grande

❷ Spoleto

Spoleto is one of the most important towns in Umbria. It occupies a striking hillside position, at the foot of Monteluco, is home to a host of fine monuments, and enjoys an international reputation. The last started with the travellers on the Grand Tour and continues today with the cosmopolitan crowd that has flocked to the famous Festival di Spoleto since 1958. The first settlement here was founded, probably by the Umbri, high up where the fortress was later built: traces of the massive 4th-century-BC walls are still visible. Spoletium, founded in 241 BC, became a major Roman colony, thanks partly to its proximity to the Via Flaminia, used by people travelling to Rome from the north. Spoleto later became the seat of a Lombard dukedom and then an important commune. Numerous monastic orders were established here and the town maintained its prosperity over the centuries.

Entrance to San Nicolò, framed by Gothic arches

The city of Spoleto, dominating the Spoletine valley

Exploring Spoleto

The main approach into the city is from the northern side, over the Ponte Sanguinario, a Roman bridge. From here, the route of the tour climbs upwards, via several sites of importance, to the highest and oldest part of the city, where both the duomo and the Rocca Albornoziana, essential sights on a visit to Spoleto, are found.

⬆ San Gregorio Maggiore
Piazza Garibaldi.
Just over Ponte Sanguinario, the gateway to the town, is Piazza Garibaldi, home to the church of San Gregorio Maggiore. It was founded in the 4th century, in the early Christian era, outside the walls, as were all the oldest churches in the city. It was renovated in the 12th century, incorporating materials from various Roman remains, and a second set of city walls were constructed around the church. The façade is adorned with statues and a

huge campanile (notice the Roman blocks used in the lower half) and has a portico modelled on that of the duomo (*see p117*). Despite frequent restoration and embellishment, the Romanesque interior still bears traces of interesting medieval frescoes.

The façade of San Gregorio with portico and bell tower

⬆ San Nicolò
Via Cecili.
From Piazza Garibaldi, Via dell' Anfiteatro heads towards the centre, past the meagre ruins of a 2nd-century-AD Roman amphitheatre. Continuing up Via Cecili you reach the deconsecrated church of San Nicolò.

What looks like a single church is, in fact, a complex of religious buildings placed one on top of the other over the course of the centuries. The imposing Gothic church, which played host to Martin Luther in 1512, is now used for plays and concerts.

⬆ San Domenico
Via Pierleone.
Via Cecili leads to Piazza della Torre dell'Olio, with the 14th-century tower of the same name. Taking Via Pierleone, which runs south, you reach the large monastic church of San Domenico (13th century), with its distinctive pink and white striped design.

Restored to its original Gothic form in the 1930s, the church has a single, unusually long nave. Here, you can admire interesting frescoes dating from the 14th and 15th centuries, some of which have come to light only in recent decades. In particular, linger over the Cappella di San Pietro Martire (the first on the left), the Cappella di Santa Maria Maddalena, on the right-hand side of the apse, and the Cappella Benedetti di Montevecchio, on the left of the presbytery.

The Roman theatre in Spoleto, dating from the 1st century AD

🔼 Santi Giovanni e Paolo

Via Filitteria.

Heading up Via Sant'Andrea from San Domenico, you pass the Teatro Nuovo, a grand theatre built over the ruins of a monastery and inaugurated in 1864. A little further on is the deconsecrated church dedicated to saints John and Paul in 1174. It is worth a visit for the frescoes inside: the oldest is the one depicting the *Martyrdom of Thomas Becket*, painted after his canonization in 1173.

🏛 Palazzo Collicola Arti Visive

Piazza Collicola 1. **Tel** 0743 464 34. **Open** mid-Mar–mid-Oct: 10:30am–1pm, 3–7pm daily; mid-Oct–mid-Mar: 10:30am– 1pm, 3–5:30pm Wed–Mon. 🎫

The collection in this modern art gallery is divided into three sections. The most interesting is the first, which has works by contemporary Italian artists, participants in the "Premio Spoleto" (Spoleto Prize), among them Arnaldo Pomodoro and Giulio Turcato.

🏛 Teatro Romano

Museo Archeologico Nazionale, Piazza della Libertà.

Piazza della Libertà is the site of a restored Roman theatre built in the 1st century AD. Excavated in the late 19th century, today the theatre forms part of the **Museo Archeologico Nazionale** and is used during festivals. It has a capacity of 3,000.

The Museo also occupies the nearby monastery of Sant'Agata, one of the oldest religious buildings in the city.

🏛 Museo Archeologico Nazionale

Via Sant'Agata 18. **Tel** 0743 223 277.
Open 8:30am–7:30pm daily.
Closed 1 Jan, 1 May, 25 Dec. 🎫

Spoleto Town Centre

① San Gregorio Maggiore
② San Nicolò
③ San Domenico
④ Santi Giovanni e Paolo
⑤ Palazzo Collicola Arti Visive
⑥ Teatro Romano
⑦ Sant'Ansano and the Crypt of Sant'Isacco
⑧ Piazza del Mercato
⑨ Palazzo Comunale
⑩ Casa Romana
⑪ Museo del Tessile e del Costume
⑫ Museo Diocesano and Sant'Eufemia
⑬ La Rocca Albornoziana
⑭ Duomo
⑮ San Ponziano
⑯ San Salvatore

0 metres   250
0 yards   250

⚐ Sant'Ansano and the Crypt of Sant'Isacco
Via Brignone.

Climbing up towards the oldest part of Spoleto, you follow the route of the "cardo maximus", one of the main roads through the Roman settlement. The church of Sant'Ansano is, in fact, built on the ruins of a 1st-century temple. What you see today dates from the 18th century, but the church has a complex architectural history. The crypt of Sant'Isacco (St Isaac) provides evidence of a 12th-century church dedicated to both saints. It contains Roman columns and striking Byzantine-style frescoes. The church above contains a *Madonna* by Spagna (first half of the 16th century).

⚐ Piazza del Mercato
This square lies at the heart of the oldest part of Spoleto. With an open market, shops and bars, it is always busy. At the far end of the piazza, along Via Arco di Druso, is the Arch of Drusus, or **Arco di Druso**. This arch marked the point where the *cardo maximus* entered the forum (now Piazza del Mercato). It was erected in AD 23 in memory of the son of Emperor Tiberius.

In terms of other monuments in Piazza del Mercato, there is a fountain built in the mid-18th century with material taken from other buildings, among them four coats of arms and a slab commemorating Pope Urban VIII.

⚐ Arco di Druso
Piazza del Mercato.

⚐ Palazzo Comunale
Via di Visiale. **Tel** 0743 234 350. **Open** 10:30am–5:30pm Wed–Mon.

To the north of Piazza del Mercato is one side of the Palazzo Comunale. This building was built in medieval times, but rebuilt in the late 1700s, after earthquake damage. Today it is used as the town hall.

⚐ Casa Romana
Via di Visiale. **Tel** 0743 234 250. **Open** 11am–7pm (winter: till 5:30pm) Tue–Sun. **Closed** Mon (Oct–Mar). ⚐

Casa Romana, which literally translates as Roman house, dates from the 1st century BC, and was

Mid 18th-century fountain in Piazza del Mercato

believed to be a stately home. It has some lovely mosaic floors.

⚐ Museo del Tessile e del Costume
Via delle Terme 5. **Tel** 0743 459 40. **Open** 3–6pm Sat & Sun. ⚐

The Museo del Tessile e del Costume is dedicated to historic textiles, and contains over 2,500 pieces spanning the 14th to the 20th centuries. These include liturgical vestments, clothing, fans, hats and folk textiles.

⚐ Museo Diocesano and Sant'Eufemia
Palazzo Arcivescovile, Via Saffi 13. **Tel** 0743 231 022. **Open** 11am–1:30pm Thu–Fri; 11am–4:30pm Sat & Sun. **Closed** Mon & Tue. ⚐

The architectural history of this palace, inside the Palazzo Arcivescovile, constitutes a virtual narrative in stone of the history of Spoleto. It began with the construction of a Roman building (still partially visible), above which it is thought that

the Palazzo dei Longobardi was built when Spoleto was a duchy. In the 12th century the building became a part of a monastery. It turned into the bishop's palace in the 16th–17th centuries.

Inside is a good collection of works of art and, in the courtyard, the 12th-century church of Sant'Eufemia. This church is Romanesque but more Lombard than Umbrian in style. It is famed for its rare women's galleries above the nave.

⚐ La Rocca Albornoziana
Piazza Campello 1. **Tel** 0743 224 952. **Open** La Rocca and Camera Pinta 9:30am–6pm Tue–Sun; Museo Nazionale del Ducato di Spoleto 9:30am–6pm Tue–Sun.

In 1359, when the city was an outpost of a Church intent on reconquering Umbria, Cardinal Albornoz, papal legate for Innocent VI, ordered the construction of a military fortress (*rocca*) at the highest point of the city. It was linked to the hill behind, Monteluco, by the Ponte delle Torri, which still straddles the Valle del Tessino (see p113). La Rocca can be visited by bus (buses run hourly from Piazza Campello) or the escalators can help cover the climb.

The fortress is built on a rectangular plan around two courtyards, the Corte d'Armi and the Cortile d'Onore, both surrounded by towers. Over the centuries, La Rocca has been home to various notable figures, among them Lucrezia Borgia, whose caprices were perhaps responsible for the naming of the tower called

Interior of the ancient Casa Romana

"della Spiritata" (the spirited one). Converted into a prison for over a century, in 1984 the Rocca underwent restoration.

Inside La Rocca today is Museo Nazionale del Ducato di Spoleto, which contains many treasures that trace the history of Spoleto. Further highlights include the frescoes in the Camera Pinta (in one of the main towers). These chivalric scenes were painted by artists from the school of Terni in the 14th–15th centuries.

Behind La Rocca is the masterly, ten-arch Ponte delle Torri, crossing the River Tessino. It is 230 m (755 ft) long and over 70 m (230 ft) high: the date of construction is uncertain and it is probable that today's bridge evolved from a Roman bridge-cum-aqueduct. In the middle of the bridge is an opening offering lovely views.

Mosaic by Solsternus on the façade of the duomo

🛈 Duomo

Piazza del Duomo. **Open** 8:30am–12:30pm, 3:30–6pm (summer: 7pm) daily.

A short climb from Piazza del Mercato leads to the sloping Piazza del Duomo, home of Spoleto's cathedral. As a backdrop to the Festival di Spoleto, this church's image is now world-famous.

The cathedral, built and consecrated at the end of the 12th century, is dedicated to Santa Maria Assunta, and rises on a site where there were at least two earlier religious buildings. The façade, one of the most superb examples of Umbrian Romanesque, is divided into three orders and is the result

The duomo's façade, backdrop to the annual Festival di Spoleto

of at least three successive phases of construction.

The original project resulted in the basilica layout, and the bell tower probably dates from the same era (12th century). A second phase of construction (early 13th century) saw the building of the façade, with the mosaic of Solsternus (1207) and the three upper rose windows, which frame the original Cosmatesque one underneath, one of the most beautiful in central Italy. The portico, with its magnificent central door, was added at the end of the 15th century. The bronze bust of Urban VIII above the central door was sculpted by Gian Lorenzo Bernini in 1640.

The interior of the church, rebuilt in Baroque style in 1648, is built on a Latin cross plan, divided into three aisles separated by a colonnade. There are various important works of art here. Just past vthe entrance, on the right, is the Cappella del Vescovo Costantino Eroli, built in 1497 and entirely decorated with frescoes by Pinturicchio. Don't miss those in the chapel altar niche, depicting *God the Father and Angels*, *The Madonna and Child* and *John the Baptist and St Stephen*. There is also a fine series of figures from the Old Testament on the vault.

Transition of the Virgin, Filippo Lippi, detail

The other important cycle of frescoes (1467–9), by the artist Filippo Lippi, is found on the walls of the apse. The subject is the life of Mary. Among the scenes are an *Annunciation*, a *Transition of the Virgin*, a *Nativity* and a *Coronation of the Virgin*. The remains of Filippo Lippi are in the right transept of the church. After his death and burial in the Duomo, the Medici dynasty commissioned a sarcophagus from Lippi's son Filippino, and it was placed in the church, by the original grave.

On the two sides of the apse, extending outwards from the main body of the church, are two chapels, the Cappella della Santissima Icona and the Cappella del Sacramento. In the first is an image of the Virgin in the form of an icon, much venerated because it is attributed to St Luke. On the left, to the side of the transept is the lovely Cappella delle Reliquie. Besides some fine frescoes and painted panels, this chapel contains a 14th- century wooden statue of a *Madonna and Child* and a letter written by St Francis to his disciple Fra Leone. On the first altar on the left, in the nave, hangs a *Crucifix* by Alberto Sotio, painted on parchment applied to board, dated 1187. Other similar treasures are kept in the Archivio Capitolare.

Detail of a Pinturicchio fresco in the duomo's Cappella Eroli

Detail of a bas-relief on the façade of the church of San Pietro Fuori le Mura

San Paolo inter Vineas

Via San Paolo.

The first of four important churches, which form a curve around the eastern side of the historic centre of Spoleto, lies south of the city, beyond the Giardino Pubblico (public gardens) and the stadium.

San Paolo inter Vineas was built on the site of an early Christian religious building, mentioned by St Gregory the Great in the 6th century. The present Romanesque church, flanked by a cloister, dates from the 12th and 13th centuries, and was skilfully restored in the latter half of the 20th century. The most important feature inside is the fresco cycle, which was painted in the early 13th century and is considered to be among the oldest in the region. It depicts the *Prophets* and *Scenes from the Creation of the World*.

The Romanesque church of San Paolo inter Vineas

San Pietro Fuori le Mura

Via Matteotti, then Via Roma, beyond main road Strada Statale Flaminia.

Whereas at San Paolo inter Vineas it is the interior frescoes which are the most important feature, here it is the decorations on the façade.

San Pietro Fuori le Mura ("outside the walls"), which lies south of the town centre, stands at the top of a flight of steps on a plateau from where there are fine views.

The building has ancient origins, probably dating back to the 5th century, when the relics of the chain of St Peter were moved here. The current church dates mainly from the 12th century. The carved stone reliefs on the façade are regarded as one of the most prized examples of Umbrian Romanesque. The reliefs on the lower, older part of the structure, produced in the 12th and 13th centuries, tell complex stories rich in symbolism. They relate lay episodes, taken from medieval encyclopedias, and other religious stories linked to the life of Christ.

Façade of San Pietro Fuori le Mura

San Ponziano

Strada Statale Flaminia, road to the cemetery.

This church lies northeast of the centre, alongside Via Flaminia, and at the foot of the Cinciano hill. It occupies the site of the tomb of the martyr Ponziano, patron saint of Spoleto, who is commemorated on 14 January. This is a convent church, first the home of Poor Clares and later Augustinian nuns, with a Romanesque exterior and an interior which was completely restructured in 1788 by Giuseppe Valadier. (He also designed the doors and altars of the cathedral.)

The main feature of interest is the crypt. Divided into three aisles, like the church above, and with five apses, this contains

The Festival di Spoleto

The most important event in Spoleto's recent history occurred when it was chosen by the Italian-American composer Gian Carlo Menotti as the venue for the Festival dei Due Mondi, which was to become a major international arts event. The choice fell on Spoleto because of its central location within Italy, its historic appeal and its plentiful theatres and cinemas. In 1958 a performance of Verdi's *Macbeth*, directed by Luchino Visconti, inaugurated the first festival. Since then, despite the controversy with which the festival has always been associated and the change of name (today it is called the "Festival di Spoleto"), every summer the event attracts an enthusiastic audience, as well as artists from all over the world, to this splendid city.

A closing concert at the Festival

Roman fragments and some pretty votive frescoes, which include one showing the *Archangel Michael* with a globe and staff, in the right-hand apse. On the left is an *Enthroned Madonna*.

The formal interior of the church of San Salvatore

⛪ San Salvatore

Via del Cimitero, off Strada Statale Flaminia. **Closed** temporarily closed

From San Ponziano, the road goes up the Cinciano hill and brings visitors to the last, and perhaps the most historically interesting, of all the religious buildings close to Spoleto.

This UNESCO-protected site, the church of San Salvatore is an exceptional example in Umbria, of a building constructed using mainly salvaged material, all dating from the Roman era. The columns, decorative elements, capitals, architraves – most of the architectural features in the three-aisled basilica church, in fact – date from the Roman period. For this reason, it has been difficult for art historians to date San Salvatore with any great precision, although it is undoubtedly one of the oldest churches in the country. Two theories circulate currently. According to the first, the church dates from the early Christian period, and bears witness to the heights of splendour achieved in late Roman art in this area (the Tempietto del Clitunno would be of the same era). According to the second theory, the building was probably designed around the 8th century.

⓿ San Pietro in Valle

Perugia. **Road Map** E5. 🚆 Rome–Ancona line, Terni, 20 km (12 miles); FCU Perugia–Terni line. 🚌 Abbey: **Tel** 0744 780 129 (hotel). **Open** summer: 10am–1pm, 3–6pm daily; winter: 10am–noon daily (call ahead). 🌐 **sanpietroinvalle.com**

It is difficult to try to rank Umbrian abbeys in order of importance, but clearly no classification could omit the Benedictine abbey of San Pietro in Valle, situated in the lower part of the Valnerina, just north of the village of Ferentillo *(see p127)*.

Set against a backdrop of wooded hills, San Pietro in Valle is of significant artistic and religious interest. The abbey's roots lie deep in legend. Its foundation, as one of the frescoes in the left-hand transept of the church testifies, traditionally dates from the 5th century AD, when the Lombard duke of Spoleto, Faroaldo II, met the Syrian hermit Lazarus. St Peter had suggested to the duke in a dream that he should transform the hermit's small chapel into a powerful abbey, and so San Pietro in Valle was built. Faroaldo later decided to stay here, becoming a monk, and he rests here still: his splendid sarcophagus can be seen in the right-hand transept. The abbey was severely

Capital, San Pietro in Valle

damaged by the Saracens in the 9th century, but was restored in around 1000 by Ottone III and then by his successor, Enrico II. In the 1930s, extensive renovation revealed the medieval linear forms which the building had managed to retain, despite all the alterations. Today, the abbey is privately owned, and has been converted into an appealing, sought-after hotel and restaurant, part of the Relais & Châteaux chain, though parts are open to the general public.

The abbey church is owned by the state and is well worth a visit. Long and formal, with a single nave ending in a short transept and three apses, the church contains some superb works of art. On the walls is a cycle of frescoes, which ranks among the finest examples of Romanesque painting in Italy in its complexity and in the precision of its execution. On the left-hand wall and on the upper right-hand side are *Stories from the Old Testament*, while in the remaining space on the right-hand side are *Scenes from the Life of Christ*. The inner façade and the transept are decorated with works from later eras.

Look out for the beautifully preserved Lombard altar (8th century), which bears the self-portrait and signature of the sculptor: "Ursus".

The medieval Benedictine abbey of San Pietro in Valle

Castellina, the impressive fortress in the centre of Norcia

⓫ Norcia

Perugia. **Road Map** 5F. 🚇 5,000. 🚌
ℹ️ Piazza San Benedetto, Via Solferino
22, 0743 828 711. 🎪 Mostra Mercato
del Tartufo Nero, Feb. **W** norcia.net

At the foot of the Monti Sibillini,
on the edge of the plain of
Santa Scolastica, and on the
borders of the ancient duchies
of Spoleto and Benevento,
Norcia was a trading city and
a staging post for centuries.
Today, the town is known for its
local produce, in particular for
its black truffles and for the
production of high-quality
meat, sausages and salami.
In fact, the word "norcino"
– from Norcia – is now
synonymous with
superior meat prod-
ucts. Browsing
around the wonder-
ful *salumerie* and
other food shops is
a highlight of any visit to
the town.

In recent years, the town of
Norcia has been affected by a
number of earthquakes,
particularly that of October
2016, which destroyed the
majority of the town's churches
and cultural heritage. Despite
the damage, Norcia, which is of
great historic importance to the
Italian people, retains its charm,
and a number of buildings do
still stand.

The walls built by the Romans
(who conquered the city in
290 BC) were replaced by
another, heart-shaped set in
the 13th century. These walls,
and the city itself, have been
damaged by disastrous

Lunette from the door of San
Benedetto, detail

earthquakes over the years.
Along the perimeter, however,
the ancient gates (eight in all)
can still be seen.

One of these gates, Porta
Romana, marks the start of
Corso Sertorio, which leads to
Piazza San Benedetto, the
heart of the town since the
Middle Ages. At its centre is a
statue of St Benedict (1880).
Facing onto the square is
Palazzo Comunale, of 14th-
century origin but partly
rebuilt after the
earthquake in 1859.
The portico is
original, while the
soaring bell tower
dates from the
18th century.

Alongside the
palazzo stood
the church of San
Benedetto, which
was founded in the
Middle Ages and extensively
rebuilt in 1389 and at various
later dates. Sadly, the church
was levelled following the
2016 earthquake, and the only
structure of the church that
remains is the 14th-century
façade, which is dominated
by a monumental doorway
(1578). Two statues
representing St Benedict and
Santa Scolastica are also still
standing. On the right side of
the church was a 16th-century
portico, the Portale delle
Misure, the front arch of which
still stands.

The cathedral of Santa
Maria Argentea, built in the
16th century and remodelled
in the 18th, was also badly

affected by the 2016 earthquake. The impressive
Castellina,is a fortress which
was built for Pope Julius III in
1554. Its square layout, centred
on a courtyard with a loggia,
was the work of the prestigious
architect Jacopo Barozzi, also
known as Vignola. The fort
houses the **Museo Civico
Diocesano**, where the highlights include two crucifixes
and a five-figured sculptural
group of the *Deposition* (13th
century). The latter is perfectly
preserved and provides
important evidence of the
popular art being done at that
time (such groups would have
been carried in processions).

🏛️ **Museo Civico Diocesano**
Piazza San Benedetto. **Tel** 0743 817
030. **Open** Jan–Jun, Oct–Dec:
10am–1pm, 3–5pm (5:30pm Sat &
Sun); Jul–Sep: 10am–1pm, 4–7:30pm
daily. 🎫 📷 ♿ 🏠

The courtyard of the Castellina with its
loggia and gallery

A Land Renowned for Saints

Two of the most important saints in Umbrian history (St Francis apart) were born in this area, just a few kilometres from each other but separated by nearly 1,000 years.

St Benedict, founder of the oldest monastic order in the West, was born (with his twin sister Santa Scolastica) in Norcia, in 480. After studying in Rome he settled at Montecassino, where he wrote his famous *Rule*. This became a major influence on medieval monastic life. The patron saint of Norcia (as well as of Europe), St Benedict's saint's day is celebrated on 21 March.

Santa Rita (born Rita Lotti, commemorated on 22 May) was born at Roccaporena, near Cascia, in around 1380, and died in the mid-15th century. The factional struggles between the Guelfs (pro the papacy) and the Ghibellines (pro the German emperors) caused

Monument to St Benedict by Giuseppe Prinzi, 1880

her much suffering. Her parents were part of the so-called "peacemakers of Christ", or mediators between the two factions. Rita carried on their work, even after the assassination of her husband and the death of her two sons, who died of dysentery after conspiring to have their revenge, much to their mother's disapproval (pious Catholics believe God took them by natural death to save them from mortal sin).

Rita entered the Augustine convent of Santa Maria Maddalena at Cascia, where she remained for 40 years, until her death in 1457. She developed a sore on her forehead, which was said to have been caused by a thorn falling from a crown of thorns as she knelt in prayer beneath a statue of Christ; it was viewed by fellow nuns as a stigmata. The miraculous story of Rita gave rise to a popular cult that has lasted for centuries. Indeed, it was thanks only to a popular campaign that Rita was eventually made a saint, on 24 May 1900.

Town of Roccaporena, with the cliff of Santa Rita behind

⑫ Cascia

Perugia. **Road Map** 5E. 🚗 3,300. 🚌
ℹ️ Piazza Garibaldi 1, 0743 711 47.
🎭 Celebrazioni per Santa Rita, 21–22 May.

Inhabited since late antiquity, because of its strategic position, high on a hill, Cascia has had a turbulent past: Umbrian, then Roman and Byzantine, then part of the Duchy of Spoleto, but independent from the 10th century. In the early Middle Ages, it was a Ghibelline city, locked in bitter struggle with Norcia and Spoleto, cities

owing allegiance to the pope. Taken by Rome in 1517, Cascia immediately acquired great importance because of its position on the border with the Kingdom of Naples. This brought great prosperity.

With the unification of Italy, Cascia lost its political relevance and fell into a long period of decline, halted in the 20th century only thanks to religious tourism, which brought large numbers of pilgrims dedicated to the memory of Santa Rita.

The cult is still a significant feature of life in Cascia today, so the focus is no longer the now-destroyed hilltop fortress, but a modern Sanctuary dedicated to the saint. It was built in 1947, replacing a church dating from 1577. To the left of the sanctuary

is the convent of Santa Rita, where the saint lived for much of her life.

Other sites to visit in the town include the Museo Civico (divided between Palazzo Santi and the church of Sant'Antonio Abate), in particular for the fine wooden sculptures, and the churches of San Francesco and Santa Maria. In the outskirts of the town is Roccaporena, Rita's birthplace, dominated by a hill known as the "scoglio" (cliff) of Santa Rita. The area's many castles and towers, which formed an effective system of fortification, are evidence of the historical importance of the region.

Cascia experienced some damage in the 2016 earthquake, with restoration work being carried out as a result..

Fresco in the lunette above the door to the church of San Francesco

⓭ Terni

The only Umbrian provincial capital apart from Perugia, Terni has always been the most developed centre for industry in the region – the result of its position: at the centre of a plain and at the confluence of the River Nera and the Serra and Tescino streams. The availability of water was crucial for the development of heavy industry during the 19th century (the famous Italian steelworks Acciaierie Breda is based here). Terni is also crossed by the Via Flaminia, an extremely important route since Roman times, linking Rome with the north and the Adriatic coast. Terni's industrial importance made it a target for heavy bombardment during World War II and today, despite its Bronze Age origins, it looks modern compared with most other Umbrian towns. With the ruined Roman town of Carsulae and man-made Marmore falls, Terni is a delight. It is the unlikely birthplace of St Valentine, the patron of lovers and one of the world's most popular saints.

Exploring Terni

Although it is a fairly large city, Terni – or at least the most important sights – can be visited in a relatively short time and on foot: the historic centre, located on the western side of the River Nera, is reasonably compact.

Visitors should leave their cars near the railway station (to the north of the centre), and then follow Viale della Stazione to Piazza Tacito, from where Corso Cornelio Tacito leads directly to the heart of Terni. This is focused around the squares of Piazza della Repubblica, where the main public buildings are located, and Piazza Europa. The latter is home to Palazzo Spada,

which was designed, according to local tradition, by Antonio da Sangallo the Younger.

⌂ San Francesco
Piazza San Francesco. **Open** 8am–12:30pm, 3:30–7:30pm daily.

It is worth making a detour to the right halfway along Corso Tacuto to look at this 13th-century church, which was originally designed in typical Franciscan style with a single nave and transept. In the course of the 15th century, the lateral aisles and the bell tower were added. Inside, the Cappella Paradisi contains a cycle of frescoes (*The Last Judgment*), painted by Bartolomeo di Tommaso, of the Giotto school. The cycle dates from the middle of the 15th century.

⌂ Sant'Alò
Via Sant'Alò. **Tel** 320 252 8895. **Open** by appt.

This Romanesque church, just off Via XI Febbraio, dates from the 11th century and is notable for the abundant re-use of Roman statuary on the exterior. It is thought that the church was built on the ruins of an earlier pagan temple.

⌂ Duomo (Santa Maria Assunta)
Piazza Duomo. **Open** 9am–noon, 3:30–7pm daily.

The Duomo, located south of the city centre, near the public gardens, was built on the site of earlier religious buildings, the first of which existed at least by the 6th century; numerous churches were later built on the same site. The current basilica is the result of reconstruction in 1653, although there are still some traces of a Romanesque church. Look out for the bird and animal reliefs on the main door as you enter. There's also Museo Diocesano e Capitolare inside the duomo, displaying works of religious art.

Detail of the decoration on the main door of the duomo

⌂ Anfiteatro Romano
Piazza Duomo, Via dell'Anfiteatro. **Open** 10am–1pm, 4–8pm (winter: 7pm) by appt.

This amphitheatre (1st century AD), not far from the duomo, is very much a ruin but is still one of the best-preserved Roman sites in Terni. Used as a quarry and later covered by buildings, it was discovered in the mid-19th century and was finally excavated in the 1930s. On the left is

A huge ladle in action in a steelworks

Industrial Terni

The industrial importance of Terni goes back to the dawn of the industrial revolution in Italy (beginning of the 19th century), when the Vatican ironworks were based here. During the 19th century the industries multiplied: foundries, saw-mills, wool mills, as well as the hugely successful Acciaierie Breda steelworks. All found an ideal environment on this plain, which is well supplied with water and in a strategic position for trade. Industry has altered both the countryside and the town itself. Today the factories are, for the most part, dismantled or converted for other use, but the industrial archaeology of Terni is still a reason to visit the area. There are other reasons, of course: this "outdoor museum" extends to cover Terni itself, the waterfalls of Marmore and the town of Narni.

Palazzo Vescovile, whose curvilinear rear façade follows the line of the old bastions. There are lovely views from the adjacent public gardens.

The circular interior of San Salvatore, also known as *Tempio del Sole*

San Salvatore
Largo San Salvatore. **Open** 9am–noon, 4–6pm daily.

The town's most interesting church, just off Piazza Europa, was erected on the ruins of Roman buildings, but it has been impossible to establish exactly when. Also known as *Tempio del Sole* (Temple of the sun), the main body of this church was built on a circular plan and thought to have been

a Roman temple to the sun. It is now believed to date from the 11th century; the rectangular avant-corps is more recent, built perhaps in the 12th century.

Inside the church are traces of frescoes; the ones in the Cappella Manassei date from the 14th century.

Centro Arti Opificio SIRI (CAOS)
Viale Campofregoso 98. **Tel** 0744 258 946. **Open** 10am–1pm, 5–8pm Tue–Sun (winter: 4–7pm).

This former chemical plant houses the Aurelio de Felice collection of modern art, including lithographs by Chagall, Miró, Picasso and Kandinsky. The museum's broad sweep also encompasses works representative of the medieval Umbrian school, such as by Benozzo Gozzoli *(The Marriage of St Catherine)*, Spagna and Nicolò Alunno. It also displays works by upcoming artists.

San Pietro
Piazza San Pietro. **Open** 8am–noon, 3:30–7:30pm daily.

This 14th-century church, not far from Palazzo Comunale,

Madonna and Saints, Benozzo Gozzoli

was enlarged and restored several times. It contains many 14th- and 15th-century frescoes representative of the local school.

Mostra Permanente di Paleontologia
Ex-chiesa di San Tommaso, Largo Liberotti. **Tel** 0744 285 946. **Open** 10am–1pm Thu, 4–7pm Sat.

A vital tool for anyone studying the early history of Umbria, this permanent exhibition has a rich collection of fossils, the remains of several ancient mammals, and a diorama of Umbria when it was covered by the waters of the ancient Tiberine Lake.

Terni Town Centre

1. San Francesco
2. Sant'Alò
3. Duomo
4. Anfiteatro Romano
5. San Salvatore
6. Centro Arti Opificio SIRI (CAOS)
7. San Pietro
8. Mostra Permanente di Paleontologia

0 metres 300
0 yards 300

⑭ Narni

Terni. **Road Map** C6. 20,000.
Rome–Ancona line. Piazza
dei Priori 3, 0744 7471. Corsa
dell'Anello, mid-May for 2 weeks.
comune.narni.tr.it

This fine and unspoilt hill town,
located dramatically above a
bend in the River Nera, is the
geographical centre of Italy.
Its origins date back to the
Umbri people, who founded
Nequinum. This settlement was
conquered by Rome in 299 BC
and was renamed *Narnia*, after
the nearby river. Its importance
under the Romans derived
from the fact that it was the
birthplace of Emperor Nerva, in
AD 32, and also a major stopping
point on the Via Flaminia. Narni
grew until it occupied the entire
rocky spur above the Nera.

Medieval Narni knew tough
years during the wars between
the papacy and the empire, but
it continued to grow, even after
the establishment of papal rule
in the mid-14th century. The
building of a great fortress, on
the orders of Cardinal Albornoz,
emphasized papal authority.
In the 16th century, Narni
was devastated by the
Lanzichenecchi on their return
north after the Sack of Rome.
During the following centuries,
the slow rate of growth kept
the town centre in the form in
which it can still be seen today.
Porta Ternana, on the Via
Flaminia, is the main point of

Bas-reliefs to the right of the door of Palazzo del Podestà

entry to Narni. From here, Via
Roma leads straight to Piazza
Garibaldi, at one time known
as Piazza del Lago because of
a great subterranean cistern,
fed by the Roman aqueduct
of Formina; this now supplies
the water for a 14th-century
fountain with a bronze basin.

Most of the sights are close
to the main axis of the
town, formed by
Via Garibaldi and Via
Mazzini. At one end is
Piazza Garibaldi, home
of Narni's duomo,
an imposing and
beautiful building
dedicated to San
Giovenale, the town's
patron saint. It was
founded in 1047,
but reconstructed in
the 12th century. The
façade has a portico and a portal
decorated with carvings. Inside,
two low arcades separate the
three aisles. On the right is the
mausoleum of the bishops of
Narni, which is dominated by a
tombstone dating from 558.

From the duomo, it is a short
walk up Via Garibaldi to the
central Piazza dei Priori, the attractive seat of civic power in Narni.
Facing the square are the Palazzo
dei Priori, with a portico and an
impressive loggia designed by
Gattapone – responsible also for
the Palazzo dei Consoli in Gubbio
(see p64) – and the Palazzo del
Podestà (or Palazzo Comunale);
both date from the 14th century.
In the atrium of the Palazzo del
Podestà is a series of Roman and
medieval archaeological stones
and finds.

The superb *Coronation of the
Virgin*, by Ghirlandaio, and

Detail of the fountain in
Piazza Garibaldi

frescoes by Benozzo Gozzoli,
among others, are housed in
the Museo Eroli, located in the
same block. Palazzo Sacripanti,
also in the square, features
three medieval bas-reliefs of
griffins and knights.

Beyond Piazza dei Priori, the
main street (now Via Mazzini)
continues north. Immediately
on the right is the façade of
the little Romanesque
church of Santa Maria
in Pensole, built in
around 1175. Of
particular interest is
the exterior, with its
attractive portico
and three doorways
carved with classical
motifs. A little further
on, where the road
widens out into
Piazza XIII Giugno, is
the church of San Domenico
(12th century). Now deconsecrated, it houses the Public
Library, Historical Archive and
the town art gallery. The main
reason to go inside is to see
some of the most interesting
medieval frescoes in Narni:
among the often faint
fragments, of particular note
are those by the Zuccari
family, found in the large
chapel off the left-hand aisle.
San Domenico also has
many other works from
other churches in the town.
In the underground areas of
the church, you can visit the
Inquisition cells, with graffiti
made by the prisoners of
the ecclesiastical court. The
intriguing underground of
the city can also be toured
now; visit www.narni
sotterranea.it for details.

The duomo, facing onto
Piazza Garibaldi

To return to Piazza dei Priori from San Domenico, make your way along the narrow streets which run parallel to Via Mazzini. This area is home to the church of San Francesco, built in the 14th century on the site where it is said that St Francis stayed during his sojourn in Narni in 1213, and where he founded an oratory. The church is Romanesque, but with some Gothic elements. Among these, the most important feature of the exterior is the doorway, with a niche above. Inside, frescoes adorn every inch of wall: of special interest are the frescoes by Mezzastris, in the first chapel, depicting *Scenes from the Life of St Francis* and *Scenes from the Life of St Benedict*, as are those by Alessandro Torresani (16th century), in the sacristy.

On top of the hill that dominates Narni is a vast fortress known as the Rocca. It was built in the 1370s by Gattapone, at the behest of Cardinal Albornoz, one of the most important figures in the history of the early Middle Ages in Umbria (*see p44*), and responsible for numerous fortresses which still bear his name. Narni's fortress was abandoned for years, but it has now been restored. It is open daily and visitors can enjoy fine views from the site.

Environs

Heading out of Narni, towards Terni, you reach, after a short detour to the left, a bridge over

The Romanesque abbey of San Cassiano, dating from the 12th century

the River Nera. Though easy to miss among the modern development of industrial Narni Scalo, this is the best possible observation point from which to admire a majestic Roman arch in the middle of the river, the only one surviving from the Ponte d'Augusto. At 160 m (525 ft) long and 30 m (98 ft) high, this must have been one of the most impressive bridges in the whole of Umbria when it was built. It is known as the Augustan bridge, because it dates from the era of the first emperor (27 BC). This bridge was one of the most popular sights on the Grand Tour.

Continuing along the same road, over the Nera, a climb leads to the Abbazia di San Cassiano, perhaps the most important of the many religious buildings that dot the Narni countryside. Set in a panoramic position, the Romanesque, 12th-century complex is enclosed by battlemented

walls and includes a pretty church with a bell tower.

To the southeast, 13 km (8 miles) from Narni, is the Convento del Sacro Speco, founded in 1213 by St Francis, who often prayed in a cave nearby. The place is imbued with a mystical atmosphere.

⑮ Santa Pudenziana

Strada di Visciano, 05035, Visciano. **Road Map** C7. **FS** Narni-Amelia. **Tel** 0744 735 213, 3495 733 175 or 3495 519 231. **Open** Apr–Sep 4–7pm Sun. **W** santapudenziana.org

Heading south from Narni, a tortuous but scenic road leads up to the hilltop hamlet of Visciano. The reason for coming here is to visit the small and simple church of Santa Pudenziana (check with the tourist office to book a visit). This is a typical example of Umbrian Romanesque, built in the 12th and 13th centuries, and making abundant use of Roman materials. It has a tall stone campanile and a sober façade with a small portico. The interior is divided into three aisles, with an inlaid floor of precious marble and fragments of Roman mosaics.

The church is famous for its frescoes. Behind the façade are *Christ*, *San Vittore* and *San Medico*, and other saints, as well as the *Madonna and Child*, all contemporary with the construction. The other figures, such as *Santa Pudenziana*, date from the 14th and 15th centuries.

The Rocca, one of many fortresses built by Cardinal Albornoz

⑯ Parco Fluviale del Nera

Known as the "water park", this natural park extends along the River Nera which begins its course from Monti Sibillini and then flows from Ferentillo to Terni , leading to the heart of the National Park of the Monti Sibillini *(see pp112–13)*, and thereby forming what is virtually a single protected reserve of huge interest. Within the park is one of the most famous and much-loved sights in Italy, the Cascata delle Marmore, the highest waterfalls in the country, where the waters from the River Velino spill over from the upland of the Marmore down into the River Nera. Visitors should note that the water for the waterfall is switched on only for brief periods, which vary from month to month, so you should call ahead if you don't want to miss the spectacle. The park has much else of interest, however, and offers excellent opportunities for watersports.

Sweet violets, found in the pasture areas in the park

Cascata delle Marmore
The tremendous spectacle of the Falls, a popular destination with travellers throughout the ages, is created by the River Velino, which reaches this point via an artificial channel. Water then cascades down in three stages, over a total height of 165 m (541 ft), to reach the River Nera below. The Falls can be seen from both the lower road (SS209) and the upper road (S79).

Terni

Key

▭ Park road

▭ Scenic road

S209

Nera

Nera

①

Marmore

Velino

S79

Constructing a Waterfall

In antiquity, the River Velino did not spill into the River Nera as it does today, but stagnated in the marshes of the Rieti plain. In 271 BC the Romans decided to link the two by digging a channel, the Cavo Curiano, which feeds today's main waterfall. Since then, the Cascata delle Marmore has been at the centre of the entire river system of central Italy, provoking bitter debate between those who wanted to close it down and others who wanted to extend it. The latter option was chosen in the 15th and 16th centuries, with the work entrusted by the popes to the great architects of the day (Antonio da Sangallo, Giovanni Fontana and Carlo Maderno), who were to transform the Falls. The latest alterations, to adapt the falls for hydroelectric power, took place in the 1920s.

The hydroelectric plant at the Marmore Falls, one of Italy's main sources of energy

Montefranco

This small village, perched in a splendid panoramic position, is a centre for mountain sports. There are numerous rock climbing schools and manageable cliff faces.

VISITORS' CHECKLIST

Practical Information

Terni. **Road Map** D6. ![i] Via Cassion Bon, 0744 423 047. Cascata delle Marmore: **Tel** 0744 629 82. **Open** Jan: 11am–5pm Sat & Sun; Feb, Nov & Dec: 11am–5pm daily (Feb: to 6pm Sat & Sun); Mar: 10am–6pm daily (to 10pm Sat & Sun); Apr & May: 10am–7pm Mon–Fri, 9am–10pm Sat & Sun; Jun–Sep: 10am–10pm daily (from 9am Sat & Sun); Oct: 10am–6pm Mon–Fri, 10am–8pm Sat & Sun. ![w] marmorefalls.it

Transport

![FS] Terni, Rome–Ancona line. 🚌

Ferentillo

Monterivoso

S209

Nera

● **Montefranco**

S209
● **Arrone**
Casteldilago

● **Forca dell'Arrone**

Ferentillo

Guarded from above by twin 14th-century citadels, Ferentillo is a major climbing centre. It owes its fame also to the church of Santo Stefano, whose crypt contains several mummified bodies.

KEY

① **The Observatory** along the upper road, in the village of Marmore, is one of many points from which to admire the falls in all their glory. It dates from 1781.

② **Piediluco** is popular because of its pretty setting on the shores of Lake Piediluco, the second-largest lake in Umbria after Trasimeno, and just outside the park. The church of San Francesco is worth a visit, and boat rides on the lake are recommended.

Lago di Piediluco

② 🏕

↓ *Rieti*

0 kilometre 1
0 mile 1

Rafting

Water is the crucial element in the park and various watersports can be practised here, including rafting, canoeing and kayaking.

For keys to symbols see back flap

The 17th-century Porta Romana, inserted into the ancient walls

⑰ Amelia

Terni. **Road Map** C6. 🏔 12,200. 🚂 Narni, 11km (7 miles), Rome–Ancona line. 🚌 ℹ Piazza Augusto Vera, 05022, 0744 981 453.

Perched on a hill between the Tiber and Nera valleys, Amelia is a city of ancient origin. In fact, it was in antiquity that the town knew its greatest importance, when it was located on the Via Amerina, one of several Roman roads linking southern Etruria with Umbria.

Still standing today are parts of the impressive Mura Poligonali (Polygonal Walls), built by the Umbri and among the oldest walls in Italy. Their age is not certain, but they date from no later than the 5th century BC. Some 8 m (26 ft) high, and 3 m (10 ft) wide, the bastions are, for the most part, made up of vast polygonal stone blocks, fitted together without mortar. The size of the walls can best be seen at Porta Romana, framed by a Classical-style 17th-century arch.

This same gate is also the main entrance to the historic centre. Close by, in Palazzo Boccarini, is the **Museo Archeologico**, home to all manner of Roman finds from tablets to sarcophagi. Of huge interest is a magnificent statue of the Roman general Germanicus; discovered locally, it was for years kept in Perugia; Amelia has won it back, for the time being at least.

A short way up Via della Repubblica is the 13th-century church of Santi Filippo e Giacomo. It contains seven tombs of the Geraldini family, one of the most important dynasties in Amelia. Cardinal Alessandro Geraldini is famous for helping to persuade the Spanish monarchy to authorize the first voyage of Christopher Columbus to the Indies. The church's funerary monuments include the 15th-century tombs of Elisabetta and Matteo Geraldini, the work of Agostino di Duccio.

Palazzo Farrattini, just off Via della Repubblica, is Amelia's most impressive private building. It was designed by Antonio da Sangallo the Younger in the 16th century

Detail from the tomb of Matteo and Elisabetta Geraldini

for the Farattini, the other family to feature large in the history of Amelia. Via della Repubblica climbs further to Piazza Marconi, the town's lovely main square, and then continues up Via Duomo to the highest point of the city and the duomo.

The cathedral's appearance today is the result of almost total reconstruction in the 17th century, which replaced the original Romanesque church, though the fine 11th-century bell tower remains. Inside are several works of importance including a panel with a *Madonna and Child* attributed to Antoniazzo Romano, and two paintings by Nicolò Pomarancio in the Oratorio del Sacramento. Returning to the lowest part of the town along Via Geraldini, you reach Piazza Matteotti, whose architectural highlight is the charming Palazzo Comunale. Beyond Porta Romana, you can visit the country church of Santa Maria delle Cinque Fonti, built on the site where St Francis is said to have given a sermon in 1213. The church is named after a fountain with five spouts that stands nearby.

🏛 Museo Archeologico
Piazza Augusto Vera.
Tel 0744 978 120. **Open** Apr–Jun & Sep: 10:30am–2pm, 4–6pm Tue–Sun; Jul & Aug: 10:30am–1:30pm, 4–7pm Tue–Sun; Oct–Mar: 10:30am–1:30pm, 3–5pm Fri–Sun. **Closed** 1 Jan, 25 Dec. 🚫 📷

Picturesque Amelia, cascading down the hillside

◄ The town of Alviano, set amidst stunning Italian countryside

Environs

The area around Amelia is dotted with abbeys and sanctuaries that are easy to reach and a delight to visit. About 4 km (2 miles) southwest of Amelia, on the road to Attigliano, is the 13th-century Monastery of the Santissima Annunziata, which belongs to the Friars Minor. There is a *Last Supper* on the wall of the refectory. Heading eastwards, past the village of Capitone – which was the castle of nearby Narni in the Middle Ages – you reach the village of La Cerqua and the Sanctuary of the Madonna della Quercia. This was built in the 16th century to hold an image of the Virgin Mary, now on the apse altar.

The Roman Via Amerina is a historical object in itself, and has maintained its role as a communication route.

Interior of Santa Maria Assunta, in Lugnano

⑱ Lugnano in Teverina

Terni. **Road Map** C6. ⛰ 1,600. ⓕⓢ Attigliano, 11km (7 miles), Milan–Rome line. 🚌 ⓘ Pro Loco, Piazza S Maria 1, 0744 902 566. 🎭 Christmas concerts and Living Nativity, 24 Dec–6 Jan.

Following the main road S205 from Amelia towards Lago di Alviano, after around 10 km (6 miles) you come to the small town of Lugnano in Teverina. Set in a panoramic position along a ridge and enclosed by medieval walls, Lugnano began life as the feudal village of a Provençal count, in around 1000.

Lago di Alviano, along the border with neighbouring Lazio

Although some way from the usual tourist trails, Lugnano is well worth visiting simply to see one of the most interesting Romanesque churches in Umbria, the church of Santa Maria Assunta. The building dates from the 12th century, although it has undergone much restoration, especially in the 15th century. In common with various other Umbrian churches of the same era, such as the cathedral of Spoleto, the façade features a beautifully decorated portico, some of which is the work of the famous Roman marble workers, the Cosmati. There is more Cosmati work inside, both in the nave (which has a Cosmatesque pavement) and in the crypt, which also has a finely sculpted screen. Other works of art include a triptych of the *Annunciation* by Niccolò Alunno, in the apse, and a *Crucifixion* of the Giotto school.

Capital in Santa Maria Assunta

Environs

A short distance southwest of the town centre are traces of the Assisi saint in the church of San Francesco (open during services). It was erected in 1229 on the spot where a miracle occurred, as shown in the fresco above the right-hand altar.

After passing ancient Roman ruins, the road descends towards the Tiber and the town of Attigliano. Proceeding north on the Via Amerina, along the banks of the Tiber, after about 8 km (5 miles) you come to the Lago di Alviano (open Sundays and public holidays). This is part of an artificial basin created to generate hydroelectricity and today is an oasis run by the World Wide Fund for Nature and part of the Parco Fluviale del Tevere (*see p137*). From the nearby medieval town of Alviano, birthplace of *condottiere* Bartolomeo di Alviano, steps lead to Santa Illuminata, a pilgrimage site linked to an order of hermits called the Camaldolese.

A lovely 10-km (6-mile) stretch of the Via Amerina runs to Montecchio, with an interesting necropolis (6th–4th centuries BC) nearby.

One of the chambers in the necropolis near Montecchio

For hotels and restaurants see pp150–51 and pp162–7

Gate at the entrance to the medieval town of San Gemini

⑲ San Gemini

Terni. **Road Map** D6. 🚹 4,300.
🚉 Rome–Ancona line, Terni, 11 km
(7 miles); FCU Perugia–Terni line. 🚌 ℹ️
Piazza San Francesco 4, 0744 630 130.

The medieval town of San Gemini was built over the ruins of an ancient Roman settlement, alongside Via Flaminia. The only traces of the Roman town are a tomb, the so-called Grotta degli Zingari and a ruined villa.

The heart of San Gemini is Piazza di Palazzo Vecchio, home to the medieval Palazzo Pubblico, whose tower was much altered in the 1700s. Under an exterior arcade is an image of St George, patron saint of the town. The 13th-century Oratorio di San Carlo, nearby, has lovely frescoes.

In the main square, outside the city walls are the churches of San Francesco, with a fine Gothic doorway, and San Giovanni Battista, with a 13th-century façade and a lovely Romanesque door decorated with mosaics. One of the façade inscriptions bears the date of its founding, 1199, with the names of the architects and sculptors, Nicola, Simone and Bernardo.

Just outside San Gemini's old gateway is the privately owned church of San Nicolò. The beautifully sculpted Romanesque portal is a copy, since the original is in the Metropolitan Museum in New York. There is more fine (and original) sculpture inside.

There's also an interactive science museum, Geolab, for children and those interested in geology.

Environs

Just to the north, on flatter ground, is the modern spa town of San Gemini Fonte, with facilities for spa water treatments. The famous mineral waters of Sangemini and Fabia are bottled here. Sangemini water, known in antiquity and exploited since the late 19th century, is rich in calcium but low in chlorine and sodium, so is approved for children. Fabia water has average levels of minerals and is today promoted as a light table water good for the digestion.

The ancient spring at the Terme di San Gemini

⑳ Carsulae

Terni. **Road Map** D6. 🚉 Rome–Ancona line, Terni, 14 km (9 miles); FCU Perugia–Terni line. 🚌 ℹ️ Soprintendenza Archeologica dell'Umbria, 0744 630 420; Sito Archeologico di Carsulae, 0744 334 133. **Open** 8:30am–7:30pm daily (Oct–Mar: 5:30pm).
🌐 carsulae.it

From San Gemini Fonte, a detour of 3 km (2 miles) along

part of the old Via Flaminia brings you to the ruined Roman town of Carsulae, founded in the 3rd century BC on the slopes of the mound bearing the pretty name of Chiccirichì.

At first merely a staging and garrison post, then a village, Carsulae eventually became a town in Augustus' Region VI. It experienced its greatest period of splendour between 30 and 10 BC, when work was being done on the Via Flaminia. The town was abandoned following the decline in importance of the road. Carsulae was attacked and raided by barbarians and marauders on a number of occasions, and was also badly damaged by earthquakes.

From the 16th century onwards, the aristocratic families of the region, in particular the Cesi family of Acquasparta, began to carry out excavations in search of objects of interest for their own private collections. The modern archaeological excavations date back to the 1950s, when a number of sites were uncovered, including a basilica, the old forum, and temples. The great value of Carsulae as an archaeological site lies in the fact that the original layout has remained complete for the most part, despite the encroachment of the modern Via Flaminia, which crosses the site.

The small church of San Damiano was built in the 11th century, using the remains of a Roman temple. From here, you can follow a stretch of the original Via Flaminia to the

The little church of San Damiano, inside Carsulae's archaeological area

Ruins of the Roman theatre at Carsulae, showing clearly the supports for the stalls

Forum, with an adjacent basilica with three aisles and an apse. In front of the forum is a public square where numerous low walls – the ruins of religious and secular buildings – can be seen: among them are the bases of the Tempietti Gemelli (twin temples) and the remains of baths.

Continuing up the old Via Flaminia, visitors arrive at the Arco di San Damiano, a monumental gate which once had three arches: only the central one survives. A burial site is also nearby. Behind the basilica, beyond the modern Via Flaminia, is the Amphitheatre, used for circus games, and the Theatre; sadly only the foundations of the stage and the supports for the stalls (orchestra seats) remain of this building.

㉑ Acquasparta

Terni. **Road Map** D6. 🚘 4,500.
🚆 Rome–Ancona line, Terni, 20 km (12 miles); FCU Perugia–Terni line. 🚌
🛈 Via Tiberina 43, 0744 943 286.
🎭 Arte estate, Jul–Aug.

The first records of Acquasparta date from the 10th century. The name derives from the local spa waters, which were known to the Romans and, it is said, taken by St Francis. Acquasparta's appearance today recalls the influence of the Cesi family, who changed the face of the town during the 15th and 16th centuries. Among the features dating from this era are a palace named after the noble family, walls and towers.

Palazzo Cesi, commissioned by the Cesi family from the architect Giovanni Domenico Bianchi, was completed in 1565. The interior of this aristocratic residence is richly decorated: Giovan Battista Lombardelli produced the first paintings, while an artist from the north was responsible for the remainder. The rooms have splendid coffered wooden ceilings; the one in the Sala di Ercole (Room of Hercules) is particularly fine. Palazzo Cesi belongs to the University of Perugia and is used for seminars and conferences as well as a summer art exhibition.

Palazzo Cesi, now part of the University of Perugia

Along Corso Umberto I, the main street, are the church of Santa Cecilia and the Oratorio del Sacramento, where a mosaic floor from the ruins of Roman Carsulae has been put into new use.

The 200,000-year-old fossil forest at Dunarobba

Environs
A detour 15 km (9 miles) west of Acquasparta skirts Casteltodino and leads to the fossil forest of Dunarobba, close to the village of Avigliano Umbro. This ancient forest, which dates from the Pliocene age, is made up of around 40 petrified trunks of large trees similar to today's sequoia. The trees were preserved for centuries under a blanket of clay on the shores of Lago Tiberino (which once filled the Tiber Valley).

A few kilometres north is the medieval castle and village of Casigliano. Within is Palazzo Atti, also known as Maniero degli Atti, designed by Antonio da Sangallo the Younger in 1519.

㉒ Todi

The city of Todi occupies a stunning spot, on a hilltop halfway between Perugia and Terni. First built on land occupied by the Umbri, Todi was later appropriated by the Etruscans (its name derives from the Etruscan word *tutere*, meaning "border") and then, in 89 BC, by the Romans. Under the Romans, Todi's two hilltops were levelled out to make Piazza del Popolo and new walls were built around the Etruscan ones. Todi today would not have looked very different during the Middle Ages, a time of great splendour, when the town expanded southwards and was divided into four districts, surrounded by a third circle of walls. The city became a papal possession, along with all the other towns of Umbria, and there was only minor subsequent modification during the Renaissance.

Exploring Todi

Todi is best approached by car and explored by foot. Parking is limited in the centre of the town so it's best to park outside of the city walls. There are a number of spaces in Porta Orvietana car park, and a lift up into the town from here.

The eagle of Todi, Palazzo dei Priori

🏛 Piazza del Popolo

The centre of the city is, as it was in Roman times, Piazza del Popolo. This truly magnificent square contains the duomo, as well as three fine monuments to temporal power: Palazzo del Popolo, Palazzo del Capitano and Palazzo dei Priori. Following years of research, this largely medieval square was chosen as the starting point for excavations which have provided the information necessary to reconstruct the layout of the ancient city.

🏛 Palazzo dei Priori

Piazza del Popolo.
Tel 075 894 4148.
Closed to the public.

This palace, situated on the southern side of Piazza del Popolo was built between 1293 and 1385. At the top left of the façade is an eagle in bronze, the symbol of the city and the work of Giovanni di Gigliaccio in 1339. (According to tradition, the original Umbrian town was built where an eagle dropped a tablecloth taken from a local family.) Over the centuries the palazzo has housed the city's various and varied rulers, including the leaders of the medieval commune and the papal governors.

🏛 Palazzo del Popolo

Piazza del Popolo. **Tel** 075 894 41 48. **Open** see Palazzo del Capitano.

This is one of the oldest buildings of its type in Italy:

construction began in 1213, though the palace has been considerably restored. Built in Lombard-Gothic form, the palace's left-hand side faces Piazza del Popolo, while the front can be admired from nearby Piazza Garibaldi. In particular, look out for the swallowtail crenellations (a Guelf motif) and the external staircase, which gave access to the hall on the first floor, above the porticoed space of the ground floor. Public assemblies were held here.

The palace shares an entrance with Palazzo del Capitano and houses part of the Museo Pinacoteca.

Three-mullioned window, Palazzo del Capitano

🏛 Palazzo del Capitano

Piazza del Popolo. Museo Pinacoteca:
Tel 075 894 4148. **Open** Apr–Oct: 10am–1:30pm, 3–6pm; Nov–Mar: 10:30am–1pm, 2:30–5pm.
Closed Mon (except hols), 25 Dec.
♿ 🖉 📷

This palace dates from the late 13th century and faces the

Piazza del Popolo, an excellent example of a well-preserved medieval square

For hotels and restaurants see pp150–51 and pp162–7

eastern side of the square. The façade has mullioned Gothic windows and a grand arched staircase which serves both the Palazzo del Capitano and the adjacent Palazzo del Popolo. In particular, it gives access to the Sala del Capitano, with remains of frescoes, medieval coats of arms and a 14th-century *Crucifixion*.

Sculptural detail from the door of the duomo

The Museo Pinacoteca, located in the adjacent palazzi, includes a decent archaeological collection, the Museo Etrusco-Romano, as well as paintings, of which the most significant is a *Coronation of the Virgin* (1507–11) by Giovanni di Pietro, known as Spagna. The palazzo also houses the Museo della Città (Civic Museum).

🏛 Duomo

Piazza del Popolo. **Tel** 075 894 30 41.
Open 8am–dusk daily.

Dedicated to Maria Santissima Annunziata, the duomo was founded in the 12th century, probably on the site of a Roman temple, but wasn't completed for another 200 years, with further additions being made after that. The simple and lovely façade is divided horizontally by cornices. An 18th-century flight of steps leads up to a carved 16th-century door set into a decorative framework, above which, as befits the façade's Romanesque simplicity, is a beautiful rose window (1515). Pilaster strips, small loggias and mullioned windows adorn the right-hand side and the tall apse.

Inside, the church has a decorative beamed roof and splendid Gothic capitals, as well as a superb 16th-century choir. The entire central space as well as the chapels contain various works of art, the most interesting of which are near the altar: two paintings by Spagna, to the sides, and, above, a painted wooden Crucifix dating from the 13th and 14th centuries. There is also a crypt, which contains

three figures originally on the façade, as well as a handful of Roman remains.

The magnificent rose window on the façade of the cathedral

Todi Town Centre

① Piazza del Popolo
② Palazzo dei Priori
③ Palazzo del Popolo
④ Palazzo del Capitano
⑤ Duomo
⑥ San Fortunato
⑦ Corso Cavour
⑧ Nicchioni
⑨ Santa Maria della Consolazione

For keys to symbols *see back flap*

Detail from the main door of the church of San Fortunato

🏛 San Fortunato

Piazza Umberto I. **Open** Nov–Mar: 10:30am–1pm, 2:30–5pm Tue–Sun; Apr–Oct: 10:30am–1pm, 3–6:30pm Tue–Sun. **Closed** 25 Dec.

Heading south along Via Mazzini, which skirts around the medieval heart of Todi, is the enormous hilltop church of San Fortunato, a sight which is not to be missed.

This is a Franciscan church, but with many anomalies: the dedication, for example, is not to the Assisi saint but to Fortunato, patron of Todi. (The reason for this was that the church replaced a building used by Benedictine monks.) The construction took place in two phases: the first from 1292–1328, the second in the 1400s. It was commissioned by the bishop of Todi, Matteo d'Acquasparta.

The unfinished façade, a mixture of Romanesque and Gothic styles, stands out at the top of an imposing flight of steps.

It has a campanile with splendid views open to the public. Through the fine Gothic central doorway lies a wonderfully airy Gothic interior, which does not follow the traditional Franciscan model. It is a rare example in Italy of a Gothic hall church; that is, in which the two side aisles are as high as (though much narrower than) the nave. Note the lovely and unusual ribbed cross vaults, the fine late 16th-century choir stalls, the raised chapels along the sides, and the Gothic baptismal font.

Frescoes decorate many of the chapels and include, in the fifth chapel on the left, some scenes from the *Life of St John the Baptist* by the Giotto school, and, in the fourth chapel on the right, a *Madonna and Child* (1432) by Masolino da Panicale.

The church is also famous for the tomb of Jacopone da Todi, in the crypt beneath the altar. Jacopone was a rich merchant who, following the death of his devout wife, Vanna, became a mystic and a poet. His devotion was reputedly so extreme that he was rejected even by the Franciscans. He was accused of heresy on a number of occasions and is mainly remembered for his *Laudi*, one of the fundamental texts in the birth of Italian literature. The great man, a native of Todi, died in 1306 and gradually became the symbol of the medieval city. He is still the best-known figure in the cultural history of Todi. Extending westwards from San Fortunato

is a large public park, where a fortress commissioned by Cardinal Albornoz stood until 1503.

🏛 Corso Cavour

Descending the steps of Via San Fortunato brings you to the steep Corso Cavour, the "Rua degli Speziali" (spice sellers' street) of medieval Todi. Halfway along is a fountain known as the Fonte Rua (1606), or Fonte Cesia (after the bishop who had it built), and, at the end, Porta Marzia, a medieval arch made out of material salvaged from other buildings.

The 17th-century Fonte Rua, in Corso Cavour

🏛 Nicchioni

Piazza del Mercato Vecchio.

Walk through Porta Marzia, and turn left into Via Mercato Vecchio. At the end of Via Mercato Vecchio, the old medieval market square (Piazza del Mercato) is dominated by four Roman arches, the so-called Nicchioni (niches). These most probably date from the Augustan era, and either supported a raised street or formed part of the wall of a Roman basilica.

🏛 Santa Maria della Consolazione

Viale della Consolazione. **Open** Apr–Jun, Sep & Oct : 9am–12:30pm, 3–6:30pm; Jul & Aug: 9:30am–12:30pm, 3:30–6:30pm; Nov–Mar: 9:30am–12:30pm, 2:30–5pm. **Closed** Tue (except during Christmas hols).

This church, located outside the city walls, is one of the masterpieces of the Umbrian

The airy interior of the church of San Fortunato

Santa Maria della Consolazione, outside Todi

Renaissance. Begun in 1508 and finished in 1607, it has been attributed by some to Bramante, one of the architects of St Peter's in Rome. In fact, there is no documentary evidence of any such project by the great architect, though it is just possible that Cola di Caprarola, who started the project, may have used drawings by Bramante.

The distinctive silhouette of the church – familiar from the covers of dozens of publications devoted to Todi – is built on a square plan and rises to a great dome. Encircling the main structure are four apses, of which one, to the north, is semicircular and three are polygonal; they have two orders of pilasters, with a mixture of capitals, and are pierced by elegant windows. The drum which supports the great dome is narrower than the main body of the church, leaving space for a raised terrace, guarded by four eagles sculpted by Antonio Rosignoli in the 17th century. There are great views from here. The Baroque doorways date from the 18th and 19th centuries.

The airy and light interior, in the form of a Greek cross, is also Baroque and contains statues of the apostles. In the apse is the venerated fresco of the *Madonna della Consolazione* (15th century). The church was built to protect the fresco.

Eagle on the terrace, Santa Maria della Consolazione

🄮 Parco Fluviale del Tevere

Terni. **Road Map** B5. 🄵🄢 Orvieto, Milan–Rome line; Todi, FCU Perugia–Terni line. 🚌 🄸 Piazza Umberto I, 16, Civitella del Lago, Baschi, 0744 951 409. 🆆 parks.it

This river park extends for some 295 ha (18,025 acres) from the bridge of Montemolino, at the gates of Todi, south as far as Lago di Alviano, and has great wildlife and lovely scenery. It includes around 50 km (31 miles) of land along the banks of the Tiber, the largest river in central Italy, and two artificial lakes (Alviano and Corbara). The main access to the park is at the medieval hill town of Baschi, about 24 km (15 miles) from Todi, close to the junction of road S448 and the motorway. The Tiber River,

one moment placid and the next turbulent, is home to a variety of birds, among them blue heron and kingfishers, as well as freshwater fish. Poplars, alders and willows, typical riverside vegetation, cloak the sides.

Steep valleys sweep away from the river and extend as far as the Apennines: the wildest is the Gole del Forello, considered one of the most interesting biotopes in the region. On the northern banks of Lago di Corbara, not far from the fortified village of Prodo, winds the Gole di Prodo, a deep gorge best suited to hikers or experienced and well-equipped mountain climbers. Diverse birds of prey, including buzzards, sparrowhawks and kites, can be seen in these inaccessible areas, where the vegetation consists mainly of trees such as holm oaks and hornbeams and shrubs such as broom and heather. The marshes in the Lago di Alviano basin (*see p131*), with its own particular birdlife and plants, are also of great interest.

Besides the natural beauty and the opportunities for outdoor sports, the park also incorporates sites of historical and archaeological interest. Digs are under way in various spots, including in the Vallone di San Lorenzo (site of several necropolises) and in the area of the ancient river port of Pagliano, at the confluence of the Paglia and Tiber rivers; the port's existence confirms the importance of the Tiber as a communication route of the central Italic peoples.

Gole del Forello, a fascinating wildlife habitat

㉔ Orvieto

A sheer tufa outcrop, the remains of ancient volcanoes fractured by millennia of ice, sun and rain, rises abruptly from the plain and supports the spectacular medieval city of Orvieto. In the Etruscan era a city called *Velzna* stood here and became rich through commerce with traders from the Tyrrhenian Sea (part of the Mediterranean) and the north. The Romans took over in 264 BC and virtually destroyed the town. Revival came only in the Middle Ages, when Orvieto developed into a free and powerful commune, albeit one troubled by civic strife. The Black Death of 1348 was devastating, however, and Orvieto eventually came under papal control. The old city, with its superb duomo (which is reached by bus from the train station or by funicular and shuttle bus), has changed little in the last 500 years, and attracts thousands of tourists every year.

The imposing tufa platform supporting Orvieto

🏛 Duomo
See pp140–41.

🏛 Museo Archeologico Nazionale

Piazza del Duomo. **Tel** 0763 341 039.
Open 8:30am–7:30pm daily.
Closed 1 Jan, 1 May, 25 Dec. 🗐 ♿

On the scenic Piazza del Duomo, next to the imposing mass of the cathedral, stands the Palazzo Papale, which includes three 14th-century buildings, commissioned by popes Urban IV, Gregory X and Martin IV and later combined into one complex.

The Museo Archeologico Nazionale, housed in the Palazzo del Martino IV, has a particularly fine Etruscan collection, including bronzes and mirrors. Several tombs and funerary objects are among the exhibits, including frescoes from 2nd-century-BC tombs and two painted 4th-century tombs from Settecamini.

🏛 Museo dell'Opera del Duomo

Piazza del Duomo. **Tel** 0763 343 592.
Open Apr–Sep: 9:30am–7pm daily; Oct & Mar: 10am–5pm daily; Nov–Feb: 10am–1pm, 2–5pm daily.
Closed Tue.

Orvieto Town Centre

① Duomo pp140–41
② Museo Archeologico Nazionale
③ Museo dell'Opera del Duomo
④ Palazzo Soliano
⑤ Palazzo Faina
⑥ San Francesco
⑦ Torre del Moro
⑧ Sant'Andrea
⑨ Palazzo del Popolo
⑩ San Domenico
⑪ Pozzo di San Patrizio
⑫ Rocca dell'Albornoz

Underground Orvieto

🏛 Parco delle Grotte

Società Speleotecnica. **Tel** 0763 344 891, 339 733 2764. **Open** tours depart from Piazza del Duomo; call ahead to book. 🅿️
W orvietounderground.it

🏛 Pozzo di Via della Cava

Trattoria Sciarra, Via della Cava 28. **Tel** 0763 342 373. **Open** 8am–8pm Tue–Sun. **Closed** Sun after Epiphany–2 Feb. 🅿️
W pozzodellacava.it

Passages below the town

The people of Orvieto are used to living with cellars: every house or shop has its own cave, and every family has its own story to tell of the underground. Marco Marino, for example, an antiques dealer in Via della Cava, found the remains of the oldest ceramics kiln known in the world by digging in his cellar. He uses it to display his collection of 15th-century ceramics.

A group of enthusiasts developed a project to open up some of Orvieto's caves to visitors, and the Società Speleotecnica is one of the groups to run tours. The caves underneath the embankment that separates the hospital from the walls of the cliff are examples of underground Orvieto: caves which were re-used over the centuries, as workshops, and storerooms for cereals, oil and wine. In addition to the intriguing Pozzo di San Patrizio (*see p142*), it is well worth visiting the Pozzo di Via della Cava, an Etruscan well. Used in the 16th century and then covered up, the well now forms part of the basement of a restaurant.

The Palazzo Papale also houses a museum dedicated to the cathedral. Exhibits include paintings, statues and other works of art that once filled the cathedral, dating from the Middle Ages up to the 18th century. Among them are paintings by Simone Martini, a series of large statues formerly

Detail from an Etruscan fresco, Museo dell'Opera del Duomo

in the cathedral and also a collection of church ornaments.

🏛 Palazzo Soliano and Museo Emilio Greco

Piazza del Duomo. **Tel** 0763 344 605. **Open** 10:30am–1pm, 2:30–6pm daily. 🅿️ ♿

Commissioned in 1297 by Pope Boniface VIII, this austere building was not completed until 1359. In the early days, it was used as a storehouse by the Fabbrica del Duomo (cathedral works). Later, from the mid-16th century onwards, the hall on the ground floor was used by Orvieto's stone-masons. The structure is very simple, consisting of two large rooms one on top of the other. The lower room has a line of pilasters and arches and opens out into a grand, monumental staircase.

Palazzo Soliano houses a substantial collection of 20th-century sculptures, drawings and lithographs given to the city by Emilio Greco, a contemporary Sicilian artist.

VISITORS' CHECKLIST

Practical Information
Perugia. **Road Map** B5. 🅿️ 22,000. 🛈 Piazza del Duomo 24, 0763 341 772. 🎭 Corpus Domini procession; Palombella Pentecoste, 30 May. **W** orvietoviva.com

Transport
🚉 Milan–Rome line, 892021. 🚌

🏛 Palazzo Faina (Museo Civico and Museo Claudio Faina)

Piazza del Duomo 29. **Tel** 0763 341 511. **Open** Apr–Sep: 9:30am–6pm daily; Oct–Mar: 10am–5pm Tue–Sun. 🅿️ ♿ **W** museofaina.it

This 19th-century palazzo opposite the duomo houses two museums. The Museo Civico, on the ground floor, is of much less interest than the Museo Claudio Faina, an extraordinarily rich private collection gathered by the Faina counts in the 19th century. Among the exhibits are beautiful Etruscan vases, superb jewellery from the 5th century BC onwards, and a series of exquisite Attic vases. There is a wonderful view of the duomo from the top floor.

Cinerary urn kept in the Museo Civico, Palazzo Faina

🏛 San Francesco

Piazza dei Febei.
The Romanesque church of San Francesco was founded in 1240, but it has been much altered over the centuries.

The large church has a tufa façade with three arched doorways and mullioned windows. Inside, the vault is supported by wooden trusses of huge dimensions given the era in which they were made.

Look out for the 14th-century wooden *Crucifixion*, attributed to Maitani (a key person involved in the construction of the duomo) or his school.

Orvieto: Duomo

Orvieto's magnificent Duomo, which dominates the skyline, was founded by Pope Nicholas IV in 1290. Things got off to a bad start and, in 1308, the Sienese architect and sculptor, Lorenzo Maitani, was brought in to save the building. It wasn't finished for another 300 years. Maitani himself was largely responsible for the 52-m (170-ft) façade, with his own magnificently detailed bas-reliefs of scenes from the Old and New Testaments, a superb rose window, 16th-century statues and multicoloured mosaics (not original). The striped design outside is carried through into the Romanesque nave, which has alabaster windows and is divided by columns with elaborate capitals. Inside, the masterpiece is the chapel of the Madonna di San Brizio, with frescoes by Fra Angelico and Luca Signorelli and portraits of famous poets such as Dante.

Stained Glass
Among the stained glass in the apse is this *Nativity* by Giovanni Bonino di Assisi.

Sanctuary
The sanctuary walls feature 14th-century frescoes by Ugolino di Prete Ilario, a local artist. Above is a detail from the *Adoration of the Magi.*

KEY

① **The exterior** is characterized by horizontal bands of white travertine and blue-grey basalt.

② **The Reliquario del Corporale**, the design of which copies the duomo's façade, contains the altar cloth associated with the Miracle of Bolsena.

③ **The rose window**, with Christ at the centre, is the work of Florentine artist Andrea Orcagna (1360). The window is encircled by sculptures.

Cappella del Corporale
This chapel contains the superb 14th-century *Madonna dei Raccomandati* (left) by the Sienese artist Lippo Memmi, and frescoes (1357–64) of the *Miracle of Bolsena* and *Miracles of the Sacrament* by Ugolino di Prete Ilario.

Frescoes by Luca Signorelli

A fascinating cycle of frescoes narrating events related to the Apocalypse unfolds on the walls of the Cappella della Madonna di San Brizio. Signorelli tackles the themes of the Last Judgment – *The Day of Judgment, The Preaching of the Antichrist, The Resurrection of the Dead, The Damned Consigned to Hell, The Blessed Entering Heaven* and *Angels Guide the Elect to Paradise* – blending spatial harmony and dynamism in a synthesis of the art of central Italy of the time. The three-dimensionality and energy emanating from the figures heighten the drama and anticipate the painting of Michelangelo in the Sistine Chapel.

Detail from the fresco of The Day of Judgment by Signorelli

VISITORS' CHECKLIST

Practical Information
Piazza Duomo.
Tel 0763 340 168, 0763 343 592 (tickets).
Duomo and Chapel:
Open Mar–Oct: 7:30am–7:30pm daily; Nov–Feb: 7:30am–1:30pm, 2:30–5:30pm daily.

★ **Cappella della Madonna di San Brizio**
The fresco cycle in this Gothic chapel, begun by Fra Angelico (1447) with the assistance of Benozzo Gozzoli, and later completed by Luca Signorelli (1499–1504), is one of the finest of the Renaissance.

★ **Façade**
Bas-reliefs and statues (the originals of some are in the Museo dell'Opera), mosaics, pilasters and arches characterize this perfect synthesis between architecture and the decorative arts. It is a stunning example of Italian Gothic.

Main Door
The decorated bronze panels of the main door were the work of Emilio Greco in the 1960s.

🏛 Torre del Moro

Corso Cavour 87. **Tel** 0763 344 567.
Open Mar, Apr, Sep, Oct: 10am–7pm;
May–Aug: 10am–8pm; Nov–Feb:
10:30am–4:30pm daily. 🅿

The 12th-century "Tower of the Moor" towers 42 m (137 ft) above Corso Cavour, Orvieto's main street, where it meets Via del Duomo. It owes its name to the figure on the coat of arms of the Pucci, a local family. Its 14th-century bell is still in working order.

Alongside the tower is the **Palazzo dei Sette** (1300), built as the seat of the seven *(sette)* magistrates in charge of the commune, and later the seat of the papal governor.

Torre del Moro rising above the roofs of old Orvieto

🏛 Sant'Andrea

Piazza della Repubblica.
This church is one of the oldest buildings in Orvieto. Founded in the 7th century, Sant'Andrea was built upon walls of probable Etruscan origin, over which a Roman temple was later built. It was then rebuilt in stages during the 12th–14th centuries. Sant'Andrea was once the most important church in

Orvieto. It was here that Pope Innocent III proclaimed the Fourth Crusade in 1201 and that Martin IV was crowned pope in 1281, in the presence of Charles of Anjou.

Important elements include the Gothic door, by Marco da Siena, designed by Maestro Vetrino (1487), and the imposing 12-sided bell tower, with three orders of two-mullioned windows and a series of coats of arms, placed here when restoration was undertaken in 1920–30. The interior is supported by great granite columns, probably Roman, and is decorated with fragments of frescoes and a 10th-century pulpit.

🏛 Palazzo del Popolo

Piazza del Popolo. **Closed** to the public.
The heart of the city in ancient times, Piazza del Popolo is home to the Palazzo del Popolo, first described in the town records at the end of the 13th century. Built from the local tufa stone and topped by a bell tower, it is an imp-

Detail from the Palazzo del Popolo

ortant example of Orvieto civic architecture from the late 13th century. Ornamentations include an external staircase, an open loggia, crenellations, and mullioned windows linked by a cornice. It is now a conference centre.

Façade of San Domenico with the original striped pilasters

🏛 San Domenico

Piazza XXIX Marzo.
It was here that the unusual striped stonework, in dark-coloured basalt and pale travertine, appeared for the first time in Orvieto, in the late 13th century. The style was then extensively used in the duomo and became a signature motif for the city. Despite substantial restoration in the Baroque era, the façade maintains its simple Romanesque-Gothic austerity, with a beautiful doorway, a tall two-mullioned window and a rose window which repeats the two-coloured motif.

Half the church was taken down in the 20th century to make room for the nearby barracks; the interior space today consists merely of the original transept and the tribune. The main work of art is the splendid tomb of Cardinal Guglielmo de Braye by Arnolfo di Cambio (1282), but there are also frescoes and other examples of sculpture.

🏛 Pozzo di San Patrizio

Viale Sangallo. **Tel** 0763 343 768.
Open daily. Jan, Feb & Nov: 10am–4:45pm; Mar, Apr & Sep: 9am–6:45pm; May–Aug: 9am–7:45pm. 🅿

Located at the eastern end of Corso Cavour is one of Orvieto's best-known monuments. Commissioned in 1527 by Pope Clement VII and designed by Antonio da Sangallo the Younger, the 62-m (203-ft)

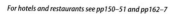

The church of Sant'Andrea with its unusual 12-sided tower

The impressive depths forming the Pozzo di San Patrizio

well is a superb piece of engineering. Crucial to the design are two 248-step spiral staircases: one was used for the descent and one for the ascent, so that donkeys carrying pitchers of water would not meet on the way. The stairways are lit by 72 windows.

Looking over the plain from the bastions of the Rocca

🏛 Rocca dell'Albornoz

Viale Sangallo. **Open** always open. 🖼

Dominating the eastern end of Orvieto, near the terminus of the funicular that connects the old city with the railway station down on the plain, is the Rocca, built by Cardinal Albornoz in 1364 to bolster the power of the papacy. The locals destroyed it soon afterwards, and not much remains today.

The Rocca is an excellent vantage point from which to enjoy superb views over the city and the plain, as well as being a tranquil spot, surrounded as it is by several pretty gardens.

Environs

Around 1.5 km (1 mile) north of Orvieto, at the foot of the tufa cliff, is the **Necropoli del Crocifisso del Tufo**. This Etruscan cemetery complex dates from the 6th–3rd centuries BC and consists of small chambered tombs built of tufa blocks and containing a stone bench for laying out the corpse. On the lintel over the entrance to each tomb is the name of the person or family buried there. The site seems to have had an essentially "urban" layout, following what would be defined today as a town plan.

The site was discovered only in the 19th century, by foreign archaeologists who passed on some of the finds to the Louvre and the British Museum. It wasn't until 1880 that the site was first explored in a scientific, non-intrusive way and finally began to arouse the interest of the Italian authorities. Over 100 tombs have now been found. The majority of the important funerary objects discovered in

the tombs are now distributed among Orvieto's museums.

On the south side of the cliff is the Necropoli della Cannicella, another burial site used by the Etruscans from the 7th–3rd centuries BC. It follows a similar layout to the necropolis at Crocifisso del Tufo.

Around 3 km (2 miles) south of Orvieto, just off SS71, is the Abbazia di Santi Severo e Martirio, a great medieval monastery complex. Now partly converted into a hotel (La Badia, see p151), the monastery belonged to the Benedictines until 1221 and then the Premonstratensians (a French Order founded in 1120 by St Norbert).

Apart from the rooms used by the hotel, several areas of the monastery can still be visited. There is much that dates from the original construction (12th–13th-centuries). The splendid 12-sided Romanesque tower dates from the 12th century. The church, reached through a great 13th-century arch, features a single nave with a ribbed vault, an inlaid marble floor in the Cosmat-esque style and several fragments of medieval frescoes. The barrel-vaulted Oratorio del Crocifisso, once the monks' refectory, is adorned with a 13th-century fresco depicting the *Crucifixion with Saints*. Also of interest is the 13th-century Abbot's House.

🏛 Necropoli del Crocifisso del Tufo

Tel 0763 343 611. **Open** 8:30am–7pm (winter: 5pm) daily. 🖼 ♿

Etruscan necropolis of the Crocifisso del Tufo, 6th century BC

TRAVELLERS' NEEDS

WHERE TO STAY

The range of accommodation in Umbria is impressively varied and caters to all tastes and pockets. While the traditional hotel is still an option in the main tourist centres, a large number of *agriturismo*, or working-farm, establishments have sprung up out of town, as have more luxurious country-house hotels, some with spas or wellness centres. Compared to similar complexes in Italian cities, these upscale rural hotels often offer excellent value for money. Bed-and-break-fast accommodation has also become more popular, and there is now a substantial network of B&Bs, both in the countryside and in the region's towns. More basic accommodation is offered by religious institutions to groups and individuals alike, while camping is another popular option in this region, often referred to as the green heart of Italy.

Hotels

Many of the hotels in Umbria's major towns are grouped into local consortiums – this is done in order to promote standards and to protect the interest of both the hotel and the guests. Lists with prices and other information are published annually by the Perugia tourist office (APT).

Grading and Prices

Hotels in Umbria are classified according to the standards followed in the rest of Italy. The categories run from one to five stars, plus a top luxury hotel category (L). Services offered are generally good. Prices vary according to the season and are higher during festivals and major cultural events. Most hotels accept credit cards.

Booking

Umbria does not really have much of a low season, although visitor numbers drop between November and February. Booking ahead is strongly advised; an email to confirm the booking is often requested when checking-in.

Historic Residences

A strong sense of the past is palpable in Umbria. For an unforgettable holiday, you might want to stay in a place that is steeped in history. The region features a wealth of centuries-old buildings, a number of which have been adapted to accommodate visitors. Standards are strictly regulated, so that the carefully refurbished interiors lose none of their character and charm; period furniture and artistic treasures abound in these establishments.

For a night or two in the peaceful environment of a monastery, try the tranquil La Badia (*see p151*), just outside Orvieto, or the equally lovely Eremo delle Grazie (*see p151*), near Spoleto.

Those with aspirations of grandeur, could opt for an actual castle. Try the opulent Relais Il Canalicchio (*see p149*), in Deruta, or, in Acquasparta, the Castello di Castigliano (*see p150*), with 16th-century cottages and rooms set inside a fortification.

Agriturismo and Country Houses

Holidaying at a working farm, or *agriturismo*, has become a tremendously popular option throughout Umbria. Also – either in rooms on B&B terms, or in independent self-catering apartments – many places offer a wide variety of facilities, including swimming pools and bikes. Horse-riding and other activities, such as cookery, pottery or yoga classes, are sometimes available, and guests are often encouraged to take an active part in farm life. Meals prepared with traditional local ingredients, some of which must be produced by the farm itself, are usually served to external diners as well as guests. The self-catering option generally requires a longer stay, paid for in advance, especially in high season.

Country-house hotels are a more upmarket option to stay in rural surroundings. A country house is usually more luxurious than an *agriturismo*, often with more sports and wellness facilities and a more refined restaurant, without the home-grown produce aspect.

Local tourist offices can provide visitors with full

Spacious apartment at Borgo Pirolino, an *agriturismo* in Orvieto

◀ Charming pavement café in Piazza IV Novembre, Perugia

listings containing information on costs and facilities.

Campsites

There are campsites all over the region: all the historic Umbrian towns have at least one, and the area around Lake Trasimeno has a range of sites suited to tents, camper vans or caravans.

All Umbrian campsites are registered with the authorities and listed in regional tourist guides issued by the Perugia and Terni tourist offices.

Sites are usually clean and well run, and often located in attractive settings. Overnight stops by camper vans are strictly regulated; overnight stays are prohibited in historic centres, while in the modern or less touristy centres there are often designated parking places.

Bed & Breakfast

Bed-and-breakfast establishments can be found throughout Umbria, both in the region's towns and in the countryside. Expect to find homely, simple accommodation and a friendly welcome. Rooms are usually limited, so if you wish to stay at a particular place, it is wise to book well in advance.

Self-Catering Apartments

One option for a longer stay in the area is to rent an apartment. Whether you want to be based in the countryside, by a lake, in the mountains or in a town, you will find there is a good choice of properties available for short-term lets. Many of them are attached to an *agriturismo* or grouped together in a holiday village, with the benefit of shared facilities.

Religious Institutions

Many religious institutions offer simple accommodation to visitors. This may be in the form of a no-frills hotel, but some convents or monasteries provide special lodgings for pilgrims. There is a wide choice

Hilltop hamlet converted into *agriturismo* accommodation

in Assisi, a major pilgrimage destination, but it is also worth looking in much smaller places, such as Bevagna or Spello. Meals are not normally provided, with the exception of the busy hostels in Assisi. The accommodation lists supplied by the tourist office are the best source of information.

Youth Hostels and Student Accommodation

Perugia, a university town, has youth hostels and student accommodation of various types. Hostel accomodations can also be found in Terni, Amelia, Magione and Assisi, although not all of them are associated with the International youth hostels. For sources of information, *see p175*.

Travellers with Disabilities

Larger hotels and religious institutions usually offer accessible rooms and services for travellers with disabilities. A list of these hostels can be found on the Turismo Senza Barriere website.

Recommended Hotels

The hotels in this section have been chosen to reflect their quality and amenities within the themes of Luxury, Historic, Rural, Boutique and Value for Money, although it is fair to say that some establishments will fall into more than one category. Umbria has a number of **luxury**

options, with the best service and settings, plus countless **historic** hotels, which are set in buildings of note. **Rural** covers hotels in remote villages or in acres of countryside, while **boutique** reflects smaller, often independent establishments with stylish interiors. Finally, Umbria has a wide selection of hotels we consider **value for money** and will stretch the budget that little bit further. The DK Choice hotels are extra special. They may have above average standards and amenities or a breathtaking location, or simply have a charm that sets them apart.

DIRECTORY

Agriturist Umbria
w agrituristumbria.com
Perugia
Via San Bartolomeo 79.
Tel 075 597 0752.

Perugia IAT
Piazza Matteotti 18.
Tel 075 573 6458.
w turismo.comune.perugia.it

Terni IAT
Via Cassian Bon 1.
Tel 0744 423 047.
w marmore.it

Travellers with Disabilities
w turismosenzabarriere.it

Umbria Bed and Breakfast
w bed-and-breakfast.it/en/region/umbria

Umbria Information
Umbrian region tourist information.
w bellaumbria.net
w lamiaumbria.it

Where to Stay

Northern Umbria

ASSISI: Tre Esse Country House
Rural   €
Map D4
Via di Valecchie 41, 06081
Tel *075 81 63 63*
W countryhousetreesse.com
Old-fashioned hotel in a centuries-old stone building reached by a steep uphill climb. Classic décor, antique furnishings and lovely gardens.

ASSISI: Fontebella
Historic   €€
Map D4
Via Fontebella 25, 06081
Tel *075 81 28 83*
W fontebella.com
Restored 17th-century building with elegant rooms and suites, many with sweeping views of the Umbrian valley. Limited parking.

ASSISI: Hotel Giotto
Luxury   €€
Map D4
Via Fontebella 41, 06081
Tel *075 81 22 09*   **Closed** *Jan–Feb*
W hotelgiottoassisi.it
Located at one of the highest points in Assisi, Giotto offers lovely views from its rooms, restaurants and terraces. Fine dining, informal dining and a day spa available.

ASSISI: Romantik Hotel Le Silve
Rural   €€
Map D4
Località Armenzano 82, Parco Regionale del Monte Subasio, 06081
Tel *075 801 90 05*
W lesilve.it
Set in a 10th-century stone farmhouse east of Assisi, this upmarket hotel, with pretty rooms and apartments, offers spa, pool, fine dining facilities and even horse riding.

BETTONA: Relais La Corte di Bettona
Rural   €€
Map C4
Via Santa Caterina 2, 06084
Tel *075 98 71 14*
W relaisbettona.com
Plush rooms, vaulted ceilings and lavish décor; this rural hotel also has a wellness suite and a gourmet restaurant.

BRUFA DI TORGIANO: Borgo Brufa
Luxury   €€€
Map C4
Via del Colle 38, 06089
Tel *075 98 52 67*
W borgobrufa.it
This tranquil rural spa resort has a well-equipped wellness centre

featuring a swim-through indoor and outdoor pool, a Finnish sauna and a host of treatments. Lavish rooms, a gourmet restaurant, horse riding and tennis complete the package.

CIGLIANO: Agriturismo Cigliano
Value for Money   €
Map D3
Frazione Colpalombo 22, 06020
Tel *333 603 3998*
W agriturismo-cigliano.it
Escape modern-day trappings at this intimate *agriturismo* that has no electric lighting and uses only candle light. Meals on request.

CITTÀ DELLA PIEVE: Hotel Relais dei Magi
Country House   €€
Map A4
Località Le Selve Nuove 45, 06062
Tel *0578 298133*
W hotelpiccoloeden.it
Ideally suited for exploring Umbria and Tuscany, this stylish 18th-century villa, high in the hills, is surrounded by woodlands as well as formal gardens. The hotel has only 14 rooms and a couple of apartments. Excellent panoramic restaurant and caring service.

DK Choice

CITTÀ DELLA PIEVE: Hotel Vannucci
Boutique   €€
Map A4
Via Icilio Vanni 1, 06062
Tel *0578 29 80 63*
W hotel-vannucci.com
Chic hotel in a 19th-century palazzo built by King Vittorio Emanuele II. Decor includes antique furniture, modern art, a walled garden with a pool, a wellness suite, a fine dining restaurant and superb rooms combine to make this place really special.

Price Guide
Prices are based on one night's stay in high season for a standard double room, inclusive of service charges and taxes.

€	up to €100
€€	€100 to 200
€€€	over €200

CITTÀ DI CASTELLO: Hotel Garden
Value for Money   €€
Map B2
Via Aldo Bologni, 06012
Tel *075 855 05 93*
W hotelgarden.com
This elegant hotel and spa pampers guests with beauty and relaxation services. Great restaurant.

CITTÀ DI CASTELLO: Hotel Tiferno
Historic   €€
Map B2
Piazza R Sanzio 13, 06012
Tel *075 855 03 31*
W hoteltiferno.it
Once a monastery, centrally located Tiferno is today a hotel with elegant rooms. The owner's Alberto Burri paintings line the walls.

CORCIANO: La Contea
B&B   €
Map C3
Via Cattaneo 25, San Mariano di Corciano, 06073
Tel *320 662 5469*
W bblacontea.it
Located next to a golf course, this cosy B&B with vaulted ceilings occupies a family house that dates back almost 500 years.

DERUTA: Antica Fattoria del Colle
Boutique   €
Map C4
Strada Colle delle Forche 6, 06053
Tel *075 97 22 01*
W anticafattoriadelcolle.it
This *agriturismo* with a sun terrace and pool has tastefully decorated rooms. Meals use products from the farm.

Relaxed setting at the poolside in Hotel Vannucci, Città Della Pieve

DK Choice

DERUTA: Relais Il Canalicchio €€
Luxury   **Map** C4
Via della Piazza 13, Collazzone, 06053
Tel *075 870 73 25*   **Closed** *Nov–Mar*
🌐 relaisilcanalicchio.it
The 1,000-year-old, castle-like structure evokes a real sense of history – stone arches and ceiling beams, an old press and millstone. The luxurious accommodation is backed by a gym, a relaxation suite and a wood-panelled dining hall.

A well-decorated room at the luxurious Relais Il Canalicchio in Deruta

GUBBIO: Relais Ducale €
Luxury   **Map** D2
Via Galeotti 19, 06024
Tel *075 922 01 57*
🌐 relaisducale.com
This annexe of the Ducal Palace, just off Gubbio's main square, offers luxurious accommodation and includes a lovely terrace garden. Child- and pet-friendly.

GUBBIO: La Rocca €
Boutique   **Map** D2
Via Monte Ingino 15, 06024
Tel *075 922 12 22*
🌐 laroccahotel.com
Stylish hotel built against a rock face high on Mount Ingino, two minutes from the medieval town of Gubbio by cable car.

GUBBIO: Park Hotel ai Cappuccini €€
Spa hotel   **Map** D2
Via Tifernate, 06024
Tel *075 92 34*
🌐 parkhotelaicappuccini.it
A short walk from the town, this hotel is set in a restored monastery and has a restaurant, art gallery, spa and sports amenities.

LAKE TRASIMENO – CASTIGLIONE DEL LAGO: Bandita €
Value for Money   **Map** B3
Localita Vitellino
Tel *075 965 3082*
🌐 labandita.eu
Restored stone house divided into comfortable apartments, each with lake views. Minimum stay is three nights.

LAKE TRASIMENO – CASTIGLIONE DEL LAGO: Isola Verde €€
Boutique   **Map** B3
Via Bruno Buozzi 74, 06061
Tel *075 95 10 39*
🌐 isolaverderesort.it
Surrounded by the lush greenery of Castiglione del Lago, Isola Verde has elegant and spacious suites furnished in country style. This pet-friendly accomodation is also wheel-chair accessible.,

LAKE TRASIMENO – ISOLA MAGGIORE: Da Sauro €
Rural   **Map** B3
Via Guglielmi 1, 06060
Tel *075 82 61 68 or 399 37 82 037*
🌐 dasauro.it
Family-run hotel in an idyllic fishing village on Isola Maggiore. Lovely rooms and an excellent fish restaurant.

LAKE TRASIMENO – PASSIGNANO: Hotel Kursaal €
Value for Money   **Map** B3
Via Europa 24, 06065
Tel *075 82 80 85*   **Closed** *Dec–Mar*
🌐 kursaalhotel.net
Set in an elegant 1930s villa, Hotel Kursaal has contemporary rooms, a popular restaurant and terrace pool, nestled among trees, on the shores of Lake Trasimeno.

MIGLIANO DI MARSCIANO: Il Casale Di Buccole €€
Luxury   **Map** B4
Vocabolo Buccole 25, 06050
Tel *075 870 81 26*
🌐 ilcasaledibuccole.it
A 19th-century farmhouse with rooms that have Italian-style décor, some with four-poster beds. Lovely views from the pool.

MONTONE: La Locanda del Capitano €€
Boutique   **Map** C2
Via Roma 5, 06014
Tel *075 930 24 28*
🌐 ilcapitano.it
Small, charming hotel located in the centre of town. Antique furnishings give it an exclusive feel. During summer, breakfast is served on the lovely verandah.

PANICALE: Villa di Monte Solare €€
Luxury   **Map** C4
Tavernelle di Panicale, 06068
Tel *075 83 23 76*
🌐 villamontesolare.com
Ivy-covered villa and farmhouse amid olive groves; offers luxurious rooms, spa centre and a celebrated restaurant.

DK Choice

PERUGIA: Etruscan Chocohotel €
Boutique   **Map** C3
Via Campo di Marte 134, 06124
Tel *075 583 73 14*
🌐 chocohotel.it
From the decor and room furnishings, including desks and headboards resembling chocolate bars, to the crockery and a breakfast menu featuring chocolate pastries, this fun hotel is all about chocolate. An outdoor pool and a restaurant that serves Umbrian classics.

PERUGIA: Hotel Rosalba €
Value for Money   **Map** C3
Via del Circo 7, 06121
Tel *075 572 82 85*
🌐 hotelrosalba.com
Centrally located and with its own parking facilities, this simple yet charming hotel is set in a 18th-century town house.

PERUGIA: Brufani Palace €€€
Luxury   **Map** C3
Piazza Italia 12, 06100
Tel *075 573 25 41*
🌐 brufanipalace.com
Five-star elegance in every detail at Brufani Palace– from the restaurant and boudoir-style rooms, to the spectacular pool built over glass-covered Etruscan ruins.

For more information on types of hotels *see pp 146–7*

Idyllic views from Le Tre Vaselle in Torgiano

PETRIGNANO DI ASSISI:
Parco dei Cavalieri   €
Historic   **Map** D3
Via Matteotti 47, 06081
Tel *075 809 80 12*
🅦 parcodeicavalieri.it
Located in a medieval building,
the hotel has richly decorated
rooms and an elegant à la carte
restaurant, surrounded by acres
of neat gardens.

PETROIA: Castello di Petroia €€
Historic   **Map** D3
Località Petroia, 06024
Tel *075 886 01 37*
🅦 petroia.it
A castle immersed in the greenery
of the Umbrian hills, here visitors
can enjoy spectacular views, a
swimming pool, and delicious
cuisine at the hotel's restaurant.

DK Choice

PIEGARO: Ca' de' Principi   €
Luxury   **Map** B4
Via Roma 43, 06066
Tel *075 835 80 40*
🅦 dimorastorica.it
Outstanding frescoes adorn the
halls of this lavish hotel housed
in an 18th-century royal palace.
Highlights include a vaulted
restaurant that uses produce
from the estate's farms and
orchards, luxurious boudoir-
style rooms furnished with
period pieces, a swimming pool
and terrace.

TORGIANO: Le Tre
Vaselle   €€€
Boutique   **Map** C4
Via Garibaldi 48, 06089
Tel *075 988 04 47*
🅦 3vaselle.it
Situated in the centre of the
city, a 17th-century villa forms

the setting for this stylish
hotel with large, comfortable
rooms. The hotel is a great
base for exploring the nearby
areas. It also has a spa and
wellness centre.

Southern Umbria

ACQUASPARTA: Agriturismo
Santomanno   €
Value for Money   **Map** D6
Strada delle Molinelle 142, 05021
Tel *338 297 5216*
🅦 santomanno.com
Five apartments within a
farmhouse at this *agriturismo*
farm, which also has a play
area for children and on-site
barbeque facilities. Minimum
stay is two nights.

ACQUASPARTA: Castello di
Casigliano Country Inn   €
Historic   **Map** D6
Piazza Corsini 1, 05021
Tel *0744 94 34 28*
🅦 castellodicasigliano.com
A tastefully converted set of 16th-
century cottages and rooms inside
a fort. Furnished to complement
the rustic features that have been
retained. It also has a gourmet
restaurant and a beautiful garden
offering panoramic views.

BASCHI: La Penisola Villa
Bellago   €
Value for Money   **Map** B6
*Località Pian delle Monache 138
(Todi-Baschi road), 05023*
Tel *0744 95 05 21*
🅦 lapenisola.com
A centuries-old hotel with a
tranquil feel, located on the
pretty banks of the Lago di
Corbara. Tennis courts and fish
restaurant too.

BEVAGNA: Residenza
Porta Guelfa   €€
Rural   **Map** D4
Via Ponte delle Tavole 2
Tel *0742 36 20 41*
Set in an old country house, this
hotel has tastefully-furnished
rooms in a country style. It also
has a swimming pool and a spa.

DK Choice

CASCIA: Casale Sant'Antonio
Agriturismo   €
Rural   **Map** E5
Casale Sant'Antonio 59, 06043
Tel *333 321 2344*
🅦 casalesantantonio.it
Working organic farm rearing
cattle and producing grains and
pulses for its restaurant. It is
located in a protected area on
the slopes of Monte Meraviglia
with numerous paths for
wandering the countryside.
Rooms and apartments are
elegant in a country-house style.

FOLIGNO: Le Mura   €
Value for Money   **Map** D4
Via Bolletta 27, 06034
Tel *0742 35 73 44*
🅦 lemura.net
Beside Foligno's medieval
walls near San Giacomo; an old-
fashioned hotel with tastefully
decorated rooms and a
restaurant serving Umbrian fare.

NARNI: Colle Abramo delle
Vigne Agriturismo   €
Rural   **Map** C6
*Strada di Colle Abramo 34, Vigne,
05035*
Tel *0744 79 64 28 or 335 52 91 135*
🅦 colleabramo.com
Cosy rooms and apartments in a
group of traditional stone farm
buildings, set in unspoilt countryside. There is an alfresco dining
area, lush gardens, sun terraces,
a swimming pool, children's
playground and riding stables.
Offers good deals for longer stays.

NARNI: Terra Umbra   €€
Modern   **Map** C6
*Strada Provinciale, Maratta Bassa 6,
05036*
Tel *0744 75 03 04*
🅦 terraumbra.it
Smart hotel with a gym and
sauna and a restaurant serving
excellent Umbrian fare.

NORCIA: Hotel La Rocca   €
Value for money   **Map** F5
Via Flaminia Ternana 508, 05035
Tel *340 887 2903*
🅦 laroccahotel.com
Housed in an 18th-century villa,
this hotel has spacious rooms

and bathrooms. The restaurant serves quality Umbrian cuisine, and there is Wi-Fi in all rooms.

ORVIETO: Agriturismo Titignano €
Rural **Map** B5
Località Titignano, 05010
Tel *0763 30 80 00*
W titignano.com
Overlooking Lake Corbara, this wine-producing *agriturismo* is set in a medieval castle. Rooms have classic Umbrian styling.

DK Choice

ORVIETO: La Badia €€
Luxury **Map** B5
Località Badia 8, 05019
Tel *0763 30 19 59*
W labadiahotel.it
This 6th century abbey with its 12-sided tower added in AD 1103, has been creatively converted into a beautiful honey-coloured landmark hotel. The romantic rooms and fine dining restaurant have period features. It also offers a state-of-the-art spa.

ORVIETO: Hotel Duomo €€
Value for Money **Map** B5
Vicolo di Maurizio 7, 05018 Orvieto
Tel *0763 34 18 87*
W orvietohotelduomo.com
This centrally located, popular hotel takes its name from the Duomo, which many of its rooms overlook. Décor tastefully combines antiques with artwork.

PARRANO: Il Poggiolo di Parrano €€
Rural **Map** B6
Contrada Bagno 43, 05010
Tel *0763 83 84 71*
W ilpoggiolo.com
Rooms and restaurant are in stylishly renovated farm buildings. The surrounding olive groves are known for their oil products.

SAN GEMINI: Albergo Duomo €
Historic **Map** D6
Piazza Duomo 4, 05029 San Gemini
Tel *0744 63 00 15*
W albergoduomosangemini.it
Once home to Italian nobility, the hotel has tasteful décor with 18th-century frescoes. Neat rooms, including one with its own spa.

SPELLO: Hotel del Teatro €€
Historic **Map** D4
Via Giulia 24, 06038
Tel *0742 30 11 40*
W hoteldelteatro.it
Del Teatro, with well-equipped rooms and tasteful interior, is located in an 18th-century

building, with some parts dating back to medieval times.

SPELLO: Terme Francescane €€
Luxury **Map** D4
Via delle Acque, 06038
Tel *0742 30 11 86*
W termefrancescane.com
This refined spa resort uses natural sulphur springs for a host of health treatments. Smart rooms and restaurants. Prices are inclusive of spa and half-board.

SPOLETO: Clitunno €
Boutique **Map** D5
Piazza Sordini 6, 06049
Tel *0743 22 33 40*
W hotelclitunno.com
A restored town house near the Duomo, this family-run hotel offers modern rooms and a popular fine-dining restaurant.

DK Choice

SPOLETO: Eremo delle Grazie €€
Historic **Map** D5
Strada per Monteluco 13, Monteluco, 06049
Tel *074 34 96 24*
W eremodellegrazie.com
Staying at this luxurious hotel in a restored 5th-century monastery is an experience. Wooden beams, wall paintings and antique furnishings add to the original architectural details visible throughout. Cosy rooms, library, restaurant and wine cellar lend charm to the atmosphere.

SPOLETO: Palazzo Leti €€
Luxury **Map** D5
Via degli Eremiti 8–10, 06049
Tel *0743 22 49 30*
W palazzoleti.com
Dating from medieval and Neo-Classical times, this palazzo,

A bright room in the historic San Lorenzo Tre, Todi

standing in lovely gardens, is one of Spoleto's finest. Lavish rooms.

TODI: Torre Sangiovanni €
Historic **Map** C5
Vocabolo Castello 26g, Collevalenza, 06059
Tel *075 88 60 134*
W torre-sangiovannii.it
Situated inside the fortress of Borgo di Collevalle, this hotel is decorated with antique furniture. The charming suites have a reading corner.

TODI: Hotel Bramante €€
Historic **Map** C5
Via Orvietana 48, 06059
Tel *075 894 83 81*
W hotelbramante.it
Upscale hotel, restaurant and spa in a restored 800-year-old convent outside Todi's city walls.

TODI: San Lorenzo Tre €€
Historic **Map** C5
Via San Lorenzo 3, 06059
Tel *075 894 45 55*
W sanlorenzo3.it
This countryside hotel, with fabulous views, is a Todi landmark. The 19th-century building displays beautiful antique furnishings and old photographs tracing the story of the Gagliardi-Pellegrini family that once lived here. Smart en-suite rooms with Wi-Fi.

TODI: Relais Todini €€€
Luxury **Map** C5
Vocabolo Cervara 24, Collevalenza, 06059
Tel *075 88 75 21*
W relaistodini.com
Todini is a charming hotel in a 14th-century manor house. Period features run throughout, complemented by lavish furnishings. Superb spa.

TREVI: Casa Giulia €
Rural **Map** D5
Località Corciano, Bovara, 06039
Tel *0742 782 57*
W casagiulia.com
Housed in a 17th-century manor house near the Clitunno Springs, Casa Giulia offers bright rooms, a restaurant and a swimming pool with panoramic views of the Umbrian valley.

**TREVI:
Antica Dimora Alla Rocca** €€
Value for Money **Map** D5
Piazza della Rocca 1, 06039
Tel *074 23 85 41*
W hotelallarocca.it
With furnishings matching the style of the 17th-century palazzo it occupies, this hotel is one of Trevi's best. Convenient central location.

For more information on types of hotels *see pp146–7*

WHERE TO EAT AND DRINK

A key draw of Umbria is its excellent food. A land of robust flavours, ancient culinary traditions and fabulous fresh produce, Umbria is brimming with cosy, family-run trattorias and traditional restaurants where you can try the local cuisine, often in atmospheric, historical surroundings. Many restaurants now offer international, fish and seafood, and vegetarian cuisine, especially in the major towns, in addition to classic Umbrian.

The region's many food-based festivals and fairs, known as *sagre*, offer an ideal opportunity to find out more about and taste some authentic local produce. These lively events are often devoted to a particular crop, such as mushrooms, chestnuts, truffles or olives. Most *agriturismo* structures (farm lodgings) provide meals for their guests, and some are open to external diners, too, the hosts often eating together with the guests.

Opening Hours and Prices

Restaurant and trattoria opening hours in Umbria are similar to those found all over central Italy. Generally, lunch is served from noon to 2:30pm, and evening meals from 7pm onwards. Closing times depend on the season and on the type of place: earlier for small trattorias and in winter; later in summer and during the holiday season, and in busy historic centres. Many restaurants close for a week or two during August for holidays.

Prices vary enormously depending on the type of establishment. In some of the most famous restaurants, the bill can easily exceed 50 euros per person, excluding wine, while in a village trattoria you can usually eat for around 20 to 30 euros per person. Most establishments charge a *coperto* (cover charge), which is usually 1–3 euros per customer; some places also add a 10 per cent service charge to the bill.

The Produce of Umbria

Umbrian cuisine consists of dishes deriving from an ancient tradition, sometimes re-interpreted

Comfortable interior of the Trillo Bar

by enterprising chefs. The region yields excellent produce of all kinds, and crops cultivated using organic methods are becoming increasingly widespread.

Umbria produces high-quality red and white wine, which are highly respected all over the country; the region also produces some of Italy's best olive oil. Mushrooms are a delicacy, and some of the finest black and white truffles in the world are found here. Cured meats are another specialty, particularly in Norcia, while good freshwater fish can be found in Lake Trasimeno and other lakes around the region. The tiny village of Castelluccio, in the Monti Sibillini, gives its

name to a renowned and tasty variety of lentil. A further popular trend is Km0, which reflects the ingredients being locally sourced, and having travelled 0 km from farm to table.

Top Restaurants

In response to the region's gastronomic traditions, some prestigious restaurants have been established in Umbria. Such places alone can make a trip to the region worthwhile.

One of the most famous is the restaurant of chef Gianfranco Vissani (*see p162*), in Baschi, on the shores of Lago di Corbara, but there are other restaurants worthy of note, including Il Postale (*see p161*) of Marco Bistarelli, in Perugia. Tables at these and other top-class restaurants are in high demand, so booking ahead as far as possible is a necessity.

Trattorias

A traditional trattoria is a good choice for an authentic taste of the local specialities. Often family-run, and sometimes incorporating an all-day bar or general store, down-to-earth trattorias can be found in every town and village around Umbria. Unpretentious and affordable, they are often the first choice among the locals when eating out with family or friends, so they make an ideal spot for people-watching, too.

Specialities of the Lake Trasimeno area, including local wine and oil

Relaxing outside the San Francesco restaurant in Assisi

Agriturismo

Agriturismo farms are obliged to use locally grown ingredients, some of which are usually produced on the farm itself. The sometimes limited choice of dishes is made up for by the genuine farmhouse flavours and the welcoming atmosphere. Furthermore, these properties often have lots of space, as well as play areas – perfect for small children.

Cookery Courses

Umbria has numerous cookery schools, where both professionals and amateurs can learn the secrets of the region's traditional cuisine. There are also plenty of *agriturismo* farms that run cookery courses.

Bars and Cafés

Bars are an important part of everyday life all over Italy, and no less so in Umbria. Although the locals will often just pop in for a quick espresso or an apéritif standing at the bar, many places also have plenty of seating – both inside and out– for you to linger and take in the view. Table service generally costs a little extra. Hot and cold snacks are usually available, and if it's a *bar-pasticceria*, the cakes will be made on the premises.

Local Festivals

The traditional fairs and festivals held all over Umbria attract visitors and locals alike, and they provide a great opportunity to try local food and wine specialities at reasonable prices. People flock to Norcia (in February) and Città di Castello (in November) to taste the precious truffle, while wine is the attraction at Todi and Torgiano, and particularly at the Sagrantino festival in Montefalco, held in September.

One event of great interest is the Mercato delle Gaite, an event usually held in two parts, one in April and the other May in Bevagna (*see p108*). The town adopts the dress and ways of the 14th and 15th centuries, and local restaurants offer tasty menus that feature ancient dishes.

A more modern event of international importance is Perugia's Eurochocolate.

Travellers with Disabilities

More and more places in Umbria, including restaurants and hotels, are upgrading their buildings by installing slopes and bathrooms in order to facilitate access for the disabled. Even so, the streets can be steep in Umbria's medieval hill towns, and steps are common.

Smoking

All restaurants and bars throughout Italy are obliged to adhere to a strict no-smoking policy. Some places do have a properly ventilated room for smokers, and the no-smoking restrictions do not apply at outside tables.

Recommended Restaurants

The restaurants in this section have been chosen to reflect their quality, amenities and variety of cuisine. Umbria has a large number of traditional restaurants and we have selected those that offer the most authentic dining experience. Similarly, Umbria has restaurants serving inter-national cuisine, although it is fair to say that many of these may also include classic local dishes on their menu. Umbria has fish restaurants, and others that offer good vegetarian menus, and we have selected the best. The DK Choice restaurants are extra special. We consider them to have historical charm, especially high standards or an above average location.

The Festa di San Benedetto in Norcia, held in March

The Flavours of Umbria

Umbria has an earthy cuisine based on what ingredients are in season. Like their Etruscan ancestors, Umbrians have an affinity with the land and enjoy hunting for edible bounty from their beautiful countryside. In spring there is wild asparagus, and in summer there are fruit and herbs to be picked and preserved. Autumn and winter have their fair share of culinary delights; as the weather turns colder, market stalls and restaurants display the hunters' catch – hare, pheasant, pigeon, woodcock and quail, as well as chestnuts, porcini mushrooms and truffles sniffed out by the hunters' dogs. Winter vegetables like *cavolo nero* are also popular.

Black truffles

Local olives mixed with tiny chillies on a market stall

Northern Umbria

Landlocked Umbria has always depended on its rivers and lakes for fish, including Lake Trasimeno. In waterside villages, the daily catch of carp, trout, perch, pike, tench and eel are made into soups and stews, or baked with herbs. Eel is simmered with fresh tomatoes, while trout is cooked with wild fennel.

The largest carp are roasted whole in a the same way as a suckling pig *(regina in porchetta)*. There is fine lamb from the hillside herds of prime beef-cattle. The regional capital, Perugia, is noted for its Chianina beef, as well as for its chocolate.

A wide variety of vegetables and cereals, like barley and spelt, are cultivated on the fertile land. Olive trees are everywhere: their oil is some of Italy's finest – light but scented, and full of flavour. Special sweets and pastries are made to mark historical and religious celebrations. Perugia's patron saint, San Costanzo, is honoured with the *torcolo*, a ring-shaped cake studded with aniseed, pine nuts and dried fruit. From Assisi, *ossi di morta* are bone-shaped marzipan sweets prepared for All Souls' day in November.

Rocket   Fennel   Artichokes   *Cavolo nero* (black chard)   Wild mushrooms
Asparagus

Typical selection of fresh Umbrian vegetables

Umbrian Dishes and Specialities

Cured meats, salami and black olives marinated with orange peel, are typical *antipasti*. Asparagus is used in tomato or cheese sauces with pasta, or fried with beaten eggs to make a *frittata*. Pastas include *ciriole* (like tagliatelle), often served with fried onions and garlic. *Porchetta* is a whole young pig, stuffed with offal and herbs, and roasted on a spit until the skin is deliciously crisp; it is sometimes served sliced, in bread rolls. Game is roasted or cooked with wine to make rich stews such as *piccione in salmi* (pigeon). *Torta al testo* is a flattish bread made with olive oil and stuffed with herbs, sausage or ham. *Pan pepato* is sweetened with sugar, candied fruit and nuts. Coffee may be accompanied by Baci (meaning "kisses") from Perugia *(see p171)*.

Baci chocolates

Teggacmaccio is a stew from Lake Trasimeno, made with perch, trout, tench and eel, in a tomato and wine broth.

Chefs prearing to serve freshly roasted *porchetta*

Southern Umbria

The south of the region has prime agricultural areas, like the Castelluccio plains, where tiny, distinctively flavoured lentils are grown and used in many local dishes, such as rustic hearty soups made with seasonal vegetables. Among these are cardoons (*cardone*), which look like giant celery and have a rather bitter taste.

Traditionally, meat is often grilled or spit-roasted with herbs, especially sage and rosemary. Norcia is an important gastronomic centre, famous for black truffles and as the home of marvellous hams (*prosciutti*), salami and sausages. Throughout Italy, *norcino* means "pork butchery". Dozens of recipes hail from the town, including *mazzafegati* (pig's liver sausages with raisins,

pine nuts and orange peel) and *beccacce alla norcina* (woodcock stuffed with sausage, herbs and truffles). Orvieto is wine country, as reflected in *gallina umbriaca* ("drunken chicken", cooked in wine). Orvieto is also known for quails (*quaglie*) baked in bread,

Black grapes, ripe and ready to be pressed to make wine

while Todi's speciality is ox tongue (*lingua di bue*) in a sweet-and-sour (*agrodolce*) sauce.

Umbrian Truffles

Truffles are part of Umbrian life and are used liberally in its cuisine, elevating even basic salads or scrambled eggs to gourmet fare. They appear in classic recipes, grated over risottos or sliced thinly onto *crostini* (bread fried in olive oil). Black truffles are added to cheese (*pecorino tartufato*) and can be frozen or preserved. Rarer white truffles are always eaten fresh.

REGIONAL WINES

Orvieto Famous for crisp, dry white wines, but there are also some lesser-known reds and dessert wines.

Torgiano Rosso Riserva Possibly Umbria's finest red, it is made from Sangiovese grapes and ages well.

Sagrantino di Montefalco This full, rich red wine has been produced for centuries in vineyards around Montefalco.

Colli Perugini Red and white wines from a number of grape varieties, including Pinot Grigio, Grechetto and Montepulciano.

Vin Santo A lusciously sweet wine, pressed from semi-dried Grechetto or Malvasia grapes.

Cinghiale alla cacciatore is wild boar cooked with red wine, herbs and vegetables until tender.

Lenticche di Castelluccio (lentils) are often served as an accompaniment to fennel-flavoured pork sausages.

Strangozzi pasta with sugar, walnuts, cinnamon, cocoa and lemon is a Christmas Eve treat in Umbria.

Where to Eat and Drink

Northern Umbria

ASSISI: La Bella Stazione €
Italian   **Map** D4
Piazza Dante Alighieri 5, Santa Maria degli Angeli, 06081
Tel 075 80 41 647   **Closed** *Tue in winters*
Traditional pizza and pasta dishes are given a modern twist with creative toppings and sauces at this intimate restaurant with great views of the city. Located on the first floor of Assisi railway station.

ASSISI: Enoteca San Pietro €
Classic Umbrian   **Map** D4
Via Borgo San Pietro 18, 06081
Tel 075 81 33 03   **Closed** *Mon D, Tue*
Surrounded by convents in a quiet hillside location, this cosy restaurant with stone walls and rattan chairs has an à la carte menu with truffles among the Umbrian classics and local artisan beer and wines. Specializes in using Km0 or local ingredients.

ASSISI: La Fortezza €
Classic Umbrian   **Map** D4
Vicolo della Fortezza/Piazza del Comune, 06081
Tel 075 81 29 93   **Closed** *Thu*
Gourmet Umbrian dishes set the tone here. The meat and pasta dishes are given special attention too.

ASSISI: Pasticceria Pizzeria Bagnoli €
Italian   **Map** D4
Via Patrono d'Italia 3, Santa Maria degli Angeli, 06081
Tel 075 80 40 611
Friendly little pizzeria with the distinct aroma of pizza fresh from

L'Antico Forziere is set in a Casalina country house, in Deruta *(see p157)*

the oven. Pizza Napoletana and Pizza Salamino Piccante are the crowd favourites.

ASSISI: Pizzeria Il Duomo €
Italian   **Map** D4
Via Porta Perlici 11, 06081
Tel 075 81 63 26   **Closed** *Wed*
Housed in a stone building with arches and gallery seating, this welcoming pizzeria is always busy. Well-known for their imaginative toppings.

ASSISI: Trattoria degli Orti €
Classic Umbrian   **Map** D4
Via Salita degli Orti, 06081
Tel 075 81 25 849   **Closed** *Wed*
Housed in a stone building in a quiet alley near the Piazza Santa Chiara, this family-run eatery offers innovative Umbrian dishes like truffle omelette and traditional *strangozzi* (handmade spaghetti) in a wide variety of sauces.

ASSISI: Trattoria Pallotta €
Classic Umbrian   **Map** D4
Vicolo della Volta Pinta 3/Via San Rufino 4, 06081
Tel 075 81 26 49   **Closed** *Tue*
Reached via a beautiful alley with original Renaissance frescoes, this pretty eatery serves antipasti platters designed to share. Typically, they precede Umbrian classics like *strangozzi* with olives.

ASSISI: Bibenda €€
Enoteca   **Map** D4
Vicolo Nepis 9, 06081
Tel 075 81 55 176
The Italian Sommelier Association has listed this as one of the best wine bars in Italy. Vaulted brick ceilings and contemporary décor are a great backdrop to the wines and tasting menus, which include cured meats, cheese platters and various gourmet snacks.

DK Choice

ASSISI: Buca Di San Francesco €€
Classic Umbrian   **Map** D4
Via Eugenio Brizi 1, 06081
Tel 075 81 22 04   **Closed** *Mon*
Traditional Umbrian fare such as succulent filet steak flavoured with local truffle, Minestrone and a variety of meats and side dishes make this elegant restaurant delightful. Located in renovated medieval cellars beneath a townhouse in central Assisi, this restaurant has a good cellar and a terrace for alfresco dining in summers.

Price Guide
Price categories include a three-course meal for one, half a bottle of wine, including cover charge, service and tax.

€	up to €30
€€	€30 to 50
€€€	over €50

ASSISI: Da Erminio €€
Classic Umbrian   **Map** D4
Via Montecavallo 19, 06081
Tel 075 81 25 06   **Closed** *Thu*
Fashionable trattoria with wild boar and rabbit with herbs, and pasta dishes like the speciality *strangozzi alla boscaiola* with walnuts on the menu. Good wine list.

DK Choice

ASSISI: La Locanda Del Cardinale €€
Fine Dining   **Map** D4
Piazza del Vescovado 8, 06081
Tel 075 81 52 45   **Closed** *Tue*
Favoured by celebs, this elegant restaurant is known as much for its menu as for its décor. Tables stand on a glass floor that covers the illuminated remains of the Domus Romana Palace of Assisi. The menu encompasses Umbrian classics with a gourmet twist, accompanied by wine from a cellar holding over one thousand vintages.

ASSISI: Medio Evo €€
International   **Map** D4
Via Arco dei Priori 4, 06081
Tel 075 81 30 68   **Closed** *Mon*
Subtly lit to enhance its 13th-century vaulted interiors, this cosy trattoria is a memorable place to enjoy authentic local dishes. Try the house special truffle risotto.

ASSISI: Osteria Plazzetta dell'Erba €€
Classic Umbrian   **Map** D4
Via San Gabriele dell'Addolorata 15A, 06081
Tel 075 81 53 52   **Closed** *Mon*
Located in a characterful corner of Assisi, just a few steps away from Piazza del Comune, this osteria offers classic Umbrian cuisine with a modern twist. Great attention is paid to detail and quality ingredients. Best to reserve in advance.

ASSISI: Ristorante Carfagna €€
Classic Umbrian   **Map** D4
Ponte San Vittorino, 06081
Tel 075 81 30 63   **Closed** *Mon*
A large restaurant situated at the foot of the hill topped by the

Basilica of Assisi. It is part of a *agriturismo* farm complex that uses home produce. Open from breakfast until late.

ASSISI: Ristorante da Cecco €€
Classic Umbrian   Map D4
Piazza San Pietro 8, 06081
Tel *075 81 24 37*   **Closed** *Thu*
This hotel restaurant celebrates the art of gastronomy with specials like *agnello al tartufo* (lamb with truffles) and *tagliata di chianina* (steak and tagliatelle with truffle). Excellent wine list.

ASSISI: Ristorante da Elide €€
Italian   Map D4
Via Patrono d'Italia 48, 06081
Tel *075 80 40 867*   **Closed** *Mon*
A cosy autumnal décor, a menu of Italian pasta favourites and an extensive selection of ice creams, combine to make this hotel trattoria a lively place. There is also a special menu for children.

ASSISI: San Francesco €€€
International   Map D4
Via San Francesco 52, 06081
Tel *075 81 23 29*   **Closed** *Wed*
Carpaccio of *porcini* mushrooms, home-made pâtés and steak with truffles are highlights on the menu at this classy eatery, located right by the Basilica in the heart of Assisi. Upmarket wines sold by the glass. Views from the terrace are delightful.

ASSISI: Il Frantoio €€€
Classic Umbrian   Map D4
Via Fontebello 25, 06081
Tel *075 81 22 42*
Elegant restaurant laid-out within set in a renovated 17th-century olive press on the grounds of the Fontebella Hotel. A superb wine list complements the Umbrian menu that offers a variety of meat dishes as well as vegetarian and gluten-free options.

ASSISI: Tuna Fish €€€
Fish & Seafood   Map D4
Via Los Angeles 83, 06081
Tel *075 80 43 433*   **Closed** *Mon*
Specializing in fish and seafood, this trendy restaurant takes great care in always offering the day's catch from the nearby Tyrrhenian Sea, cooked following local Italian recipes. To please the palate, order one of the artfully presented desserts.

BETTONA: Il Poggio degli Olivi
La Veranda €€
Fine Dining   Map C4
Località Montebalacca, 06084
Tel *075 98 69 023*
This *agriturismo* restaurant, housed in a 16th-century farm,

The elegant La Locanda Del Cardinale, Assisi, is a favourite with celebs *(see p156)*

offers creative dishes that use locally produced truffles, olive oil, honey and beans. Risotto with pigeon, followed by ragout of rabbit flavoured with orange and olive oil are frequent items on the menu.

BETTONA: Osteria
Straccagnasse €€
Classic Umbrian   Map C4
Corso Marconi 3, 06084
Tel *075 46 57 095 or 338 67 17 599*
Closed *Mon*
Stylish, intimate restaurant occupying the vaulted cellar of a centuries-old building. Menu includes a great variety of home-made pastas, lots of desserts and good wine.

DK Choice

BETTONA: La Taverna Del
Giullare €€
Fine Dining   Map C4
Vicolo del Forte 11, 06084
Tel *075 98 72 54*   **Closed** *Nov–Mar*
Popular taverna set in a beautifully restored olive oil mill complete with stone arches and a terrace for alfresco dining. The menu is classic Umbrian with a gourmet twist. A typical dinner here includes omelette with black truffle and asparagus cream, pasta dishes and mains of lamb or roasted rabbit. Excellent wine selection.

CITTÀ DELLA PIEVE: Trattoria
Bruno Coppetta €€
Classic Umbrian   Map A4
Via Pietro Vannucci 90, 06062
Tel *057 82 98 108*   **Closed** *Mon*
Located near the Church of Santa Maria dei Bianchi, this elegant place with pretty frescoes specializes in inexpensive char-grilled meats, served between starters like goose ragout and home-made desserts.

CITTÀ DI CASTELLO:
Trattoria da Noi €
Classic Umbrian   Map B2
Via XI Settembre 12, 06012
Tel *075 372 0342*   **Closed** *Mon & Tue*
With pavement tables outside on the road, this popular trattoria has a good wine list and makes its own bread and pasta. Menu includes *agnolotti al ragu* (mince sauce), *beef tagliata*, salumi and cheese platters, bruschetta, pasta and meats.

CITTÀ DI CASTELLO:
Trattoria Lea €
Classic Umbrian   Map B2
Via San Florido, 06012
Tel *075 85 21 678*
Located in the town centre, this traditional restaurant focuses on Umbrian cuisine, namely home-made *cappelletti* pasta in a chicken broth, lamb and pasta with *ceci*, all accompanied by a great wine selection.

CITTÀ DI CASTELLO:
La Miniera di Galparino €€
Classic Umbrian   Map B2
Vocabolo Galparino 35, Sansecondo, 06010
Tel *075 85 40 784*   **Closed** *summer: Sun; winter: Sun D, Mon–Wed*
Serving Umbrian fare at wooden tables in converted stables, this local favourite is housed in an *agriturismo*. It produces its own honey, wine and olive oil.

DERUTA: L'Antico
Forziere €€
Classic Umbrian   Map C4
Via della Rocca 2, Casalina, 06053
Tel *075 97 24 314*   **Closed** *Mon*
This elegant yet rustic Casalina country house offers a creative menu of chargrilled meat and fish dishes, pasta, stews and home-made desserts. Good wine selection.

For more information on types of restaurants *see page 155*

DERUTA: Il Chicco di Grano €€
Gourmet   Map C4
Vocabolo La Torre, 06053
Tel *370 34 52 142*   **Closed** *Tue*
Set inside a country house, this
pleasant restaurant serves
creative and artfully presented
Umbrian dishes and a variety of
fish specialities. Tasting events
take place frequently.

DERUTA: Osteria Il Borghetto €€
Classic Umbrian   Map C4
Via Garibaldi 102, 06053
Tel *075 97 24 264*   **Closed** *Sun*
Attractive and informal family-
run eatery serving classics
including sheep-milk cheeses
from their own farm, and stews
of lamb and wild boar cooked to
time-honoured recipes.

GUBBIO: Alcatraz €
Classic Umbrian   Map D2
Località Santa Cristina 53, 06020
Tel *075 92 29 938*
Food prepared in the restaurant
of this friendly *agriturismo* is
healthy, colourful and mostly
100 per cent organic. Meals are
served buffet-style. Open by
reservation only.

GUBBIO: Grotta Dell'Angelo €€
Italian   Map D2
Via Gioia 47, 06024
Tel *075 92 71 747*   **Closed** *Tue*
Wide choice of pizzas, from
Neapolitan to seafood, as well as
pasta and meat dishes are served
at this traditional hotel trattoria
set in 13th-century rooms.
Terrace for alfresco dining.

**GUBBIO: Locanda Del
Cantiniere** €
Classic Umbrian   Map D2
Via Dante 30, 06024
Tel *075 927 6851*
Friendly, old-fashioned crowd-
pleaser, this elegant restaurant
with exposed brick and wood
beams even bakes its own bread
and makes pasta by hand.

GUBBIO: Bosone Garden €€
Fine Dining   Map D2
Via Galeotti 18, 06024
Tel *075 92 21 246*
Located in the beautiful Palazzo
Raffaelli that was once home
to a wealthy family, this
refined restaurant serves
exquisite Umbrian dishes,
most of which feature truffles,
with a modern twist.

GUBBIO: Taverna del Lupo €€
Classic Umbrian   Map D2
Via Ansidei 21, 06024
Tel *075 92 74 368*
With medieval stone walls
and elegant décor, this

Elegant setting of Taverna del Lupo restaurant, in Gubbio

charming restaurant offers
an innovative Umbrian menu.
Tagliatelle with truffles and
guinea fowl with juniper
are specials.

DK Choice

**GUBBIO: Villa
Montegranelli** €€€
Gourmet   Map D2
Località Monteluiano, 06024
Tel *075 92 20 185*
Famous for its legendary
truffle creations, the Villa
Montegranelli uses Gubbio's
white variety to prepare
delicious pasta dishes and
to flavour Umbrian *pecorino*
or *formaggio di fossa* cheese
which is served with *crostini*
(toasts). Good wine cellar.
The 18th-century villa
offers great views of the
rural countryside.

**LAKE TRASIMENO –
CASTIGLIONE DEL LAGO:
La Cantina** €
Fish & Seafood   Map B3
Via Vittorio Emanuele 93, 06061
Tel *075 96 52 463*
An attractive *agriturismo*
restaurant with outside dining,
La Cantina has a creative menu
of Umbrian lakewater fish dishes.
Try the *tegamaccio*, a stew of
fish from the lake.

**LAKE TRASIMENO –
CASTIGLIONE DEL LAGO:
L'Acquario** €€
Fish & Seafood   Map B3
Via Vittorio Emanuele 69, 06061
Tel *075 96 52 432*   **Closed** *Wed*
Said to be the town's oldest
eatery, L'Acquario is located
inside the city walls. Try the fish
flavoured with herbs and
flowers. Trasimeno caviar is a
speciality. Good wine cellar.

**LAKE TRASIMENO –
CASTIGLIONE DEL LAGO:
La Badiaccia** €€
Fish & Seafood   Map B3
Località La Badiaccia, 06061
Tel *075 95 31 80*
A variety of fish dishes dominate
the menu at this countryside rest-
aurant. There are plenty of meat
options too, with a special focus
on wild boar. There is a terrace for
dining alfresco in summer.

**LAKE TRASIMENO –
CASTIGLIONE DEL LAGO:
Porta Senese** €€
Italian   Map B3
Via vittorio Emanuele 4, 06061
Tel *075 95 33 31*
Meat dishes are the speciality
at this trendy restaurant and
bistrot-cum-butcher's shop –
the menu includes everything
from steaks and burgers to
other options, such as tartares
and even raw beef sashimi.
There's also an extensive menu
of pastas and soups.

DK Choice

**LAKE TRASIMENO – ISOLA
MAGGIORE: Da Sauro** €€
Fish & Seafood   Map B3
Via Guglielmi 1, 06060
Tel *075 82 61 68*
Part of the hotel with the
same name Da Sauro is
reachable only by boat,
this is certainly a romantic
restaurant. Fresh fish from
the lake is transformed into
creative dishes. Try the *Tartine
di Pesce* (fish canapés) with
chilled wine, before enjoying
specials such as *Gnocchetti
alla Trasimeno* (gnocchi with
perch) or *lattarini fritti* (fried
Atherines). There is also a
delicious array of home-made
desserts to choose from.

Basilica of Assisi. It is part of a *agriturismo* farm complex that uses home produce. Open from breakfast until late.

ASSISI: Ristorante da Cecco €€
Classic Umbrian   Map D4
Piazza San Pietro 8, 06081
Tel *075 81 24 37*   **Closed** *Thu*
This hotel restaurant celebrates the art of gastronomy with specials like *agnello al tartufo* (lamb with truffles) and *tagliata di chianina* (steak and tagliatelle with truffle). Excellent wine list.

ASSISI: Ristorante da Elide €€
Italian   Map D4
Via Patrono d'Italia 48, 06081
Tel *075 80 40 867*   **Closed** *Mon*
A cosy autumnal décor, a menu of Italian pasta favourites and an extensive selection of ice creams, combine to make this hotel trattoria a lively place. There is also a special menu for children.

ASSISI: San Francesco €€€
International   Map D4
Via San Francesco 52, 06081
Tel *075 81 23 29*   **Closed** *Wed*
Carpaccio of *porcini* mushrooms, home-made pâtés and steak with truffles are highlights on the menu at this classy eatery, located right by the Basilica in the heart of Assisi. Upmarket wines sold by the glass. Views from the terrace are delightful.

ASSISI: Il Frantoio €€€
Classic Umbrian   Map D4
Via Fontebello 25, 06081
Tel *075 81 22 42*
Elegant restaurant laid-out within set in a renovated 17th-century olive press on the grounds of the Fontebella Hotel. A superb wine list complements the Umbrian menu that offers a variety of meat dishes as well as vegetarian and gluten-free options.

ASSISI: Tuna Fish €€€
Fish & Seafood   Map D4
Via Los Angeles 83, 06081
Tel *075 80 43 433*   **Closed** *Mon*
Specializing in fish and seafood, this trendy restaurant takes great care in always offering the day's catch from the nearby Tyrrhenian Sea, cooked following local Italian recipes. To please the palate, order one of the artfully presented desserts.

BETTONA: Il Poggio degli Olivi
La Veranda €€
Fine Dining   Map C4
Località Montebalacca, 06084
Tel *075 98 69 023*
This *agriturismo* restaurant, housed in a 16th-century farm,

The elegant La Locanda Del Cardinale, Assisi, is a favourite with celebs *(see p156)*

offers creative dishes that use locally produced truffles, olive oil, honey and beans. Risotto with pigeon, followed by ragout of rabbit flavoured with orange and olive oil are frequent items on the menu.

BETTONA: Osteria Straccagnasse €€
Classic Umbrian   Map C4
Corso Marconi 3, 06084
Tel *075 46 57 095 or 338 67 17 599*
Closed *Mon*
Stylish, intimate restaurant occupying the vaulted cellar of a centuries-old building. Menu includes a great variety of home-made pastas, lots of desserts and good wine.

DK Choice

BETTONA: La Taverna Del Giullare €€
Fine Dining   Map C4
Vicolo del Forte 11, 06084
Tel *075 98 72 54*   **Closed** *Nov–Mar*
Popular taverna set in a beautifully restored olive oil mill complete with stone arches and a terrace for alfresco dining. The menu is classic Umbrian with a gourmet twist. A typical dinner here includes omelette with black truffle and asparagus cream, pasta dishes and mains of lamb or roasted rabbit. Excellent wine selection.

CITTÀ DELLA PIEVE: Trattoria Bruno Coppetta €€
Classic Umbrian   Map A4
Via Pietro Vannucci 90, 06062
Tel *057 82 98 108*   **Closed** *Mon*
Located near the Church of Santa Maria dei Bianchi, this elegant place with pretty frescoes specializes in inexpensive char-grilled meats, served between starters like goose ragout and home-made desserts.

CITTÀ DI CASTELLO: Trattoria da Noi €
Classic Umbrian   Map B2
Via XI Settembre 12, 06012
Tel *075 372 0342*   **Closed** *Mon & Tue*
With pavement tables outside on the road, this popular trattoria has a good wine list and makes its own bread and pasta. Menu includes *agnolotti al ragu* (mince sauce), *beef tagliata*, salumi and cheese platters, bruschetta, pasta and meats.

CITTÀ DI CASTELLO: Trattoria Lea €
Classic Umbrian   Map B2
Via San Florido, 06012
Tel *075 85 21 678*
Located in the town centre, this traditional restaurant focuses on Umbrian cuisine, namely home-made *cappelletti* pasta in a chicken broth, lamb and pasta with *ceci*, all accompanied by a great wine selection.

CITTÀ DI CASTELLO: La Miniera di Galparino €€
Classic Umbrian   Map B2
Vocabolo Galparino 35, Sansecondo, 06010
Tel *075 85 40 784*   **Closed** *summer: Sun; winter: Sun D, Mon–Wed*
Serving Umbrian fare at wooden tables in converted stables, this local favourite is housed in an *agriturismo*. It produces its own honey, wine and olive oil.

DERUTA: L'Antico Forziere €€
Classic Umbrian   Map C4
Via della Rocca 2, Casalina, 06053
Tel *075 97 24 314*   **Closed** *Mon*
This elegant yet rustic Casalina country house offers a creative menu of chargrilled meat and fish dishes, pasta, stews and home-made desserts. Good wine selection.

For more information on types of restaurants *see page 155*

DERUTA: Il Chicco di Grano €€
Gourmet   **Map** C4
Vocabolo La Torre, 06053
Tel *370 34 52 142*   **Closed** *Tue*
Set inside a country house, this
pleasant restaurant serves
creative and artfully presented
Umbrian dishes and a variety of
fish specialities. Tasting events
take place frequently.

DERUTA: Osteria Il Borghetto €€
Classic Umbrian   **Map** C4
Via Garibaldi 102, 06053
Tel *075 97 24 264*   **Closed** *Sun*
Attractive and informal family-
run eatery serving classics
including sheep-milk cheeses
from their own farm, and stews
of lamb and wild boar cooked to
time-honoured recipes.

GUBBIO: Alcatraz €
Classic Umbrian   **Map** D2
Località Santa Cristina 53, 06020
Tel *075 92 29 938*
Food prepared in the restaurant
of this friendly *agriturismo* is
healthy, colourful and mostly
100 per cent organic. Meals are
served buffet-style. Open by
reservation only.

GUBBIO: Grotta Dell'Angelo €€
Italian   **Map** D2
Via Gioia 47, 06024
Tel *075 92 71 747*   **Closed** *Tue*
Wide choice of pizzas, from
Neapolitan to seafood, as well as
pasta and meat dishes are served
at this traditional hotel trattoria
set in 13th-century rooms.
Terrace for alfresco dining.

**GUBBIO: Locanda Del
Cantiniere** €
Classic Umbrian   **Map** D2
Via Dante 30, 06024
Tel *075 927 6851*
Friendly, old-fashioned crowd-
pleaser, this elegant restaurant
with exposed brick and wood
beams even bakes its own bread
and makes pasta by hand.

GUBBIO: Bosone Garden €€
Fine Dining   **Map** D2
Via Galeotti 18, 06024
Tel *075 92 21 246*
Located in the beautiful Palazzo
Raffaelli that was once home
to a wealthy family, this
refined restaurant serves
exquisite Umbrian dishes,
most of which feature truffles,
with a modern twist.

GUBBIO: Taverna del Lupo €€
Classic Umbrian   **Map** D2
Via Ansidei 21, 06024
Tel *075 92 74 368*
With medieval stone walls
and elegant décor, this

Elegant setting of Taverna del Lupo restaurant, in Gubbio

charming restaurant offers
an innovative Umbrian menu.
Tagliatelle with truffles and
guinea fowl with juniper
are specials.

DK Choice

**GUBBIO: Villa
Montegranelli** €€€
Gourmet   **Map** D2
Località Monteluiano, 06024
Tel *075 92 20 185*
Famous for its legendary
truffle creations, the Villa
Montegranelli uses Gubbio's
white variety to prepare
delicious pasta dishes and
to flavour Umbrian *pecorino*
or *formaggio di fossa* cheese
which is served with *crostini*
(toasts). Good wine cellar.
The 18th-century villa
offers great views of the
rural countryside.

**LAKE TRASIMENO –
CASTIGLIONE DEL LAGO:
La Cantina** €
Fish & Seafood   **Map** B3
Via Vittorio Emanuele 93, 06061
Tel *075 96 52 463*
An attractive *agriturismo*
restaurant with outside dining,
La Cantina has a creative menu
of Umbrian lakewater fish dishes.
Try the *tegamaccio*, a stew of
fish from the lake.

**LAKE TRASIMENO –
CASTIGLIONE DEL LAGO:
L'Acquario** €€
Fish & Seafood   **Map** B3
Via Vittorio Emanuele 69, 06061
Tel *075 96 52 432*   **Closed** *Wed*
Said to be the town's oldest
eatery, L'Acquario is located
inside the city walls. Try the fish
flavoured with herbs and
flowers. Trasimeno caviar is a
speciality. Good wine cellar.

**LAKE TRASIMENO –
CASTIGLIONE DEL LAGO:
La Badiaccia** €€
Fish & Seafood   **Map** B3
Località La Badiaccia, 06061
Tel *075 95 31 80*
A variety of fish dishes dominate
the menu at this countryside rest-
aurant. There are plenty of meat
options too, with a special focus
on wild boar. There is a terrace for
dining alfresco in summer.

**LAKE TRASIMENO –
CASTIGLIONE DEL LAGO:
Porta Senese** €€
Italian   **Map** B3
Via vittorio Emanuele 4, 06061
Tel *075 95 33 31*
Meat dishes are the speciality
at this trendy restaurant and
bistrot-cum-butcher's shop –
the menu includes everything
from steaks and burgers to
other options, such as tartares
and even raw beef sashimi.
There's also an extensive menu
of pastas and soups.

DK Choice

**LAKE TRASIMENO – ISOLA
MAGGIORE: Da Sauro** €€
Fish & Seafood   **Map** B3
Via Guglielmi 1, 06060
Tel *075 82 61 68*
Part of the hotel with the
same name Da Sauro is
reachable only by boat,
this is certainly a romantic
restaurant. Fresh fish from
the lake is transformed into
creative dishes. Try the *Tartine
di Pesce* (fish canapés) with
chilled wine, before enjoying
specials such as *Gnocchetti
alla Trasimeno* (gnocchi with
perch) or *lattarini fritti* (fried
Atherines). There is also a
delicious array of home-made
desserts to choose from.

LAKE TRASIMENO – PASSIGNANO: Il Fischio del Merlo
€€
Fish & Seafood **Map** B3
Località Calcinaio 17a, 06065
Tel *075 82 92 83* **Closed** *Tue*
This homely restaurant overlooks its garden and the lake beyond. Trasimeno fish such as perch, eel and carp is the speciality here, each presented with imaginative sauces.

LAKE TRASIMENO – PASSIGNANO: Trattoria del Pescatore
€€
Fish & Seafood **Map** B3
Via San Bernardino 5, 06065
Tel *075 82 96 063*
Enjoy fresh fish from the lake and interact with locals at this homely trattoria inside a hotel in the old town. Among the specials is the *tagliatelle alla crema di persico* (pasta with perch cream).

LISCIANO NICCONE: Ristorante da Gianna
€€
Fish & Seafood **Map** B3
Village centre, Lisciano Niccone, Via del Palazzo, 06060
Tel *075 84 43 58* **Closed** *Mon*
Popular family-run restaurant with home-made pasta dishes and crispy pizzas with a host of toppings, including seafood from nearby Lake Trasimeno.

MAGIONE: Il Contadino
€
Italian **Map** B3
Via Giacomo Leopardi 2, 06063
Tel *075 84 15 64*
Simple and informal, this restaurant offers a wide variety of pizzas as well as classic Umbrian specialities such as pastas and meats. Try the *tagliata*.

MAGIONE: Rosso di Sera
€
Fish & Seafood **Map** B3
Via Fratelli Papini 81, 06063
Tel *075 84 76 277* **Closed** *Tue & Wed*
Tasteful décor and an imaginative menu that majors on fish from Lake Trasimeno ensure the restaurant's popularity. Try the ravioli stuffed with perch.

MAGIONE: L'Umbricello del Coccio
€
Classic Umbrian **Map** B3
Via dei Montemelini 22, 06063
Tel *075 84 18 29*
Maialino, a dish of oven-cooked suckling pig with herbs, accompanied by home-made pasta and desserts to finish is the draw at this popular restaurant in the heart of Magione.

MONTONE: Taverna del Verziere
€€
Classic Umbrian **Map** C2
Via dell'Ospedale 25, 06014
Tel *075 93 06 512*
Traditional tavern, with panoramic views from its terrace. Serves home-made *strangozzi* with truffles among other Umbrian dishes handed down through the generations.

NOCERA UMBRA: La Costa
€€
Classic Umbrian **Map** D3
Frazione Costa di Salmata 3, 06025
Tel *074 28 10 042* **Closed** *Sun: dinner; Mon: lunch*
Traditional dishes such as *cinghiale alla cacciatora* (wild boar with red wine and herbs) are served at this *agriturismo* restaurant, a medieval farmhouse outside Nocera Umbra.

DK Choice

PACIANO: La Loggetta
€€
Classic Umbrian **Map** B4
Via Guglielmo Marconi 27, 06060
Tel *075 83 0144* **Closed** *Tue*
Dine indoors or alfresco on the terrace. The recipes here have a Tuscan as well as Umbrian slant and include dishes such as the freshly made *pici* (pasta with choice sauces) that incorporate leek and pork cheek, amaretti and peach tart or choose between Chianian beef and guinea fowl stuffed with vegetables and cannelini beans flavoured with orange. Great wine selection.

PANICALE: Lillo Tatini
€€
Fine Dining **Map** B4
Piazza Umberto I 3/14, Panicale, 06064
Tel *075 83 7771* **Closed** *Mon*
Overlooking the medieval Panicale's village square, this supremely popular and elegant restaurant serves classics that major on pasta. Ravioli with

truffle is the signature dish. Excellent wine list.

PANICALE: Masolino
€€
Classic Umbrian **Map** B4
Via del Filatoio 4
Tel *075 83 71 51* **Closed** *Tue*
Situated in the picturesque Borgo Panicale, this restaurant boasts splendid views of Lake Trasimeno. Umbrian food is cooked to perfection and includes all the classics ranging from home-made pasta with truffle to a variety of cured meats.

PANICALE: Villa Di Monte Solare
€€€
Fine Dining **Map** B4
Via Montali 7, 06068
Tel *075 83 23 76* **Closed** *Jan–Mar*
One of the finest in the region, this restaurant is housed in a charming 18th-century villa standing in magnificent grounds. The menu is à la carte and comprises Umbrian dishes, each with a unique gourmet touch.

PERUGIA: La Bottega di Perugia
€
Italian **Map** C3
Piazza Francesco Morlacchi 4, 06123
Tel *075 57 32 965* **Closed** *Sun*
Street food meets gourmet at this small eatery serving sandwich-based meals made with quality ingredients, including Umbrian cured meats and cheeses, local vegetables and steak. The perfect place for a lunch on the go.

PERUGIA: Il Falchetto
€
Classic Umbrian **Map** C3
Strada Fontana La Trinita 2/d, 06132
Tel *075 57 31775* **Closed** *Mon*
This superb trattoria with a pleasant terrace is situated in the lush greenery of the Umbrian hills. It offers six different menus – traditional Umbrian, truffle-based, gluten-free, vegetarian, fish-based and a special game menu.

Wine bottles line the walls of Paciano restaurant La Loggetta

For more information on types of restaurants *see page 155*

PERUGIA: Les Cre Fantastique €
Café Map C3
Via San Ercolano 1, 06100
Tel *392 57 42 917* **Closed** *Mon*
Serving savoury, sweet and gluten-free crêpes as well as *piadine*, this restaurant with a rustic and relaxed vibe is popular with locals and kids.

PERUGIA: Osteria Il Gufo €
Classic Umbrian Map C3
Via della Viola 18, 06122
Tel *075 57 34 126*
Friendly restaurant with light meat and vegetarian meals, salads, cheeses and delicious desserts. Offers a fixed menu too.

PERUGIA: Osteria a Priori €
Classic Umbrian Map C3
Via dei Priori 39, 06123
Tel *075 57 27 098* **Closed** *Sun*
Housed in a stone building near the Palazzo dei Priori, this popular eatery specializes in local fare. Gourmet lunch menu is available for €10 on weekdays at noon.

PERUGIA: Osteria del Turreno €
Classic Umbrian Map C3
Piazza Danti 16, 06122
Tel *075 57 21 976* **Closed** *Eve, Sat all day*
Popular restaurant that serves imaginative healthy food mostly using Km0 ingredients. Freshly made local dishes are laid out as buffet in the pretty room or on tables outside in the main square near the fountain.

PERUGIA: Pizzeria Mediterranea €
Italian Map C3
Via Guglielmo Marconi 11, 06121
Tel *075 57 24 021*
A huge wood-fired oven dominates the space in this lively pizzeria. Choose from different toppings, from Neapolitan to versions with pepper and seafood.

PERUGIA: Pizzeria La Romantica €
Italian Map C3
Borgo Venti Giugno 9, 06121
Tel *075 372 14 06* **Closed** *Mon*
A favourite among locals, this pizzeria has a lively ambiance and good service. It serves delicious Neapolitan-style pizzas and a great variety of fried starters. Ask for the craft beer menu for some truly special local brews.

PERUGIA: Ristorante Il Bacio €
Italian Map C3
Via Boncambi 6, 06123
Tel *075 57 20 909*
With tables outside on the lovely pedestrianized Corso Vanucci and in the intimate dining room, Il Bacio offers innovative pizzas, freshly prepared and cooked in its wood-fired oven. Great pasta dishes, salads and desserts too.

PERUGIA: Ristorante Dal Mi'Cocco €
Umbrian Map C3
Corso Garibaldi 12, 06123
Tel *075 57 32 511* **Closed** *Mon*
Locally sourced ingredients served as imaginative starters, main, side and dessert dishes as per a set menu that changes daily. Remarkable value.

PERUGIA: Altromondo €€
Classic Umbrian Map C3
Via Cesare Caporali 11, 06100
Tel *075 572 6157* **Closed** *Sun*
This city centre trattoria has a daily changing menu with emphasis on using only quality ingredients. Try the *arrosto misto* (mix of roast lamb and other meats).

PERUGIA: Antica Trattoria San Lorenzo €€
Fine Dining Map C3
Piazza Danti 19a, 06122
Tel *075 572 19 56* **Closed** *Sun*
Umbrian gourmet cuisine featuring home-made pasta and sauces at a lovely location, right by the cathedral. Excellent wine selection and speciality ice creams.

PERUGIA: Caffè Di Perugia €€
Italian Map C3
Via Giuseppe Mazzini 10, 06121
Tel *075 57 31 863* **Closed** *Tue*
There's something for everyone at this restaurant spread over several floors. Delectable pizzas

A plateful of delicate crêpes served with lemon slices

and traditional Umbrian fare. There is a café and a bar too.

PERUGIA: Da Cesarino €€
Classic Umbrian Map C3
Piazza IV Novembre 4–5, 06123
Tel *075 57 28 974* **Closed** *Wed, Thu L*
Old fashioned décor and alfresco dining sets the tone for the classic local cuisine served at Da Cesarino.

PERUGIA: Enone Enoteca Cucina €€
Fine Dining Map C3
Corso Cavour 61, 06121
Tel *075 57 21 950* **Closed** *Mon*
Imaginative dishes are served at this trendy eaterie-cum-bar. Truffle risotto, flavoured gnocchi and sushi are popular specials.

PERUGIA: L'Opera €€
Fish & Seafood Map C3
Via dell'Allodola 9, Ponte San Giovanni, 06135
Tel *075 393 337* **Closed** *Sun*
Run by a couple from Agrigento, this eatery serves Sicilian fish specialities followed by home-made Sicilian desserts. Options for non-fish eaters too. Superb wines.

PERUGIA: Osteria I Birbi €€
Classic Umbrian Map C3
Via Campo di Battaglia 10, 06121
Tel *075 98 89 041* **Closed** *Wed; Thu lunch*
Popular for its excellent steaks, tagliatelle and rich home-made pasta dishes, this restaurant has a modern ambiance but still retains its traditonal charm.

DK Choice

PERUGIA: Ristorante Del Sole €€
Fine Dining Map C3
Via della Rupe 1, 06121
Tel *075 57 35 031* **Closed** *Mon*
Located in Perugia's medieval old town, this upmarket restaurant offers the chance to dine enjoying wonderful views of the city, both on its alfresco dining terrace and inside. Umbrian meat, fish and pasta dishes are given a modern twist with combinations like cheese ravioli with oranges, and lamb with figs. Excellent wine cellar.

PERUGIA: La Taverna €€
Classic Umbrian Map C3
Via delle Streghe 8, 06123
Tel *075 57 32 536*
This classy restaurant, with vaulted brick ceilings, offers great Italian staples and Umbrian flavours. Menu highlights include home-made tagliatelle and a wide variety of meat and fish dishes.

Dining area at the very stylish Le Melograne in Torgiano

PERUGIA: Ubu Re €€
Classic Umbrian **Map** C3
Via Baldeschi 8a, 06123
Tel *075 57 35 461* **Closed** *Mon eve, Sun*
A warm, rustic ambiance and a menu of authentic Umbrian cuisine combine to make this upmarket eatery a constant for gourmands. Try the ravioli made with *caciocavallo* cheese.

PERUGIA: Giò Arte e Vini €€€
International **Map** C3
Via Ruggero d'Andreotto 19, 06124
Tel *075 57 31 100* **Closed** *Sun*
Beautifully prepared and presented Umbrian dishes, and a lengthy wine list to choose from at this stylish and 'arty' restaurant located inside the Gio Jazz Hotel, a little way out of Perugia.

PERUGIA: La Rosetta €€€
Fine Dining **Map** C3
Piazza Italia 19, 06123
Tel *075 57 20 841*
Delicious lamb, wild boar and steak cooked in the red wine *Sagrantino di Montefalco* are among the dishes on the menu at this elegant restaurant near the Fontana Maggiore. Good wine list.

PETRIGNANO: Locanda ai Cavalieri €€
International **Map** D3
Via Matteotti 47, 06086
Tel *075 803 00 11*
The stylish restaurant of Hotel Locanda ai Cavalieri makes its own pasta and bread to accompany its international dishes. Taster menus, home-made desserts and top wines too.

TORGIANO: I Tempi Antichi €
Classic Umbrian **Map** C4
Via Vittorio Emanuele II 72, 06089
Tel *075 46 57 141* **Closed** *Tue*
Simple and traditional Umbrian cuisine defines this small restaurant in the heart of Torgiano. The antipasti are abundant and very popular while the tagliatelle are hand-made by the chef and is served with truffles and porcini mushrooms.

TORGIANO: Ristorante Siro €€
Classic Umbrian **Map** C4
Via Giordano Bruno 16, 06089
Tel *075 98 20 10*
A cosy hotel restaurant that has been thrilling diners for several decades with *antipasti* dishes featuring white truffles, and mains cooked in authentic Umbrian-style . It has a fine wine selection.

TORGIANO: Il Toscanino €€
Classic Umbrian **Map** C4
Località Signoria di Torgiano, 06089
Tel *075 98 52 80* **Closed** *Sun*
The menu is a mix of Umbrian and Tuscan cuisine at this attractive eatery. *Antipasti* dishes typically include *strangozzi* (spaghetti) with sauces freshly made and rich in taste, followed by creative mains of game. Speciality is the *fiorentina* steak. Good pizzas too.

TORGIANO: Le Melograne €€€
Gourmet **Map** C4
Via Giuseppe Garibaldi 48, 06089
Tel *075 98 80 447*
Try the mixed fish antipasti platter followed by Catalan lobster at this stylish eatery inside the boutique-style Tre Vaselle Hotel. A top-notch wine list and the rural setting is a draw.

UMBERTIDE: C'era Una Volta €
Classic Umbrian **Map** C2
Via Martiri del Lager 2, 06019
Tel *075 94 12 641*
Service is friendly and attentive at this simple, family-run restaurant serving traditional yet creative Umbrian fare. The menu includes a variety of fresh pastas, all home-made and a great selection of meaty second courses.

UMBERTIDE: La Chiusa €
Classic Umbrian **Map** C2
SS 146 del Niccone, near Umbertide
Tel *075 94 10 848*
La Chiusa is an organic restaurant that uses meat from its own farm and produce that has been grown in its garden, to create wholesome dishes. Wines are from speciality vintners.

DK Choice

UMBERTIDE: Poggiomanente €
Classic Umbrian **Map** C2
SS 219, E45 exit Umbertide/ Gubbio, 06019
Tel *075 92 52 00*
Crispy pizzas fresh from the oven, along with hearty soups, stews and truffle-based mains are served in this refined yet rustic restaurant set in the cellar of a 15th-century farmhouse.

UMBERTIDE: La Rocca €€
Fish & Seafood **Map** C2
Piazza Caduti del Lavoro 4, 06019
Tel *075 94 11 828* **Closed** *Mon*
Attractive little restaurant located just across from Umbertide's fortress. It specializes in fish. Try the large portions of *carpaccio* and the tasty pastas.

UMBERTIDE: Locanda Di Nonna Gelsa €€
Classic Umbrian **Map** C2
Via Caduti di Pentola 31, Niccone, 06019
Tel *075 94 10 699* **Closed** *Tue*
Elegant trattoria with a traditional décor, crisp linens and a menu of Umbrian dishes that features game and rabbit. Good choice of local and Tuscan wines. Picturesque countryside setting.

UMBERTIDE: Vigne di Pace €€
Classic Umbrian **Map** C2
Via Case Sparse 64, 06019
Tel *333 77 10 059* **Closed** *Mon*
A family-run *agriturismo* located in the countryside. Set in an old country house with vaulted ceilings and terracotta floors, it provides the perfect background to the home-made local dishes.

UMBERTIDE: Zibú 2.0 €€
Italian **Map** C2
Via Leopoldo Grilli 63, 06019
Tel *075 941 1952* **Closed** *Mon*
Elegant and modern restaurant with retro furnishings and a romantic ambiance. The chef uses local ingredients to prepare inventive versions of traditional Italian recipes.

For more information on types of restaurants *see page 155*

Southern Umbria

AMELIA: Anita €
Classic Umbrian **Map** C6
Via Roma 31, 05022
Tel *074 49 82 146* **Closed** *Mon*
A family-run restaurant with an
exhaustive range of home-made
pasta dishes, slow-cooked meat
casseroles, roasts and desserts.

ARRONE: Il Grottino Del Nera €
Classic Umbrian **Map** D6
*SS Valnerina 209, Vocabolo
Colleporto 21, 05031*
Tel *074 43 89 104* **Closed** *Wed*
One of the region's oldest
eateries, this osteria serves
classic Umbrian cuisine in the
form of game, wild boar and
trout. Tagliatelle with truffle is a
special. Terrace for dining alfresco.

ARRONE: La Locanda €
Fine Dining **Map** D6
Via Pié di Arrone 1, 05031 Arrone
Tel *074 43 89 961* **Closed** *Mon*
Located in the Residence Fiocchi
and offering spectacular views
of the Parco Fluviale del Nera
Valley, Locanda uses local
produce including fish from
the Nera river, local cheese,
truffles and olive oil. The truffle-
scented trout is one of the
main specialities. Home-made
desserts and pasta. Excellent
wine list.

ARRONE: Rossi €€
Classic Umbrian **Map** D6
Vocabolo Isola 7, 05031
Tel *074 43 88 372* **Closed** *Fri &
Sun eve*
A lengthy menu of *antipasti*
dishes precede the chargrilled
meats and pasta at Rossi. The
Southern Umbrian crusted veal is
a special. Located near the
Cascata delle Marmore.

DK Choice

BASCHI: Vissani €€€
Fine Dining **Map** B6
*Strada Statale 448, km 606, Todi-
Baschi, 05020*
Tel *074 49 50 206* **Closed** *Mon:
lunch; Wed; Thu: lunch; Sun:
dinner*
Elegant, contemporary place
with dark oak furniture teamed
with vibrant orange. The
Southern Umbrian cuisine
specials served here include
gourmet game and meat
creations. The menus are
devised by owner Gianfranco
Vissani, a celebrity chef known
throughout Italy for his
exquisite cuisine.

The rustic dining area at Ottavius in Bevagna

**BEVAGNA: Il Poggio Dei
Pettirossi** €€
Classic Umbrian **Map** D4
Via del Poggio 1, 06031
Tel *074 23 61 744* **Closed** *Tue*
Dishes such as *cinghiale alla
cacciatora* (wild boar with red
wine and herbs) are served to the
loyal following that frequents this
elegant restaurant. Wine is from
Montefalco. Panoramic views of
the rural countryside.

**BEVAGNA: Osteria del
Podestà** €€
Classic Umbrian **Map** D4
Corso Giacomo Matteotti 67, 06031
Tel *0742 360 222* **Closed** *Wed*
Richly-decorated with antique-
style furniture, this popular
restaurant serves traditional
Umbrian cuisine. The house
speciality is the prized *gnocchi al
Sagrantino* (in red wine sauce).

BEVAGNA: Ottavius €€
Classic Umbrian **Map** D4
Via del Gonfalone 1, 06031
Tel *074 23 60 555* **Closed** *Mon*
The seasonal menu always uses
fresh local produce. Truffles are a
speciality, along with home-made
gnocchi. Good wine selection.
Welcoming rustic décor.

BEVAGNA: Spirito Divino €€
Classic Umbrian **Map** D4
Via Onofri 2, 06031
Tel *074 23 61 926* **Closed** *Wed*
Housed in a 12th-century building
with vaulted ceilings and an open
fireplace, this trattoria specializes
in local pasta dishes, cheese and
fabulous wines. It has about 500
different vintages in its cellar.

BEVAGNA: Redibis €€€
Fine Dining **Map** D4
Via dell'Anfiteatro, 06031
Tel *074 23 62 120* **Closed** *Tue*
Part of Bevagna's Roman theatre,
Redibis is one of the few places

in Umbria where you can find
dishes cooked to authentic age-
old recipes. Veal braised in
Montefalco wine is a special.

DK Choice

**CAMPELLO SUL CLITUNNO:
Fonti Del Clitunno** €
International **Map** D5
*Via Flaminia 11, Località Fonti
Clitunno, 06042*
Tel *074 32 75 057* **Closed** *Wed*
Located inside the Fonti del
Clitunno Park, this restaurant
serves meat, fish and vege-
tarian dishes from a menu
that changes most days.
Gorgeous views over the
water, and a charming,
rustic interior.

**CAMPELLO SUL CLITUNNO:
Parco del Clitunno** €€
Fish and Seafood **Map** D5
Viale Fonti del Clitunno 3, 06042
Tel *074 35 21 052*
Located inside a lush park
amidst idyllic surroundings,
Parco del Clitunno specializes
in offering Italian fish cuisine
such as spaghetti with seafood, grilled fish and
crustaceans. It also includes
a local menu with truffle pasta
and meat dishes.

**CAMPELLO SUL CLITUNNO:
Trattoria Pettino** €€
Classic Umbrian **Map** D5
*Frazione Pettino 31, S.P. 458 (strada
provinciale), Km 15.5, 06042*
Tel *074 32 76 021* **Closed** *Tue; Sat &
Sun in winters*
A local favourite, the Trattoria
Pettino is a warmly decorated
place in the mountains.
The menu changes daily
but, typically, features pasta
and *agnello al tartufo* (lamb
with truffles).

CANNARA: Perbacco €€
Classic Umbrian   **Map** D4
Via Umberto I 16, 06033
Tel *074 27 20 492*   **Closed** *Mon*
Cannara is famous for a variety
of red onion, which is used to
good effect in the flavoursome
Umbrian dishes served at
Perbacco, a charming trattoria
with traditional décor. Great
selection of pasta dishes.

CIVITELLA DEL LAGO:
Trippini €€€
Fish & Seafood   **Map** C5
Via Italia 14, 05023
Tel *0744 950 316*   **Closed** *Mon*
An attractive restaurant with a
cottage feel, Trippini changes its
menu according to fresh local
availability, but presents with
considerable flair. Breathtaking
views and attentive service.

FABRO: La Bettola del
Buttero Fabro €
Classic Umbrian   **Map** B5
Via dei Pini 2, 05015
Tel *076 38 32 063*   **Closed** *Sun eve*
The huge wood-fired oven
and fireplace, on which meats
flavoured with local herbs,
potatoes and onions are cooked
to order, dominates this idyllic
country hotel restaurant.
Alfresco dining in summers.

FERENTILLO: Osteria
del Trap €
Fish & Seafood   **Map** D6
Località Casale Carocci, 05034
Tel *328 49 34 535*   **Closed** *Wed*
A variety of fish antipasti and
delicious pizzas make this a
popular destination for locals.
It is located just a short distance
outside town with a simple
setting. Serving portions are
large and tasty.

DK Choice
FERENTILLO:
Piermarini €€
Classic Umbrian   **Map** D6
23 Vosso Ancaiano, 05034
Tel *074 47 80 714*   **Closed** *Sun eve, Mon*
The location of Piermarini in
the Parco Fluviale del Nera,
not far from the Marmore
Waterfalls, along with its
country house décor, charms
its guests. Its lengthy menu
of Umbrian dishes focuses
on natural produce and
vegetables from its own farm,
including black truffles and
olives. Dine inside or
alfresco on its terrace that
offers pleasing views of
the countryside.

FOLIGNO:
Pizzeria Vesuv io €
Italian   **Map** D4
Via Monte Acuto 19, 06034
Tel *074 23 21 250*
Vesuvio is one of the few
pizzerias in the area that offer
the thick-crusted Neapolitan
pizza, cooked to perfection. Also
on offer are fish specialities and
fried antipasti.

DK Choice
FOLIGNO: Ristorante Via
del Forno €€
Fine Dining   **Map** D4
Piazza Matteotti/Via Colombia Antonietti, 06034
Tel *074 235 0412*
This hotel restaurant tucked
behind Foligno's pretty Palazzo
Comunale has a pretty dining
room in a noble old house.
The sober décor and classy
feel make for a relaxing dining
experience. Serves fresh pasta,
grilled meats, scrambled eggs
with truffle, lamb from
Colfiorito (a natural park
nearby) and other upmarket
versions of Foligno cuisine.
A taste of the walnut and
liquorice digestif is a great way
to end the meal.

FOLIGNO: La Spagnola €€
Classic Umbrian   **Map** D4
Via Rinaldi 14i, 06034
Tel *0742 351281*
Its vaulted stone building
dating from the 1600s serving
as backdrop, this elegant
restaurant specializes in offering
a wide variety such as *gnocchi al
sagrantino*, wild boar medallions
or lamb inn juniper, pizzas as
well as fresh fish daily. The
chef's Spanish origins ensure

Fresh lobster risotto with lemon
and herbs

that the *paella alla valenciana*
and *crème catalane* are also
represented on the menu.

FOLIGNO: Villa Roncalli €€€
Fine Dining   **Map** D4
Via Roma 25, 06034 Foligno
Tel *074 23 91 091*   **Closed** *Mon*
The bread is home-made, the
eggs and fresh produce come
from the garden while the beef is
the local-bred Chianina, at this
refined restaurant set in a 17th-
century palazzo.

DK Choice
MONTEFALCO:
Coccorone €€
Classic Umbrian   **Map** D4
Largo Tempesti 11, Vicolo Fabbri 7, 06036
Tel *074 23 79 535*   **Closed** *Wed*
Charming restaurant where
traditional country recipes that
have been saved from being
lost in time, have been given a
modern twist. Menu favourites
include home-made *strangozzi*
(spaghetti) and *gnocchi*, meat
cooked over charcoal as well as
local dishes such as *cinghiale in
umido con fagioli* (wild boar
served with beans). Excellent
Montefalco wines.

MONTEFALCO: Villa
Pambuffetti €€
Fine Dining   **Map** D4
Via della Vittoria 20, Montefalco, 06036
Tel *074 23 79 417*   **Closed** *Mon*
Olive oil and produce from its
own farm, as well as Montefalco
wines, are featured on the
restaurant's gourmet menu.
Quite popular with celebs,
Pambuffetti is housed in a
19th-century mansion.

MONTELEONE DI SPOLETO:
Trattoria da Gigetto €
Classic Umbrian   **Map** E5
Statale 471, Km 12,800, Ruscio, 06045
Tel *074 37 01 11*   **Closed** *Tue*
This traditional trattoria serves
hearty soups, pasta and meat
dishes from lunch to supper.
Agnello alla cacciatora, an
Umbrian lamb dish, is a special.

NARNI: Cavallino €
Classic Umbrian   **Map** C6
Via Flaminia Romana 220, Località Testaccio, 05035
Tel *074 47 61 020*   **Closed** *Tue*
Traditional trattoria where pasta
creations and wholesome dishes
of game, meat and fish are
prepared to Umbrian recipes.
The team prides itself on using
only seasonal local produce.

For more information on types of restaurants *see page 155*

NARNI: Gastronomia Terra & Arte €
Classic Umbrian Map C6
Vicolo Belvedere 1, 05035
Tel *074 47 26 385*
A local favourite, this gourmet deli has a seasonal menu and is famous for its sandwiches, cured meat and cheese platters. It also serves simple soups, *crostini* and lasagne. Fabulous views and pleasant outdoor space.

NARNI: Il Gattamelata €
International Map C6
Via Pozzo della Comunità 4, 05035
Tel *074 47 17 245* **Closed** *Sun eve, Mon*
Located in Narni's main square, near the cathedral, this cosy eatery celebrates local cuisine. *Carpaccio d'anatra* (duck) and *tagliata di manzo di pura razza* (pure bred beef) are specials. Good wine list.

NORCIA: Dal Francese €
Classic Umbrian Map F5
Via Riguardati 16, 06046 Norcia
Tel *074 38 16 290* **Closed** *Wed*
Local delicacy *beccacce alla norcina* (woodcock stuffed with herbs, truffles and sausage) is one of the dishes on this rustic trattoria's popular truffle-based *menù degustazione* (tasting menu).

NORCIA: Il Cenacolo €€
Classic Umbrian Map F5
Via Marconi 4, 06046
Tel *074 38 17 119* **Closed** *Sun eve*
A variety of meat specialities and delicious home-made pastas are served at this small, characterful restaurant. Try the local cured meats and cheeses.

NORCIA: Il Granaro del Monte €€
Classic Umbrian Map F5
Via Alfieri 6
Tel *074 38 16 153*
Perhaps the oldest Umbrian restaurant and part of the Hotel

Grotta Azzurra, Il Granaro serves classic gastronomic dishes such as the *mazzafegati* (pig's liver sausage with raisons, nuts and orange peel). Superb desserts and wines. The dining room is beautiful and has a huge fireplace.

DK Choice

NORCIA: Taverna De' Massari €€
Classic Umbrian Map F5
Via Roma 13, 06046
Tel *074 38 16 218* **Closed** *Tue*
Carpaccio di cinghiale del parco tartufato (wild boar carpaccio with mushrooms and truffles) and gnocchetti alla Norcina *tartufati* (potato gnocchi with cream and truffle) are just two of the exciting dishes served at this old town tavern. Beneath its dining hall is a Roman stone cellar where a wide selection of Italian wines are stored. The terrace has alfresco dining.

ORVIETO: Cantina Foresi €
Enoteca Map B5
Piazza Duomo 2, 05018
Tel *076 33 41 611*
Popular with the trendy, this bistro-style place has over 110 wine labels from Umbria, Tuscany and Lazio, which it serves with a gourmet-standard selection of dipping olive oils, cheeses and cold meats. Sip a glass gazing at the town's magnificent duomo.

ORVIETO: Charlie Pizzeria €
Italian Map B5
Via Loggia dei Mercanti, 14, 05018
Tel *076 33 44 766*
Renowned in Orvieto for its pizzas, there are also fresh pasta and succulent meat dishes on offer with a fine range of local wines and artisan beers. Its pizzas are made with sour dough and topped with seasonal ingredients

such as fresh fungi. Pretty courtyard with tables outside. Centrally located and popular with locals and tourists alike.

DK Choice

ORVIETO: La Badia €€
Fine Dining Map B5
Località Badia 8, 05019
Tel *076 33 01 959* **Closed** *Mon & Tue lunch*
Housed in a gorgeous former abbey that traces its origins back to the 6th century, this romantic restaurant tempts with Umbrian classics which have a gourmet twist. Dishes are artfully presented on the plate. Home-made *tagliolini* with black truffles and juniper-infused grilled meats are among the specials. Extensive wine list with Italian vintages.

ORVIETO: Duca Di Orvieto €€
Classic Umbrian Map B5
Via della Pace 5, 05018
Tel *076 33 44 663* **Closed** *Wed, Sun*
The theme of the menu at this cosy trattoria is 'our culture on a plate' and it draws from a stock of well-researched, old Orvieto recipes. Umbrichelle pasta is a menu staple here.

ORVIETO: Le Grotte del Funaro €€
International Map B5
Via Ripa Serancia 41, 05018
Tel *076 33 43 276*
Housed in the 12th-century workshop of a *funaro* (ropemaker), this cave-like restaurant has menus that typically feature beef with truffle and porcini mushrooms, and Umbrian game. Good fish and pasta selection, pizzas fresh from the wood-fired oven and an excellent wine list.

DK Choice

ORVIETO: I Sette Consoli €€
Classic Umbrian Map B5
Piazza Sant'Angelo 1a, 05018
Tel *076 33 43 911* **Closed** *Wed, Sun eve*
I Sette Consoli sources top notch ingredients from Europe that come together as exquisite plates. *Ravioli di anatra* (duck-filled ravioli), Scottish salmon and pigeon in marsala sauce are specials. Dine inside in this cottage-style restaurant or outside on the canopied terrace. The wine cellar has over 800 labels from around the world, and over a hundred liquors.

The wine cellar at the cottage-style I Sette Consoli, in Orvieto, has over 800 labels

Key to Price Guide *see page 156*

CANNARA: Perbacco €€
Classic Umbrian   Map D4
Via Umberto I 16, 06033
Tel *074 27 20 492*   **Closed** *Mon*
Cannara is famous for a variety
of red onion, which is used to
good effect in the flavoursome
Umbrian dishes served at
Perbacco, a charming trattoria
with traditional décor. Great
selection of pasta dishes.

CIVITELLA DEL LAGO:
Trippini €€€
Fish & Seafood   Map C5
Via Italia 14, 05023
Tel *0744 950 316*   **Closed** *Mon*
An attractive restaurant with a
cottage feel, Trippini changes its
menu according to fresh local
availability, but presents with
considerable flair. Breathtaking
views and attentive service.

FABRO: La Bettola del
Buttero Fabro €
Classic Umbrian   Map B5
Via dei Pini 2, 05015
Tel *076 38 32 063*   **Closed** *Sun eve*
The huge wood-fired oven
and fireplace, on which meats
flavoured with local herbs,
potatoes and onions are cooked
to order, dominates this idyllic
country hotel restaurant.
Alfresco dining in summers.

FERENTILLO: Osteria
del Trap €
Fish & Seafood   Map D6
Località Casale Carocci, 05034
Tel *328 49 34 535*   **Closed** *Wed*
A variety of fish antipasti and
delicious pizzas make this a
popular destination for locals.
It is located just a short distance
outside town with a simple
setting. Serving portions are
large and tasty.

DK Choice

FERENTILLO:
Piermarini €€
Classic Umbrian   Map D6
23 Vosso Ancaiano, 05034
Tel *074 47 80 714*   **Closed** *Sun
eve, Mon*
The location of Piermarini in
the Parco Fluviale del Nera,
not far from the Marmore
Waterfalls, along with its
country house décor, charms
its guests. Its lengthy menu
of Umbrian dishes focuses
on natural produce and
vegetables from its own farm,
including black truffles and
olives. Dine inside or
alfresco on its terrace that
offers pleasing views of
the countryside.

FOLIGNO:
Pizzeria Vesuv io €
Italian   Map D4
Via Monte Acuto 19, 06034
Tel *074 23 21 250*
Vesuvio is one of the few
pizzerias in the area that offer
the thick-crusted Neapolitan
pizza, cooked to perfection. Also
on offer are fish specialities and
fried antipasti.

DK Choice

FOLIGNO: Ristorante Via
del Forno €€
Fine Dining   Map D4
*Piazza Matteotti/Via Colomba
Antonietti, 06034*
Tel *074 235 0412*
This hotel restaurant tucked
behind Foligno's pretty Palazzo
Comunale has a pretty dining
room in a noble old house.
The sober décor and classy
feel make for a relaxing dining
experience. Serves fresh pasta,
grilled meats, scrambled eggs
with truffle, lamb from
Colfiorito (a natural park
nearby) and other upmarket
versions of Foligno cuisine.
A taste of the walnut and
liquorice digestif is a great way
to end the meal.

FOLIGNO: La Spagnola €€
Classic Umbrian   Map D4
Via Rinaldi 14i, 06034
Tel *0742 351281*
Its vaulted stone building
dating from the 1600s serving
as backdrop, this elegant
restaurant specializes in offering
a wide variety such as *gnocchi al
sagrantino*, wild boar medallions
or lamb inn juniper, pizzas as
well as fresh fish daily. The
chef's Spanish origins ensure

Fresh lobster risotto with lemon
and herbs

that the *paella alla valenciana*
and *crème catalane* are also
represented on the menu.

FOLIGNO: Villa Roncalli €€€
Fine Dining   Map D4
Via Roma 25, 06034 Foligno
Tel *074 23 91 091*   **Closed** *Mon*
The bread is home-made, the
eggs and fresh produce come
from the garden while the beef is
the local-bred Chianina, at this
refined restaurant set in a 17th-
century palazzo.

DK Choice

MONTEFALCO:
Coccorone €€
Classic Umbrian   Map D4
*Largo Tempesti 11, Vicolo Fabbri
7, 06036*
Tel *074 23 79 535*   **Closed** *Wed*
Charming restaurant where
traditional country recipes that
have been saved from being
lost in time, have been given a
modern twist. Menu favourites
include home-made *strangozzi*
(spaghetti) and *gnocchi*, meat
cooked over charcoal as well as
local dishes such as *cinghiale in
umido con fagioli* (wild boar
served with beans). Excellent
Montefalco wines.

MONTEFALCO: Villa
Pambuffetti €€
Fine Dining   Map D4
*Via della Vittoria 20, Montefalco,
06036*
Tel *074 23 79 417*   **Closed** *Mon*
Olive oil and produce from its
own farm, as well as Montefalco
wines, are featured on the
restaurant's gourmet menu.
Quite popular with celebs,
Pambuffetti is housed in a
19th-century mansion.

MONTELEONE DI SPOLETO:
Trattoria da Gigetto €
Classic Umbrian   Map E5
Statale 471, Km 12,800, Ruscio, 06045
Tel *074 37 01 11*   **Closed** *Tue*
This traditional trattoria serves
hearty soups, pasta and meat
dishes from lunch to supper.
Agnello alla cacciatora, an
Umbrian lamb dish, is a special.

NARNI: Cavallino €
Classic Umbrian   Map C6
*Via Flaminia Romana 220, Località
Testaccio, 05035*
Tel *074 47 61 020*   **Closed** *Tue*
Traditional trattoria where pasta
creations and wholesome dishes
of game, meat and fish are
prepared to Umbrian recipes.
The team prides itself on using
only seasonal local produce.

For more information on types of restaurants *see page 155*

**NARNI: Gastronomia
Terra & Arte** €
Classic Umbrian **Map** C6
Vicolo Belvedere 1, 05035
Tel *074 47 26 385*
A local favourite, this gourmet
deli has a seasonal menu and is
famous for its sandwiches, cured
meat and cheese platters. It also
serves simple soups, *crostini* and
lasagne. Fabulous views and
pleasant outdoor space.

NARNI: Il Gattamelata €
International **Map** C6
Via Pozzo della Comunità 4, 05035
Tel *074 47 17 245* **Closed** *Sun eve,
Mon*
Located in Narni's main square,
near the cathedral, this cosy
eatery celebrates local cuisine.
Carpaccio d'anatra (duck) and
tagliata di manzo di pura razza
(pure bred beef) are specials.
Good wine list.

NORCIA: Dal Francese €
Classic Umbrian **Map** F5
Via Riguardati 16, 06046 Norcia
Tel *074 38 16 290* **Closed** *Wed*
Local delicacy *beccacce alla
norcina* (woodcock stuffed with
herbs, truffles and sausage) is one
of the dishes on this rustic
trattoria's popular truffle-based
menù degustazione (tasting menu).

NORCIA: Il Cenacolo €€
Classic Umbrian **Map** F5
Via Marconi 4, 06046
Tel *074 38 17 119* **Closed** *Sun eve*
A variety of meat specialities and
delicious home-made pastas are
served at this small, characterful
restaurant. Try the local cured
meats and cheeses.

**NORCIA: Il Granaro del
Monte** €€
Classic Umbrian **Map** F5
Via Alfieri 6
Tel *074 38 16 153*
Perhaps the oldest Umbrian
restaurant and part of the Hotel

Grotta Azzurra, Il Granaro serves
classic gastronomic dishes such
as the *mazzafegati* (pig's liver
sausage with raisons, nuts and
orange peel). Superb desserts
and wines. The dining room is
beautiful and has a huge fireplace.

DK Choice

**NORCIA: Taverna
De' Massari** €€
Classic Umbrian **Map** F5
Via Roma 13, 06046
Tel *074 38 16 218* **Closed** *Tue*
Carpaccio di cinghiale del
parco tartufato (wild boar
carpaccio with mushrooms
and truffles) and gnocchetti
alla Norcina *tartufati* (potato
gnocchi with cream and
truffle) are just two of the
exciting dishes served at this
old town tavern. Beneath its
dining hall is a Roman stone
cellar where a wide selection
of Italian wines are stored. The
terrace has alfresco dining.

ORVIETO: Cantina Foresi €
Enoteca **Map** B5
Piazza Duomo 2, 05018
Tel *076 33 41 611*
Popular with the trendy, this
bistro-style place has over 110
wine labels from Umbria, Tuscany
and Lazio, which it serves with a
gourmet-standard selection of
dipping olive oils, cheeses and
cold meats. Sip a glass gazing at
the town's magnificent duomo.

ORVIETO: Charlie Pizzeria €
Italian **Map** B5
Via Loggia dei Mercanti, 14, 05018
Tel *076 33 44 766*
Renowned in Orvieto for its pizzas,
there are also fresh pasta and
succulent meat dishes on offer
with a fine range of local wines
and artisan beers. Its pizzas are
made with sour dough and
topped with seasonal ingredients

such as fresh fungi. Pretty
courtyard with tables outside.
Centrally located and popular
with locals and tourists alike.

DK Choice

ORVIETO: La Badia €€
Fine Dining **Map** B5
Località Badia 8, 05019
Tel *076 33 01 959* **Closed** *Mon &
Tue lunch*
Housed in a gorgeous former
abbey that traces its origins
back to the 6th century, this
romantic restaurant tempts
with Umbrian classics which
have a gourmet twist. Dishes
are artfully presented on the
plate. Home-made *tagliolini*
with black truffles and juniper-
infused grilled meats are
among the specials. Extensive
wine list with Italian vintages.

ORVIETO: Duca Di Orvieto €€
Classic Umbrian **Map** B5
Via della Pace 5, 05018
Tel *076 33 44 663* **Closed** *Wed,
Sun*
The theme of the menu at this
cosy trattoria is 'our culture on
a plate' and it draws from a stock
of well-researched, old Orvieto
recipes. Umbrichelle pasta is a
menu staple here.

**ORVIETO: Le Grotte del
Funaro** €€
International **Map** B5
Via Ripa Serancia 41, 05018
Tel *076 33 43 276*
Housed in the 12th-century
workshop of a *funaro* (ropemaker),
this cave-like restaurant has
menus that typically feature
beef with truffle and porcini
mushrooms, and Umbrian game.
Good fish and pasta selection,
pizzas fresh from the wood-fired
oven and an excellent wine list.

DK Choice

ORVIETO: I Sette Consoli €€
Classic Umbrian **Map** B5
Piazza Sant'Angelo 1a, 05018
Tel *076 33 43 911* **Closed** *Wed,
Sun eve*
I Sette Consoli sources top notch
ingredients from Europe that
come together as exquisite
plates. *Ravioli di anatra* (duck-
filled ravioli), Scottish salmon
and pigeon in marsala sauce are
specials. Dine inside in this
cottage-style restaurant or
outside on the canopied terrace.
The wine cellar has over 800
labels from around the world,
and over a hundred liquors.

The wine cellar at the cottage-style I Sette Consoli, in Orvieto, has over 800 labels

Key to Price Guide *see page 156*

Orvieto's elegant Villa Ciconia is set in a 15th-century country palazzo

ORVIETO: Trattoria del Moro Aronne €€
Classic Umbrian   Map B5
Via San Leonardo 7, 05018
Tel *076 33 42 763*   **Closed** *Tue*
This delightful trattoria, minutes from the duomo, welcomes diners with Umbrian-style home cooking. Try its signature dish *nidi di rondine, pecorino e miele caldo* (nest with pecorino cheese and warm honey). Very popular, reservations advised.

ORVIETO: Altarocca €€€
Fine Dining   Map B5
Località Rocca Ripesena 62, 05010
Tel *076 33 44 210*
The restaurant of this upscale wine resort, with its crisp linens and terraces that overlook vines and olives, is famous for its exquisite gourmet creations. Fish comes from the Lakes, meat is served in wine and desserts are home-made.

ORVIETO: Villa Ciconia €€€
Fine Dining   Map B6
Via dei Tigli 69, 05018
Tel *076 33 05 582*   **Closed** *Wed*
A hotel restaurant housed in a delightful country palazzo dating from the 15th century, Villa Ciconia stands in magnificent grounds full of ancient trees. The dining room with wood panelling and a huge stone fireplace is as handsome as its menu of gastronomy-standard meat and fish dishes and upscale pizzas. Well-stocked wine cellar.

PORANO: Il Boccone del Prete €€
Classic Umbrian   Map B5
Via Eugenio Bellini 12, 05010
Tel *076 33 74 772*   **Closed** *Mon–Fri in winters; Thu in summers*
Located in the village of Porano, close to Orvieto, this trattoria with stone walls and a rustic interior serves Umbrian dishes. The cellar has over 300 labels. The dining rooms are a series of old Etruscan grottoes and the ground floor has tables outside.

DK Choice

PRECI: Al Porcello Felice €€
Classic Umbrian   Map E5
Frazione Castelvecchio, 06047
Tel *074 39 39 005*
Part of an agriturismo set in rolling countryside, the restaurant excels in home-cooked dishes that use vegetables and herbs from its gardens, olive and fruit from its groves and meat from its farm, all produced per organic traditions and methods. Dishes are traditional, including pasta with creative sauces and pizzas cooked in a wood-burning oven. Best to book during high season.

SAN GEMINI: Il Colle €€
Italian   Map D6
Viale Garibaldi 6, 05029
Tel *074 630428*
Gourmet-style pizzas from a wood-fired oven, along with meat and fish dishes, are served on the terrace of this superb restaurant set high on a hill over San Gemini. Fine wine cellar. Popular party venue.

SCHEGGINO: Del Ponte €€
Fish & Seafood   Map E5
Via di Borgo 15, 06040
Tel *074 36 12 53*
Located in the eponymous hotel, Del Ponte serves a range of special dishes from the Valnerina valley. The emphasis is on fish, such as trout paired with local almonds, and black truffles with tagliatelle or used as a *crostini* topping.

DK Choice

SPELLO: Il Molino €
Classic Umbrian   Map D4
Piazza Giacomo Matteotti 6, 06038
Tel *074 26 51 305*   **Closed** *Tue*
Housed in a gorgeous 14th-century olive oil mill that has been tastefully converted while retaining its dramatic stone architecture, the Molino is a romantic place to dine and its passion about Umbrian cuisine shows clearly. Truffles and game dominate the menu, along with porcini mushrooms, wild asparagus and local herbs. The terrace is ideal for dining in summers.

SPELLO: La Bastiglia €€
Fine Dining   Map D4
Via Salnitraria 15, 06049
Tel *074 26 51 823*   **Closed** *Wed*
Modern upscale cuisine and an excellent wine selection has won over many a local afficionado at the elegant La Bastiglia. This gourmet restaurant is housed in a 17th-century antique-filled restored mill as its setting.

SPOLETO: Il Panciolle €
Classic Umbrian   Map D5
Vicolo degli Ebri, Via del Duomo 3, 06049
Tel *074 34 56 77*
An attractive trattoria with a shaded terrace looking out over the city. Here, truffles give flavour to meat and pasta dishes. There are a range of options for fish eaters too. Try the popular linguine pasta on creamed peppers.

SPOLETO: Al Palazzaccio Da Piero €€
Classic Umbrian   Map D5
Località Palazzaccio 33, Poreta, 06049
Tel *074 35 20 168*   **Closed** *Mon*
This attractive, family-run stone eatery in Poreta, just outside Spoleto specializes in serving delicious Umbrian dishes made with selected local ingredients. Diners will enjoy eating by a lovely log fire in winter and out on the terrace in summer.

For more information on types of restaurants *see page 155*

SPOLETO: Apollinare €€
International **Map** D5
Via Santa Agata 14, 06049
Tel *074 32 23 256* **Closed** *Tue*
Housed in a historic building
dating, in part, from Roman
times, Apollinare excels in both
international and local cuisine.
There are both taster and à la
carte menus to choose from.
Fine wine selection.

SPOLETO: Il Capanno €€
Classic Umbrian **Map** D5
Località Torrecola 6, 06049
Tel *074 35 41 19* **Closed** *Mon*
Sitting amidst a garden full of
mature trees in a rural setting,
Il Capanno serves hearty steaks
and game. Apart from offering
local cuisine, it also has many
gluten-free options.

DK Choice

SPOLETO:
Le Casaline €€
Classic Umbrian **Map** D5
Località Poreta di Spoleto,
Frazione Casaline, 06142
Tel *074 35 21 113* **Closed** *Mon*
Cinghiale alla cacciatora (wild
boar in a wine sauce) is just one
dish to tempt at this elegant
restaurant set in a mill dating
from the 1700s. Ingredients
ranging from the olive oil and
vegetables from its garden to
the lamb from the Campello
mountains, are all organic. The
meat is cooked in a wood-
burning fireplace. Pasta and
bread are home-made.
Good local wine list.

SPOLETO: Sabatini €€
Classic Umbrian **Map** D5
Corso Mazzini 54, 06049
Tel *074 347230* **Closed** *Mon*
Sabatini is an elegant place
known for its creative
presentation of classic Umbrian
dishes. *Strangozzi* with truffles,
and home-made ravioli with
ricotta and pistachios are
among the different specialities
on offer. Excellent wine
selection too.

SPOLETO: Il Tartufo €€
Classic Umbrian **Map** D5
Piazza Garibaldi 24, 06049
Tel *074 34 02 36* **Closed** *Sun eve*
& Mon
Il Tartufo opened in early
1900s and has been run by
the same family ever since.
It is best known for occupying
a Roman building considered a
national monument as much
as it is known for its love of
black and white truffles.

Serene settings at the classic Le Casaline in Spoleto

Try the courgette flowers stuffed
with truffle and cheese.

SPOLETO:
Il Tempio Del Gusto €€
International **Map** D5
Via Arco di Druso 9, 06049
Tel *074 34 71 21* **Closed** *Thu*
Known as the Temple of Taste,
this cosy eaterie stands on
architectural remains dating
back to around 2,000 years. Its
cellar, housing dozens of fine
Umbrian wines, is thought to
be much older. Its innovative
menu majors on local recipes
like home-made ravioli stuffed
with foie gras, apple and truffle
with herbs.

SPOLETO:
Trattoria del Festival €€
Italian **Map** D5
Via Brignone 8, 06049
Tel *074 32 20 993*
Del Festival is a traditional, cosy
trattoria set in a 16th-century
building. Old, vintage photos
adorn its walls and its menu
features Italian staples, such as
pizza, hand-made pasta and
plenty of local truffles.

DK Choice

SPOLETO: Cuore e
Sapore €€€
Fine Dining **Map** D5
Via Benedetto Egio 5, 06049
Tel *074 38 40 134* **Closed** *Mon*
This family-run restaurant
in the heart of Spoleto offers
excellent food and a relaxing
ambiance. The chef personally
chooses good quality local
ingredients and combines
them to create specialities like
beef fillet with white truffle,
home-made pasta dishes
and breads. The desserts
are a must-try including
biscuits and the delicious
chocolate fondue.

TERNI: Gelateria Gustoso €
Café **Map** D6
Via Mazzini 17, 05100
Tel *33 56 43 61 93*
Very famous and popular,
Gustoso is near the San
Francesco Church. Its ice
cream comes in dozens of
flavours, including pistachio,
almond and ricotta with
cinnamon. There are lactose-
free options too.

TERNI: Lu Somaru €
Italian **Map** D6
Viale Cesare Battisti 106, 05100
Tel *074 43 04 787* **Closed** *Tue*
Cosy pizzeria in central Terni,
very well-known for its excellent
pizzas. Toppings include the
classic Margherita or Napoli and
there is a whole separate menu
of specials.

TERNI: Oste della
Mal'Ora €
Café **Map** D6
Via Tre Archi 5, 05100
Tel *074 44 06 683* **Closed** *Sun*
This historic yet trendy café
is a place where locals meet,
drink and dine on simple
yet flavoursome food,
typically *crostini* with truffle
and soups.

TERNI: Osteria Garibaldi €
Classic Umbrian **Map** D6
Via Garibaldi 27, 05100
Tel *074 44 29 511* **Closed** *Sun*
Lively spot where locals go for
authentic Umbrian cuisine.
There is no menu and the
owner offers specials of the
day according to what's
in season.

TERNI: Trattoria Da
Carlino €
Classic Umbrian **Map** D6
Via Piemonte 1, 05100
Tel *074 44 20 163*
Popular with locals and
located near the Terni railway

Orvieto's elegant Villa Ciconia is set in a 15th-century country palazzo

ORVIETO: Trattoria del Moro Aronne €€
Classic Umbrian **Map** B5
Via San Leonardo 7, 05018
Tel *076 33 42 763* **Closed** *Tue*
This delightful trattoria, minutes from the duomo, welcomes diners with Umbrian-style home cooking. Try its signature dish *nidi di rondine, pecorino e miele caldo* (nest with pecorino cheese and warm honey). Very popular, reservations advised.

ORVIETO: Altarocca €€€
Fine Dining **Map** B5
Località Rocca Ripesena 62, 05010
Tel *076 33 44 210*
The restaurant of this upscale wine resort, with its crisp linens and terraces that overlook vines and olives, is famous for its exquisite gourmet creations. Fish comes from the Lakes, meat is served in wine and desserts are home-made.

ORVIETO: Villa Ciconia €€€
Fine Dining **Map** B6
Via dei Tigli 69, 05018
Tel *076 33 05 582* **Closed** *Wed*
A hotel restaurant housed in a delightful country palazzo dating from the 15th century, Villa Ciconia stands in magnificent grounds full of ancient trees. The dining room with wood panelling and a huge stone fireplace is as handsome as its menu of gastronomy-standard meat and fish dishes and upscale pizzas. Well-stocked wine cellar.

PORANO: Il Boccone del Prete €€
Classic Umbrian **Map** B5
Via Eugenio Bellini 12, 05010
Tel *076 33 74 772* **Closed** *Mon–Fri in winters; Thu in summers*
Located in the village of Porano, close to Orvieto, this

trattoria with stone walls and a rustic interior serves Umbrian dishes. The cellar has over 300 labels. The dining rooms are a series of old Etruscan grottoes and the ground floor has tables outside.

DK Choice

PRECI: Al Porcello Felice €€
Classic Umbrian **Map** E5
Frazione Castelvecchio, 06047
Tel *074 39 39 005*
Part of an agriturismo set in rolling countryside, the restaurant excels in home-cooked dishes that use vegetables and herbs from its gardens, olive and fruit from its groves and meat from its farm, all produced per organic traditions and methods. Dishes are traditional, including pasta with creative sauces and pizzas cooked in a wood-burning oven. Best to book during high season.

SAN GEMINI: Il Colle €€
Italian **Map** D6
Viale Garibaldi 6, 05029
Tel *074 630428*
Gourmet-style pizzas from a wood-fired oven, along with meat and fish dishes, are served on the terrace of this superb restaurant set high on a hill over San Gemini. Fine wine cellar. Popular party venue.

SCHEGGINO: Del Ponte €€
Fish & Seafood **Map** E5
Via di Borgo 15, 06040
Tel *074 36 12 53*
Located in the eponymous hotel, Del Ponte serves a range of special dishes from the

Valnerina valley. The emphasis is on fish, such as trout paired with local almonds, and black truffles with tagliatelle or used as a *crostini* topping.

DK Choice

SPELLO: Il Molino €
Classic Umbrian **Map** D4
Piazza Giacomo Matteotti 6, 06038
Tel *074 26 51 305* **Closed** *Tue*
Housed in a gorgeous 14th-century olive oil mill that has been tastefully converted while retaining its dramatic stone architecture, the Molino is a romantic place to dine and its passion about Umbrian cuisine shows clearly. Truffles and game dominate the menu, along with porcini mushrooms, wild asparagus and local herbs. The terrace is ideal for dining in summers.

SPELLO: La Bastiglia €€
Fine Dining **Map** D4
Via Salnitraria 15, 06049
Tel *074 26 51 823* **Closed** *Wed*
Modern upscale cuisine and an excellent wine selection has won over many a local afficionado at the elegant La Bastiglia. This gourmet restaurant is housed in a 17th-century antique-filled restored mill as its setting.

SPOLETO: Il Panciolle €
Classic Umbrian **Map** D5
Vicolo degli Ebri, Via del Duomo 3, 06049
Tel *074 34 56 77*
An attractive trattoria with a shaded terrace looking out over the city. Here, truffles give flavour to meat and pasta dishes. There are a range of options for fish eaters too. Try the popular linguine pasta on creamed peppers.

SPOLETO: Al Palazzaccio Da Piero €€
Classic Umbrian **Map** D5
Località Palazzaccio 33, Poreta, 06049
Tel *074 35 20 168* **Closed** *Mon*
This attractive, family-run stone eatery in Poreta, just outside Spoleto specializes in serving delicious Umbrian dishes made with selected local ingredients. Diners will enjoy eating by a lovely log fire in winter and out on the terrace in summer.

For more information on types of restaurants *see page 155*

SPOLETO: Apollinare €€
International **Map** D5
Via Santa Agata 14, 06049
Tel *074 32 23 256* Closed *Tue*
Housed in a historic building
dating, in part, from Roman
times, Apollinare excels in both
international and local cuisine.
There are both taster and à la
carte menus to choose from.
Fine wine selection.

SPOLETO: Il Capanno €€
Classic Umbrian **Map** D5
Località Torrecola 6, 06049
Tel *074 35 41 19* Closed *Mon*
Sitting amidst a garden full of
mature trees in a rural setting,
Il Capanno serves hearty steaks
and game. Apart from offering
local cuisine, it also has many
gluten-free options.

DK Choice

SPOLETO:
Le Casaline €€
Classic Umbrian **Map** D5
Località Poreta di Spoleto,
Frazione Casaline, 06142
Tel *074 35 21 113* Closed *Mon*
Cinghiale alla cacciatora (wild
boar in a wine sauce) is just one
dish to tempt at this elegant
restaurant set in a mill dating
from the 1700s. Ingredients
ranging from the olive oil and
vegetables from its garden to
the lamb from the Campello
mountains, are all organic. The
meat is cooked in a wood-
burning fireplace. Pasta and
bread are home-made.
Good local wine list.

SPOLETO: Sabatini €€
Classic Umbrian **Map** D5
Corso Mazzini 54, 06049
Tel *074 347230* Closed *Mon*
Sabatini is an elegant place
known for its creative
presentation of classic Umbrian
dishes. *Strangozzi* with truffles,
and home-made ravioli with
ricotta and pistachios are
among the different specialities
on offer. Excellent wine
selection too.

SPOLETO: Il Tartufo €€
Classic Umbrian **Map** D5
Piazza Garibaldi 24, 06049
Tel *074 34 02 36* Closed *Sun eve*
& *Mon*
Il Tartufo opened in early
1900s and has been run by
the same family ever since.
It is best known for occupying
a Roman building considered a
national monument as much
as it is known for its love of
black and white truffles.

Serene settings at the classic Le Casaline in Spoleto

Try the courgette flowers stuffed
with truffle and cheese.

SPOLETO:
Il Tempio Del Gusto €€
International **Map** D5
Via Arco di Druso 9, 06049
Tel *074 34 71 21* Closed *Thu*
Known as the Temple of Taste,
this cosy eaterie stands on
architectural remains dating
back to around 2,000 years. Its
cellar, housing dozens of fine
Umbrian wines, is thought to
be much older. Its innovative
menu majors on local recipes
like home-made ravioli stuffed
with foie gras, apple and truffle
with herbs.

SPOLETO:
Trattoria del Festival €€
Italian **Map** D5
Via Brignone 8, 06049
Tel *074 32 20 993*
Del Festival is a traditional, cosy
trattoria set in a 16th-century
building. Old, vintage photos
adorn its walls and its menu
features Italian staples, such as
pizza, hand-made pasta and
plenty of local truffles.

DK Choice

SPOLETO: Cuore e
Sapore €€€
Fine Dining **Map** D5
Via Benedetto Egio 5, 06049
Tel *074 38 40 134* Closed *Mon*
This family-run restaurant
in the heart of Spoleto offers
excellent food and a relaxing
ambiance. The chef personally
chooses good quality local
ingredients and combines
them to create specialities like
beef fillet with white truffle,
home-made pasta dishes
and breads. The desserts
are a must-try including
biscuits and the delicious
chocolate fondue.

TERNI: Gelateria Gustoso €
Café **Map** D6
Via Mazzini 17, 05100
Tel *33 56 43 61 93*
Very famous and popular,
Gustoso is near the San
Francesco Church. Its ice
cream comes in dozens of
flavours, including pistachio,
almond and ricotta with
cinnamon. There are lactose-
free options too.

TERNI: Lu Somaru €
Italian **Map** D6
Viale Cesare Battisti 106, 05100
Tel *074 43 04 787* Closed *Tue*
Cosy pizzeria in central Terni,
very well-known for its excellent
pizzas. Toppings include the
classic Margherita or Napoli and
there is a whole separate menu
of specials.

TERNI: Oste della
Mal'Ora €
Café **Map** D6
Via Tre Archi 5, 05100
Tel *074 44 06 683* Closed *Sun*
This historic yet trendy café
is a place where locals meet,
drink and dine on simple
yet flavoursome food,
typically *crostini* with truffle
and soups.

TERNI: Osteria Garibaldi €
Classic Umbrian **Map** D6
Via Garibaldi 27, 05100
Tel *074 44 29 511* Closed *Sun*
Lively spot where locals go for
authentic Umbrian cuisine.
There is no menu and the
owner offers specials of the
day according to what's
in season.

TERNI: Trattoria Da
Carlino €
Classic Umbrian **Map** D6
Via Piemonte 1, 05100
Tel *074 44 20 163*
Popular with locals and
located near the Terni railway

station, this eatery has a menu of local dishes like *crostini* (toasts) and tagliatelle with truffles.

TERNI: Il Convivio €€
Classic Umbrian   Map D6
Via del Leone 37, 05100
Tel *074 44 71 180*
Located in the centre of the town, a varied menu of meat and fish dishes are served at this friendly restaurant with a relaxed vibe. During summer, the tables move outdoors to the adjacent piazza, with a fresh breeze flowing. Good wine list.

TERNI:
Nascosto Posto €€
International   Map D6
Via Sant'Alò 10, 05100
Tel *333 39 62 435*   **Closed** *Sun eve, Mon*
The ultra-contemporary décor goes hand-in-hand with the modern menu at this Stroncone restaurant. Specialities include ravioli with clams and sea asparagus, and lobster with gazpacho.

TERNI: Piazzetta €€
Classic Umbrian   Map D6
Via Cavour 9, 05100
Tel *342 840 65 42*
Very pleasant restaurant Piazzetta has a menu based on classic Umbrian specialities, which are cooked with a varied combination of ingredients. Good wine selection and attentive staff.

DK Choice

TERNI: Unto €€
Fish & Seafood   Map D6
Viale Giacomo Leopardi 38, 05100
Tel *074 40 33 331*
This small restaurant serves fresh fish from the nearby Tyrrhenian Sea, prepared in a variety of ways. Tartares and ceviches are frequent finds on the daily menu, as are fried appetizers, lobster and grilled fish specialities.

TERNI: Lu Pilottu €€€
Fish & Seafood   Map D6
Strada delle Grazie 5, 05100
Tel *074 42 74 412*   **Closed** *Sun eve, Mon*
Tasteful, family-run restaurant Lu Pilottu specializes in pasta, fish and pastry creations. Its *tonnarelli* (pasta), served with seafood or a wild boar sauce are both signature dishes on the frequently updated menu.

TODI: Dige's Pizza €
Italian   Map C5
Piazza Jacopone 7, 06059
Tel *075 89 42 307*   **Closed** *Wed*
Great place for a quick bite or takeaway. Pizza and focaccia with a choice of toppings, paninis and pastries plus lots of delicious fruit tarts. It has tables outside too.

TODI: La Mulinella €
Classic Umbrian   Map C5
Località Pontenaia 29, 06059
Tel *075 89 44 779*   **Closed** *Wed*
Stone farmhouse with a chic country décor serving fresh bread baked in a wood-burning oven, pasta that is made by hand and succulent grilled meats.

DK Choice

TODI: Le Roi de la Crepe €
Café   Map C5
Corso Cavour 37, 06059
Tel *075 89 45 297*   **Closed** *Tue*
Host of snacks are cooked fresh to order and be eaten at its counter or taken away. Savory and sweet crepes top the menu favourites, along with paninis and hamburgers. Drinks and small bottles of wine too. Very popular with locals.

TODI:
Pizzeria Pozzo Beccaro €
Italian   Map C5
Via Menecali Abdon 6, 06059
Tel *075 89 48 473*   **Closed** *Wed*
Lingua di bue (ox tongue) is a speciality and used imaginatively in pasta dishes and for topping pizzas at this popular pizzeria. It also offers lovely views of Todi from its terrace.

The cosy La Vecchia Posta, in Trevi, serves a fine selection of Umbrian wines

TODI: Antica Hosteria della Valle €€
Classic Umbrian   Map C5
Via Ciuffelli 19, 06059
Tel *075 89 44 848*   **Closed** *Mon*
Cosy osteria, not far from the duomo, known for its variety of hearty, top quality dishes and home-made pasta. Try the ravioli with truffle. The desserts here are works of art. Friendly service.

DK Choice

TODI: Bramante €€
Fine Dining   Map C5
Via Orvietana 48, 06059
Tel *075 89 48 381*   **Closed** *Tue*
Housed in an elegant room of a restored 12th-century convent, the restaurant of the Hotel Bramante has a huge terrace for serving their exquisite gourmet creations. The tastefully-decorated restaurant has a seasonal menu with vegetarian, vegan and gluten-free options. Breakfast through to dinner. Excellent wine cellar.

TODI: Pane e Vino €€
Classic Umbrian   Map C5
Via Augusto Ciuffelli 33, Todi, 06059
Tel *075 89 45 448*   **Closed** *Wed*
Generous *antipasti* platters of cold meats, followed by pasta dishes and meats such as *regina in porchetta* (suckling pig) cooked on the fire are favourites at this charming restaurant. Nice wine bar.

TODI: Ristorante Umbria €€
Classic Umbrian   Map C5
Via San Bonaventura 13, 06059
Tel *075 89 42 737*   **Closed** *Tue*
A 500-year-old town centre mansion with beamed ceilings and a dramatic décor is the setting for this lovely eatery. Specializes in serving traditional Umbrian cuisine and has vegetarian options too. The terrace has a panoramic view.

TREVI: La Vecchia Posta €
Classic Umbrian   Map D5
Piazza Mazzini 14, 06039
Tel *074 23 81 690*
Truffle-stuffed *cappelletti* and wild boar *sagrantino* (in red wine) are some of the dishes featured on the menu at this cosy, family-run osteria. Apart from regional delicacies, La Vecchia Posta also offers home-made desserts and a fine selection of Umbrian wine.

For more information on types of restaurants *see page 155*

SHOPPING IN UMBRIA

The narrow streets of Umbria's characterful towns and villages are packed with charming shops, perfect for an afternoon or morning's exploration, while both permanent and weekly street markets are also excellent sources for both handicrafts and local delicacies. Aside from shopping for souvenirs in these tempting settings, the region has countless workshops that produce modern interpretations of traditional crafts, including textiles and ceramics, created by real Italian masters. The fame is such that there are many schools for artisans in Umbria, which are attended by students from all over the world. For foodies, there are a myriad of gourmet treasures available from the region, from oils and wines to preserves and truffles.

Vibrant, patterned ceramics, popular Umbrian souvenirs

Opening hours

Shops usually operate from 9am to 1pm, and 3.30 to 8pm Monday through to Saturday. In major tourist centres, such as Perugia and Assisi, shops are often open non-stop *(orario cintinuato)* from 9am to 8pm, and also on Sundays.

Payment

Credit cards are accepted almost everywhere, but some shop owners in smaller towns might set a minimum purchase of about €10. Smaller village shops tend to prefer cash payment.

Handicrafts

Pottery-making is one of the most traditional of Umbrian crafts. First practised by the Etruscans, today the ceramics of Deruta are among the most famous in Umbria, known for their bright colours and excellent quality. **L'Antica Deruta** and **Biagioli** sell classic ceramics, while **Ceramiche Rometti** is known for its modern designs.

Umbria is also known for its traditional furniture and artistic metalwork. Most workshops are keen to produce bespoke items for individual customers, but custom-made pieces can be costly. For a mix of modern and traditional wooden pieces, visit **Gualtiero Michelangeli**'s workshop in Orvieto, and head to **Artigianato Ferro Artistico** and **La Fucina** for cast-iron objects.

Umbria's classic hand-woven fabrics, made using methods and designs dating back as far as the Middle Ages, can be found throughout the region. Rugs, bedspreads and household linens, all with an antique feel, and sometimes embroidered according to the Assisi or Panicale traditions, can be purchased in stores such as **Laboratorio Tela Umbra**, **Tele Umbre**, **La Spola** and the gorgeous **Tessuto Artistico Umbro** in Montefalco.

Handmade stationery such as marbled paper or leather notebooks can be bought at **Officina Libris** in Gubbio.

Markets and Fairs

Antique books, statues, furniture, jewellery, carpets and icons are common finds at Umbria's antique markets. The market in Rocca Paolina, held every fourth weekend of the month is not to be missed, while the annual fairs of **Assisi Antiquariato** (late April) and the **Rassegna Antiquaria d'Italia** in Todi (late March) attract visitors from all over the region.

Food and Drink

Umbrian wine companies vary considerably in size, from the small vineyard owner to large modern industrial units. Vineyards are popular tourist attractions, as they're an authentic way to try local flavours while enjoying the beautiful countryside. Advance booking is encouraged.

The most famous wineries include **Lungarotti** in Torgiano, **Antinori**, near Orvieto, and **Decugnano dei Barbi**, near Corbara. For smaller wine co-operatives, head to beautiful **L'Agricola Goretti**, housed in an ancient tower not far from Perugia, or **Cantina Terre de'**

Bottles of Chianti for sale

Trinci in Foligno, which produces and serves great wines in a modern bar. For a more urban wine experience, **Gió Arte e Vini** in Perugia and **Bottega Barbanera** in Foligno, both provide a good overview of the region's best wines.

The production of olive oil is an ancient and revered Umbrian tradition. Much of the oil made in Umbria is bottled with the quality mark DOP (*Denominazione di Origine Protetta* – meaning protected denomination of origin), guaranteeing the origin of the olives used and the method of pressing. The best places to buy oil are at the olive presses (*frantoi*), which can be visited in November and December; here one can see how the olive oil is made. One such olive press is that of **Frantoio di Spello**, whose shop also delivers other Umbrian delicacies. The town of Trevi is known as Umbria's olive oil capital, and its Museo della Civiltà dell'Ulivo is worth a visit. Trevi also celebrates the harvest of olive oil every autumn with a festival, Festa

A grocery shop in the town of Norcia, Southern Umbria

dell Olio Nuovo. Among the region's top delicacies are the famous cured meats from Norcia. These can be found almost everywhere in Umbria, but **Fratelli Ansuini** in Norcia is said to be one of the best shops around. The variety is impressive – salami, hams and sausages, cured or fresh, to name but a few.

The range of famously delicious Umbrian specialities also include vegetables in oil or brine, locally made jams, and sheep's milk cheeses, both mature and fresh. Deli shops around the region sell

all of this and more. Reliable places to go to stock up are **Pasticceria Muzzi** in Foligno and **La Spezieria Bavicchi** in Perugia. The latter also carries a large variety of Perugina chocolate including the famous Baci.

Cereals and vegetables are another important Umbrian staple, and are often grown organically. In addition to the lentils of Catelluccio, look for spelt (*farro*) and chickling (*cicerchia*), a type of pea. For the white truffles, visit **La Buca del Tartufo** in Gubbio, or **Urbani Tartufi** near Spoleto.

DIRECTORY

Crafts

L'Antica Deruta
SS E45, 73.8 km, Deruta.
W anticaderuta.com

Artigianato Ferro Artistico
Via Baldassini 22, Gubbio.

Biagioli
Piazza della Signoria 3, Gubbio.
W ceramichebiagioli. com

Bottega del Legno di Gualverio Michelangeli
Via Michelangeli 3, Orvieto.
W michelangeli.it

Ceramiche Artigianali
Via Storelli 42, Gualdo Tadino.

Ceramiche Rometti
Via Canavelle 5, Umbertide.
W rometti.it

La Fucina
Via dei Muratori, Orvieto.

Laboratorio Tela Umbra
Via Sant'Antonio 3, Città di Castello.
W telaumbra.it

Officina Libris
Via dei Consoli 39, Gubbio.

La Spola
Via Garibaldi 66, Torgiano.

Tele Umbre
Via Piccotti 1, Gubbio.
W teleumbre.it

Tessuto Artistico Umbro
Piazza del Comune 1, Montefalco.
W tessutoartistico montefalco.it

Markets and Fairs

Assisi Antiquariato
Centro Umbriafiere Bastia Umbria.
W assisiantiquariato.it

Rassegna Antiquaria d'Italia
Palazzo Landi Corradi, Todi.

Food and Drink

L'Agricola Goretti
Strada del Pino 4, Pila (nr Perugia).
W vinigoretti.it

Antinori
Località Sala, 05016, Fisulle.
W antinori.it

Bottega Barbanera
Piazza della Repubblica 34, Foligno.

La Buca del Tartufo Bartolini
33 Via XX Settembre, Gubbio.

Cantina Terre de' Trinci
Via Fiammenga 57, Foligno.
W terredetrinci.it

Cantine Lungarotti
Viale Giorgio Lungarotti 2, Torgiano.
W lungarotti.it

Decugnano dei Barbi
Località Fossatello 50, Orvieto. W decugnano deibarbi.com

Drogheria Bavicchi
Via dei Priori 15, Perugia.
W drogheriabavicchi.it

Frantoio di Spello
Via Banche 1/B, Spello.
W frantoiodispello.it

Fratelli Ansuini
Viale della Stazione, Norcia.
W ansuininorcia.it

Giò Arte e Vini
Via Ruggero d'Andreotto 19, Perugia.
W hotelgio.it

Pasticceria Muzzi
Via Roma 38, Foligno.
W patticceriamuzzi.com

La Spezieria Bavicchi
Piazza Matteotti 37, Perugia.

Urbani Tartufi
SS Valnerina, 31.3 km, Santa Anatolia di Narco.
W urbanitartufi.it

What to Buy in Umbria

The varied crafts of Umbria, derived from tradition but still open to new ideas, can be found either in shops or actually at the artists' own workshops. Old-fashioned ceramics sit side by side with works by great contemporary artists such as Cagli and Leonardi. Antique linen, lovingly produced by hand on a loom, is piled up next to more up-to-date and fashionable knitwear produced by Umbrian factories. It would also be impossible to ignore the delicious food of the region. Salami, of course, but also preserves, lentils, black truffles and chocolate, enabling visitors to take home something of the flavour of Umbria.

Potter at work in his studio

Ceramics

Ceramics production – of which Deruta is the capital – is inspired by techniques and designs from a centuries-old tradition. An interesting new and flourishing trend is for new artists to make modern pieces, which have been inspired by their own imagination and by the study of new production methods.

Whistle from Ficulle

Vases and jars in painted majolica

Basket and lid

Basket for fruit

Baskets

The reeds that grow around Lake Trasimeno are gathered for use today, as they were in centuries past. A sturdy but flexible plant material, the reed is used to make all kinds of objects. Baskets, mats and traps for fishing on the lake are on sale in the towns of Passignano, Castiglione del Lago and Tuoro.

Textiles and Embroidery

In several studios in Perugia, and in a few other towns, it is possible to buy household linen, fabrics and carpets, woven on a loom according to ancient methods. Umbrian embroidery and lace (made in Assisi, Panicale and Orvieto) are still widely available.

Detail from antique fabric

Cashmere wool is used to make high-quality garments. The most famous company name is that of Brunello Cucinelli.

Ars panicalensis is the name given to the technique of embroidering on tulle, originating in Panicale and now done throughout Umbria. The pieces have the delicacy of lace.

Knitwear

Umbria is a region with a series of small but dedicated knitwear companies producing garments using different types of wool. Clothes made from cashmere wool are particularly desirable.

Bookbinding

Book plate

The old traditions of bookselling, bookbinding and book restoration are by no means dead in Umbria. Bookplates, diaries, notebooks, and albums are made with paper that reproduces the designs and colours of the Renaissance, a tradition that began with the followers of St Francis.

Wood

Hand-made wooden aeroplane

A man called Michelangeli launched the trend for good-quality woodwork in Orvieto. There is now a small but flourishing trade in wooden statues and animals, as well as garden sculptures. Items made from olive wood are now a tourist attraction in Assisi.

Pork Sausages and Salami

The meat and salami of Norcia are superb. You can choose from hams (made from pig or wild boar), fresh sausages, cured pork sausage, *capocollo* (made with neck of pig), and wild boar salami among many other delicacies. Good salami from small producers is found all over the region.

Shop selling a selection of fine hams, sausages and salamis

The prized black truffle

White truffle

Truffles

The world's most prized type of black truffle (*tartufo nero*) grows in the Valnerina, especially around Norcia, and is gathered from November to March. The white truffle, gathered from October to December, is rare, prized and expensive.

Chocolate and Sweets

The manufacture of chocolate in the city of Perugia dates back to the early 1900s. Traditional sweets can be found all over the region, and a chocolate festival is held in Perugia every October.

Perugina

Baci Perugina, individually wrapped hazelnut chocolates, are the bestselling line of a business established in 1907. Their introduction led to a fresh appreciation of Italian confectionery. "*Baci*" means kisses and each sweet wrapper contains a little quotation about love, in four languages. Historic Perugina adverts are on display in Perugia's Museo Storico.

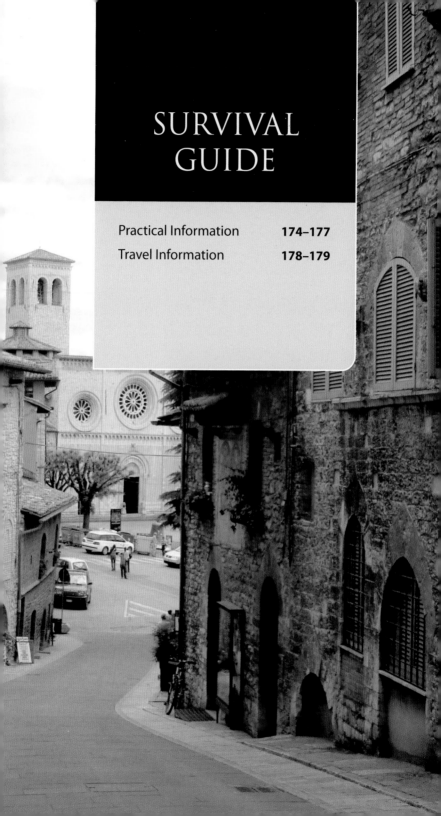

SURVIVAL
GUIDE

PRACTICAL INFORMATION

Along with an exceptional variety of landscapes, museums and places of historical and artistic interest, Umbria can offer a good range of services. The distances between the main centres are not great, making this, therefore, an ideal place for visitors eager to explore. The museums and galleries are, in general, modern, well run, welcoming and accessible to all (an increasing number have access for people with disabilities). The regional authority, Regione dell'Umbria, can offer a wide range of maps and lists of events through the various tourist offices. Banks and medical services are widely available throughout the region.

Lush, green hills around the town of Gubbio

When to Visit

Umbria is one of the richest regions in Italy in terms of its attractions (natural and manmade) and its calendar of traditional, cultural and religious events. As a result, Umbria attracts large numbers of visitors between May and September. If you have the option, it is certainly best to arrange to visit either in May and June or September and October, thereby avoiding the crowded peak summer months. In summer, Umbria can also be exceedingly hot. In winter, when snow falls in the mountains, temperatures are low and the winds cold.

Tourist Information

The two provinces that form Umbria – Perugia and Terni – each have their own **Azienda di Promozione Turistica** (APT), responsible for the promotion of tourism in that specific province.

There is a tourist office in every town of a decent size. In smaller centres, offices called Pro Loco are able to supply historical or cultural information, in addition to information about restaurants and lodgings. Specialist tour guides providing individual attention are available in some towns, too. In addition, there are numerous organizations which deal with all kinds of sporting events and activities (see pp26–7). For those planning a cycling holiday, and for lovers of mountain biking, the APT provides a booklet called *Umbria in bicicletta* (Umbria by bicycle).

Informa Giovani, set up by the Comune di Perugia (the Perugia town council), is aimed at young people, and can provide suggestions as well as addresses relating to culture, sport, music, wildlife, holidays, work opportunities and youth associations.

Tourist office
(APT) sign

AZIENDA
PROMOZIONE
TURISTICA

Sightseeing

Museums in Umbria are run either by the local town council or by the Italian government. In general, state museums are open from 9am to 7pm, and often close on Monday and on Sunday afternoon. Winter hours tend to be shorter. Museums run by the local authority have more varied timetables, and may even close over lunch. The use of a flash or a tripod is forbidden in most museums.

Church opening hours are unpredictable, but many close between noon and 3 or 4pm. When visiting churches, you should dress suitably. Tourists are discouraged from touring churches during services, and may be excluded from special religious festivals. Many areas affected by earthquakes may have sites closed for restoration, or may close without notice if structural damage is suspected.

Communications

Post offices can be found in all towns and there is often more than one branch. Main post offices are usually open from 8:30am to 7:30pm Monday to Saturday. Smaller offices, however, are often open in the morning only, from 8:30am to 1:30pm; on Saturday and the last day of the month, these post offices close at noon. If all you want is stamps (francobolli) for postcards and normal letters, you can buy these at any tobacconist (tabacchi) with the black and white "T" sign.

The number of public telephones has fallen. Those that remain take coins, although there are some credit card operated phones in train stations and they can be expensive. European mobile phones work on Italian networks, but Americans will need a tri-band phone. The EU ended roaming charges in 2017, meaning European visitors travelling within the continent

◀ A typical street in Assisi, leading down to San Pietro

Dialling Codes

- To phone another number in Italy, you must include the full area code.
- For international calls, country codes are: UK & Ireland 00 39; USA & Canada 0 11 39; Australia 00 11 39.
- For directory enquiries, dial 1240 (for Italy) or 176 (international).
- For the British Operator, dial 17200 44.
- US Operators: 172 10 11 (AT&T); 172 10 22 (MG Worldphone); 172 18 77 (Sprint).
- Australian Operators: 1225 (Telstra); 172 11 61 (Opus).

can use their mobile data abroad without incurring charges. Those travelling from outside the EU might find it cheaper to buy an Italian SIM card. The main operators are TIM, Vodafone and Wind.

Many hotels offer internet access, but it is advisable to ask before reserving. Bars and restaurants in tourist areas may have free Wi-Fi.

Travellers with Disabilities

Travelling in the smaller Italian towns can be a challenge for disabled visitors. The roads are often uneven and the pavements are frequently occupied by parked cars. Gradually, lifts and ramps are being added to museums and public institutions.

Tax Exemption

Value added tax (IVA in Italy) ranges from 12 to 35 per cent. Non-EU citizens can claim an IVA rebate, provided the total expenditure is over €155. It is easiest to get a refund if you shop where you see the "Euro Free Tax" sign. Show your passport, complete a form, and the IVA will be deducted from your bill. Or show your purchases and their receipts at customs upon departure; they will stamp the receipts. Send these to the vendor and a refund should then be sent to you.

Student Information

An International Student Identity Card (ISIC) can be used to get a reduction on admission charges to many museums and other tourist attractions. The ISIC card also gives access to a 24-hour phone helpline. For discount travel and information, visit any branch of the **Centro Turistico Studentesco** (CTS).

Electrical Adaptors

The voltage in Italy is 220 volts, with two-pin round-pronged plugs. It is worth buying adaptor plugs before you leave as they are difficult to find in Italy. Most hotels with three or more stars have hairdryers and shaving points in all bedrooms, but check the voltage first, to be safe.

Italian Time

Italy is 1 hour ahead of Greenwich Mean Time (GMT). The time difference is: London: −1 hour; New York: −6 hours; Perth: +7 hours; Auckland: +11 hours. These figures may vary briefly in summer with local time changes. Italy uses the 24-hour clock (e.g. 10pm = 22:00).

DIRECTORY

Italian State Tourist Offices Abroad

Canada
110 Yonge Street, Toronto MSC 1T4.
Tel 416-925-4882.

Ireland & United Kingdom
1 Princes St, London W1B 2AY.
Tel 020 7408 1254.

United States
686 Park Ave, New York, NY 10065.
Tel 212-245-5618.

State Tourist Offices in Umbria

Regional Tourist Office (APT)
Via Mazzini 21, Perugia.
Tel 075 572 8937.

Assisi
Tel 075 813 8680
info@iat.assisi.pg.it

Orvieto
Tel 0763 341 772.
info@iat.orvieto.tr.it

Perugia
Tel 075 573 6458.
info@iat.perugia.it

Spoleto
Tel 0743 218 620.
info@iat.spoleto.pg.it

Trasimeno
Tel 075 965 2738.
info@iat.castiglione dellago.pg.it

Other Tourist Information

Associazione Guide Turistiche (tour guides)
Via Dono Doni 18, Assisi.
Tel 075 815 228.
🔲 assoguide.it

Centro Turistico Studentesco (CTS)
Piazza del Mercato 60, Terni. **Tel** 0744 425 764.
🔲 cts.it

Informa Giovani
Piazza del Melo, Perugia.
Tel 075 577 2496.
🔲 comune.perugia.it/ informagiovani

Embassies and Consulates

Canada
Via Salaria 243, Rome.
Tel 06 854 441.

Ireland
Villa Spada, Via Giacomo Medici, Rome.
Tel 06 585 2381.

United Kingdom
Via XX Settembre 80a, Rome. **Tel** 06 4220 0001.

United States
Via Vittorio Veneto 121a, Rome. **Tel** 06 46 741.

Websites

Regione Umbria
🔲 umbriatourism.it
🔲 italian touristboard. co.uk
🔲 italiantourism.com

Emergencies

General Emergencies
Tel 113.

Carabinieri (Police)
Tel 112.

Fire Service
Tel 115.

Car Breakdown
Tel 116.

Ambulance
Tel 118.

Hospital
Via Bonacci Brunamonti 51, Perugia.
Tel 075 57 81.

Health and Safety

With low levels of reported crime, Umbria is generally a safe region. Earthquakes occur every few years, but this shouldn't deter travellers. Visitors should be sensible and vigilant when travelling here, as anywhere. If you are in difficulties, each town has a police headquarters, open 24 hours a day. Medical care in Umbria is good, but be sure to take out medical insurance.

Police vehicle, equipped for off-road use

A firefighter truck used by the Vigili del Fuoco

Travel Safety

Visitors can get up-to-date travel safety information from the **Foreign and Commonwealth Office** in the UK, the **State Department** in the US, and the **Department of Foreign Affairs and Trade** in Australia.

Hospitals and Pharmacies

Pharmacies are open 9am–1pm and 4–8pm, Monday to Friday, and mornings only on Saturdays.

Every Umbrian city has a hospital. In emergencies, go to the *Pronto Soccorso* (Casualty) or telephone for help. EU citizens are entitled to free treatment if they have a European Health Insurance Card (EHIC), but making a claim is a bureaucratic process. Always ensure travel insurance includes medical cover.

Police

In Italy the forces of law and order are organized into two divisions: the *Carabinieri* and the police *(Polizia)*, to which can be added, at urban level, the municipal police, including traffic police *(Vigili Urbani)*. Traffic police can also deal with minor matters and can provide information and deal with emergency situations. They wear a dark uniform in winter and a light one in summer, with the city coat of arms usually on the pocket. *Carabinieri* are responsible for public order. They wear black trousers with a red stripe down the side, and a white band across the body. Patrols are often seen on the streets. The duties of the *Polizia* are more wide-ranging and are, in general, concerned with criminal investigations. The uniform is blue, with a white belt and hat. To report a theft or other serious problem, go to the nearest police station or dial 113.

Firefighters

In such a green and wooded region as Umbria, problems with fires are perhaps inevitable, even if the fairly damp climate and the scarcity of winds do not favour the spread of fire. Even so, particularly if you are planning an outdoor holiday, be sure to observe all the standard countryside code practices, especially with regard to not lighting a fire outside the designated areas.

The region has many fire stations, and fire engines respond rapidly to alarm calls. Firefighters also attend to other kinds of emergencies.

Personal Safety

Municipal policeman

Use common sense to keep safe. Do not carry large sums in cash and, if you have valuables, leave them in a safe if possible. Pickpockets frequent main railway stations and crowded tourist sights. If travelling by car, lock the vehicle and don't leave any items in view.

It is essential to arrange full insurance cover before travelling, and you may wish to keep a separate photocopy of personal documents in the event of theft.

In Umbria, there are no areas that need to be avoided. It is safe to walk around town streets in the evenings, and even late at night; of course, make sure you are always aware of your surroundings and use your common sense if you feel any unease.

DIRECTORY

Travel Safety

Australia Department of Foreign Affairs and Trade
w dfat.gov.au
w smarttraveller.gov.au

UK Foreign and Commonwealth Office
w gov.uk/government/organisations/foreign-commonwealth-office

US Department of State
w travel.state.gov

Banking and Local Currency

Foreigners arriving in Umbria may change currency in a number of ways, but it is still wise to arrive with euros in your pocket. Credit cards are widely accepted for purchases and can be used to withdraw money.

Sign at a cash machine, useful for withdrawing cash with a debit card

Banks and Currency Exchange

In the larger towns there are bureaux de change as well as currency-converting machines. It is also possible to change money in hotels and in travel agencies, but you'll get a better exchange rate in the banks. Commission charges can be hefty, so it's worth shopping around.

Italian banks are normally open from 8:30am to 1:30pm, and then from 3pm to 4pm,

from Monday to Friday, but these hours may vary from place to place; banks often close early the day before a public holiday. Your hotel reception or the tourist office should be able to help with information. Opening hours of bureaux de change and other places are much more variable. Some form of identification will be needed for all kinds of money transactions.

All towns have cashpoint (ATM) machines (bancomat), which allow you to take money out with a debit card or a credit card and a PIN number.

VISA, American Express, MasterCard and Diners Club are the most commonly seen credit cards and there should be no problems getting them accepted.

The Euro

The euro (€) is the common currency of the European Union. It went into general circulation on 1 January 2002, initially for 12 participating countries. Italy was one of those 12 countries, and the lira was phased out in February 2002. EU members using the Euro as their sole official currency are known as the Eurozone. Several EU members have opted out of joining this common currency.

Euro notes are identical throughout the Eurozone, each one including designs of fictional architectural structures and monuments. The coins, however, have one side identical (the value side) and one side with an image unique to each country. Both notes and coins are exchangeable in each participating country.

When travelling, it is best not to carry euro notes of large denominations, since not all businesses have large amounts of change.

Logo of the Banca dell'Umbria

Banknotes and Coins

Banknotes come in seven denominations. The €5 note is grey, €10 is pink, €20 is blue, €50 is orange, €100 is green, €200 is yellow and €500 is purple. There are eight different coins. The €1 and €2 coins are silver and gold; those worth 50, 20 and 10 cents are gold, while the 5-, 2- and 1-cent coins are bronze.

TRAVEL INFORMATION

Umbria lies at the geographical heart of Italy. Despite the hills and the mountains of the Apennines, road and rail infrastructures are well maintained and well organized; this, combined with the relatively small size of the region, makes it easy and straightforward to travel from one place to another by car. Road and tourist signs are helpful and up-to-date. Driving and parking can be difficult in towns, but buses and taxis are plentiful, and most towns are small enough to be explored easily on foot. The railway network has few branch lines but there are frequent and reliable connections by coach where there are no trains. Umbria itself is easily reached by air or coach. Ferries link the villages on the shores of Lake Trasimeno as well as the lake islands.

Hiring a car, a practical and convenient way of getting around Umbria

Arriving by Air

The Umbrian Regional Airport of Sant'Egidio is 12 km (7 miles) from both Perugia and Assisi. Scheduled Alitalia flights arrive here from Milan Malpensa and the main Italian international airports; in high season there are also some charter flights. Ryanair flies to Perugia daily from London Stansted. Buses between the airport and the centre of Perugia are timed to coincide with the arrival of scheduled flights. Taxis are also available at the airport, as is car hire: the major companies (**Avis**, **Europcar** and **Hertz**) offer pre-booked fly-drive arrangements.

One option is to fly to Rome or another nearby airport, such as Ancona, Pisa or Florence, and take the train or drive from there. Rome to Perugia by car, for example, takes 2 hours.

Travelling by Car

A car is by far the best way to explore Umbria, enabling you to reach the most remote villages and making it easier to enjoy the scenery.

Car hire is expensive and should be booked ahead. You must be over 21 and have held a licence for at least a year. Visitors from outside the EU may need to show an international licence.

A toll is payable for use of the motorways (autostrade). Tolls are high, but you can usually pay by credit card.

Note that petrol stations may close at lunchtime and rarely stay open late.

The Autostrada del Sole (A1) from Milan, via Florence, skirts Umbria along the Tuscan border before continuing on to Rome. At the Val di Chiana exit, a road runs east to Perugia. Other useful exit points are Chiusi Chianciano, Orvieto and Orte, from where a fast road runs to Terni and links up with the Via Flaminia. The latter is the most important state road in Umbria, running from north to south. The condition of the roads is good; only within the Apennines does driving become more challenging.

Travelling by Train

Umbria has two railway lines: **Ferrovie dello Stato** (FS) and the private **Ferrovia Centrale Umbra** (FCU). FS operates the main routes, and its stations do not sell FCU tickets.

The FS Milan–Rome line stops at Orte, Orvieto and the rail junction at Terentola. From here there is another FS line running to Perugia and Foligno, stopping at a few places on Lake Trasimeno and passing close to Assisi. Two Eurostar (ES) and four regional trains provide a daily direct link between Perugia and Rome. Other useful FS lines are the one linking Florence to Perugia and the Rome–Ancona (stopping at Terni, Foligno, Spoleto and Orte).

The FCU Terni–Perugia line serves Todi and then goes on to Città di Castello and Sansepolcro, in Tuscany. Perugia has two stations: Sant'Anna and San Giovanni. The former is used only by FCU trains; the latter by both the FCU and FS.

Train stations may be some distance from the hill town after which they are named. Give yourself enough time to make your way back to the station to catch the return train.

You must buy tickets before departure. Be sure to validate both outward and return tickets

A train run by the state company Ferrovie dello Stato

in the machines provided on the platform, before boarding the train, or you will be fined. Always check before doing so that the train you plan to board stops at the station you want: InterCity and Eurostar trains stop only at major stations. Most InterCity and all Eurostar trains have a compulsory seat-reservation policy included in the fare.

Fares are still among the cheapest in Europe, but check in advance with **Rail Europe** for details of money-saving passes. Visit www.umbriamobilita.it for detailed information on trains and buses.

Travelling by Coach

Intercity coach travel can be faster than travelling by train. Perugia is the main hub for coach services. It has direct links to several Italian cities, with stops in various Umbrian towns en route. A daily service from Roma Tiburtina, Rome's main coach station, stops in Todi, Assisi and Deruta en route to Perugia. There are daily coaches between Rome and Gubbio and Città di Castello, as well as Norcia. Perugia is accessible by coach from Florence; many coaches also stop at Città di Castello (via Arezzo).

Coaches from Perugia to Assisi run six or seven times a day, while Todi has around five services a day and Gubbio ten. Coach services are often reduced at weekends, particularly on Sundays, and also vary between summer and winter.

Town Buses

In Perugia the Azienda Perugina di Mobilità operates services within the city and out to the suburbs, among them buses linking the train terminal with the coach station. Tickets are valid for different lengths of time, and prices vary accordingly. Bus tickets can be purchased from newspaper kiosks and *tabacchi*. Season tickets are also available, including tourist tickets that are valid for 24 or 48 hours.

In Assisi, regular buses link the railway station, 5 km (3 miles) away at Santa Maria degli Angeli, to the centre. In Todi, too, the railway station is linked to the town by bus. At Terni, buses run by the **Azienda Trasporti Pubblici** (ATC) serve the town and also travel as far as the Cascata delle Marmore.

Ferry logo

Taxis

Hire a cab only from an official taxi stand or else reserve it by phone. If you telephone, the meter will run from the time of your call. Extra is charged for each piece of luggage put in the boot, for rides at night, on Sundays and public holidays, and for airport trips (fix a price before you set off).

Ferries

On Lake Trasimeno, ferries link Castiglione del Lago, the islands of Isola Polvese, Isola Maggiore and Isola Minore, as well as Tuoro sul Trasimeno and Passignano sul Trasimeno.

Ferries linking the islands and towns on Lake Trasimeno

General Index

Acknowledgments

Dorling Kindersley would like to thank all those whose contribution and assistance have made the preparation of this book possible.

Special Thanks
Archivio Electa-Milano, Assessorato del Turismo Regione Umbria, APT di Perugia, APT di Assisi, APT di Foligno, APT di Spoleto, Consorzio del Parco del Lago Trasimeno, Consorzio del Parco del Monte Cucco, Ente Parco dei Monti Sibillini, Guido Stecchi for consultation and help with pages 154–5, and all the companies who have assisted with their products.

Photography
Ghigo Roli (Modena)

Translator
Fiona Wild

Editor
Emily Hatchwell

Revisions and Relaunch
Ashwin Raju Adimari, Beverley Ager, Hansa Babra, Marta Bescos Sanchez, Uma Bhattacharya, Gadi Farfour, Anna Freiberger, Carole French, Vinod Harish, Mohammad Hassan, Jasneet Kaur, Sumita Khatwani, Vincent Kurien, Sarah Lane, Leonie Loudon, Tanya Mahendru, Sam Merrell, Rebecca Milner, Deepak Mittal, Daniel Mosseri, Helen Partington, Sangita Patel, Gillian Price, Rada Radojicic, Lucy Richards, Ellen Root, Sands Publishing Solutions, Collette Sadler, Farah Sheikh, Azeem Siddiqui, Ellie Smith, Susana Smith, Nikky Tywman, Conrad Van Dyk, Vinita Venugopal, Ajay Verma.

Additional Photography
John Heseltine, Ian O'Leary, Rough Guides/Chris Hutty Helena Smith, Christine Webb, Kate Whitaker.

Photography Permissions
The publisher would like to thank all the churches, museums, hotels, restaurants, art galleries, parks and all those who supplied material and contributed to the publication of this guide, too numerous to be named individually. While every effort has been made to contact the copyright holders, we apologize for any omissions and will be happy to include them in subsequent editions of this publication.

Picture Credits
a = above; b = below/bottom; c = centre; f = far; l = left; r = right; t = top.

123RF.com: Frank Bach 179bl.

Alamy Images: Bildagentur-online / Moreno 14t; Tibor Bognar 1c; Michele Castellani 39cl; Cubo Images srl/Enrico Caracciolo 155c; Domenico Farone 100; Norma Joseph 154cl, 155tl; LMR Group 38br; Chuck Pefley 15tc; Prisma by Dukas Presseagentur Gmb 24bl; REDA &CO srl 158tr; Ian Trower 116br; Unlisted Images, Inc. 11br; Christine Webb 13cr, 21t. Fabrizio Ardito (Rome): 20tl, 37bl, 65tl, 65cr, 73tc, 75tr, 90br, 93clb, 135cr, 138cl, 139tc, 141cr. The Art Archive: Galleria Nazionale dell'Umbria Perugia/Dagli Orti 92tr; Palazzo Trinci Foligno/Dagli Orti 106cl. AWL Images: Francesco Iacobelli 18; Ian Trower 4tc.

Adriano Bacchella (Milan): 20cl. The Bridgeman Art Library: Galleria Nazionale dell'Umbria, Perugia, Italy Altarpiece: Annunciation; Madonna and Child with Saints; Miracles of St. Anthony, St. Francis and St. Elizabeth Piero della Francesca 92cl.

David Capasso (Modena): 46bl, 107cl, 108tl, 109cr. Corbis: Elio Ciol 21b; JAI / Peter Adams 144–145.

Dreamstime.com: Antonella865 176tc; Frank Bach 97tl; Jennifer Barrow 172–173; Elisa Bistocchi 71bc, 96cl; Eugene Bochkarev 163br; Valeria Cantone 83br; catiamadio 26tr; Roberto Caucino 127tl; Claudio Giovanni Colombo 11crb; Andrea La Corte 69tr; Steven Corton 12bl; Gianluca Curti 37cr; Deniskelly 12tc; Fede-candoniphoto 176c; Flaviano Fabrizi 15br; Freesurf69 4c, 19b, 56cl, 174cl Gkuna 10bc; Kaspargallery 25br; Krefografie 2–3; Sergey Lisov 117tc; Alberto Masnovo 127br; Milla74 5cl, 11tl; minnystock 5cr, 13t; Konstantinos Papaioannou 136bl, 169tr; Patronestaff 10cl, 24cl; Enrico Della Pietra 57br; Marco Saracco 25c; Stevanzz 50–51; Travelbook 57tr; Dan Vik 25tr, 70cl, Leon Viti 96tr.

Ferrovie Dello Stato: 178br; Fondazione Festival dei Due Mondi: 49bc; Giovanni Francesio (Mantua): 59cla, 59cr, 60 all photos, 61 all photos, 67tc, 67br, 68 all photos, 69 all photos, 70bl, 71tl, 71cr, 86c, 86br, 87cl, 87cra, 98 all photos.

Getty Images: DEA / M. Borchi 120tl; Layne Kennedy 146bl; Photodisc/Buena Vista Images 49cb.

Hotel Vannucci: 148br, 152c

I Sette Consoli: 164br. iStockphoto.com: clodio 128–129; FrankvandenBergh 168cl; Tanja_G 26cl; ToolX 27bl; ValerioMei 39br.

L'Antico Forziere: 156bl. La Locanda Del Cardinale: 157tr. La Loggetta: 159br. La Vecchia Posta: 167bc. Le Casaline: 166tl. Le Tre Vaselle: 150tl, 161tl.

Marco Mandibola (Milan): 55b, 65bc, 82c, 104bl, 106tl, 109bl, 134b; Marka (Milan): D. Donadoni 153br, R. Gropozzo 153tl.

Peter Noble: 176b.

Ottavius: 162tr. Relais Il Canalicchio: 149tr.

Robert Harding Picture Library: T. Gervis 20br.

San Lorenzo Tre: 151bc. Anna Serrano (Rome): 22tr, 22crb, 23bl, 36cr. Guido Stecchi (Milan): 154cra, 154bl. SuperStock: age fotostock / Phil Robinson 116tc; Marka 38cl; Tips Images 54.

Villa Ciconia: 165tr.

Front End Paper – Alamy Images: Domenico Farone bl; SuperStock: Tips Images tr
Jacket – Front and Spine: 4Corners: Maurizio Rellini. Back: Dreamstime.com: Photopips

All other images © Dorling Kindersley. For further information see: **www.dkimages.com**

Phrase Book

In an Emergency

Help!	Aiuto!	eye-**yoo**-toh
Stop!	Ferma!	fair-**mah**
Call a doctor.	Chiama un medico.	kee-**ah**-mah oon **meh**-dee-koh
Call an ambulance	Chiama un' ambulanza	kee-**ah**-mah oon am-boo-lan-tsa
Call the police.	Chiama la polizia.	kee-**ah**-mah lah pol-ee-**tsee**-ah
Call the fire brigade.	Chiama i pompieri.	kee-**ah**-mah ee pom-pee-**air**-ee
Where is the telephone?	Dov'è il telefono?	dov-**eh** eel teh-**leh**-foh-noh?
The nearest hospital?	L'ospedale più vicino?	loss-peh-**dah**-leh pee-oovee-**chee**-noh?

Communication Essentials

Yes/No	Sì/No	see/noh
Please	Per favore	pair fah-**vor**-eh
Thank you	Grazie	**grah**-tsee-eh
Excuse me	Mi scusi	mee **skoo**-zee
Hello	Buon giorno	bwon **jor**-noh
Goodbye	Arrivederci	ah-ree-veh-**dair**-chee
Good evening	Buona sera	**bwon**-ah sair-ah
morning	la mattina	lah mah-**tee**-nah
afternoon	il pomeriggio	eel poh-meh-**ree**-joh
evening	la sera	lah sair-ah
yesterday	ieri	ee-**air**-ee
today	oggi	**oh**-jee
tomorrow	domani	doh-**mah**-nee
here	qui	kwee
there	la	lah
What?	Quale?	**kwah**-leh?
When?	Quando?	**kwan**-doh?
Why?	Perchè?	pair-**keh**?
Where?	Dove?	**doh**-veh?

Useful Phrases

How are you?	Come sta?	**koh**-meh stah?
Very well, thank you.	Molto bene, grazie.	**moll**-toh **beh**-neh, **grah**-tsee-eh
Pleased to meet you.	Piacere di conoscerla.	pee-ah-**chair**-eh dee coh-**noh**-shair-lah
See you soon.	A più tardi.	ah pee-oo **tar**-dee
That's fine.	Va bene.	va **beh**-neh
Where is/are …?	Dov'è/Dove sono …?	dov-**eh**/doveh **soh**-noh?
How long does it take to get to …?	Quanto tempo ci vuole per andare a …?	**kwan**-toh **tem**-poh chee voo-**oh**-leh pair an-**dar**-eh ah…?
How do I get to …?	Come faccio per arrivare a …?	**koh**-meh **fah**-choh pair arri-**var**-eh ah…?
Do you speak English?	Parla inglese?	**par**-lah een-**gleh**-zeh?
I don't understand.	Non capisco.	non ka-**pee**-skoh
Could you speak more slowly, please?	Può parlare più lentamente, per favore?	pwoh par-**lah**-reh pee-oo len-ta-**men**-teh pair fah-**vor**-eh?
I'm sorry.	Mi dispiace.	mee dee-spee-**ah**-cheh

Useful Words

big	grande	**gran**-deh
small	piccolo	**pee**-koh-loh
hot	caldo	**kal**-doh
cold	freddo	**fred**-doh
good	buono	**bwoh**-noh
bad	cattivo	kat-**tee**-voh
enough	basta	**bas**-tah
well	bene	**beh**-neh
open	aperto	ah-**pair**-toh
closed	chiuso	kee-**oo**-zoh
left	a sinistra	ah see-**nee**-strah
right	a destra	ah **dess**-trah
straight on	sempre dritto	**sem**-preh **dree**-toh
near	vicino	vee-**chee**-noh
far	lontano	lon-**tah**-noh
up	su	soo
down	giù	joo
early	presto	**press**-toh
late	tardi	**tar**-dee
entrance	entrata	en-**trah**-tah
exit	uscita	oo-**shee**-ta
toilet	il gabinetto	eel gah-bee-**net**-toh
free, unoccupied	libero	**lee**-bair-oh
free, no charge	gratuito	grah-**too**-ee-toh
out of order	guasto	**gwass**-to
strike (train etc.)	sciopero	**sho**-pay-ro

Making a Telephone Call

I'd like to place a long-distance call.	Vorrei fare una interurbana.	vor-**ray far**-eh oona in-tair-oor-**bah**-nah
I'd like to make a reverse-charge call.	Vorrei fare una telefonata a carico del destinatario.	vor-**ray far**-eh oona teh-leh-fon-**ah**-tah ah **kar**-ee-koh dell dess-tee-nah-**tar**-ree-oh
I'll try again later.	Ritelefono più tardi.	ree-teh-**leh**-foh-noh pee-oo **tar**-dee
Can I leave a message?	Posso lasciare un messaggio?	**poss**-oh lash-**ah**-reh oon mess-**sah**-joh?
Hold on.	Un attimo, per favore.	oon **ah**-tee-moh, pair fah-**vor**-eh
Could you speak up a little please?	Può parlare più forte, per favore?	pwoh par-**lah**-reh pee-**oo for**-teh, pair fah-**vor**-eh?
local call	la telefonata locale	lah teh-leh-fon-**ah**-ta loh-**kah**-leh

Shopping

How much does this cost?	Quant'è, per favore?	kwan-**teh** pair fah-**vor**-eh?
I would like …	Vorrei…	vor-**ray**
Do you have …?	Avete …?	ah-**veh**-teh…?
I'm just looking.	Sto soltanto guardando.	stoh sol-**tan**-toh gwar-**dan**-doh
Do you take credit cards?	Accettate carte di credito?	ah-chet-**tah**-teh **kar**-teh dee **creh**-dee-toh?
What time do you open/close?	A che ora apre/ chiude?	ah keh or-ah **ah**-preh/kee-**oo**-deh?
this one	questo	**kweh**-stoh
that one	quello	**kwell**-oh
expensive	caro	**kar**-oh
cheap	a buon prezzo	ah bwon **pret**-soh
size, clothes	la taglia	lah **tah**-lee-ah
size, shoes	il numero	eel **noo**-mair-oh
white	bianco	bee-**ang**-koh
black	nero	**neh**-roh
red	rosso	**ross**-oh
yellow	giallo	**jal**-loh
green	verde	**vair**-deh
blue	blu/azzurro	bloo/at-**zoo**-row
brown	marrone	mar-**roh**-neh

Types of Shop

antique dealer	l'antiquario	lan-tee-**kwah**-ree-oh
bakery	la panetteria	lah pah-net-tair-**ree**-ah
bank	la banca	lah **bang**-kah
bookshop	la libreria	lah lee-breh-**ree**-ah
butcher's	la macelleria	lah mah-chell-eh-**ree**-ah
cake shop	la pasticceria	lah pas-tee-chair-**ee**-ah
chemist's	la farmacia	lah far-mah-**chee**-ah
delicatessen	la salumeria	lah sah-loo-meh-**ree**-ah
department store	il grande magazzino	eel **gran**-deh mag-gad-**zee**-noh
fishmonger's	la pescheria	lah pess-keh-**ree**-ah
florist	il fioraio	eel fee-or-**eye**-oh
greengrocer	il fruttivendolo	eel froo-tee-**ven**-doh-loh
grocery	alimentari	ah-lee-men-**tah**-ree
hairdresser	il parrucchiere	eel par-oo-kee-**air**-eh
ice-cream parlour	la gelateria	lah jel-lah-tair-**ree**-ah
market	il mercato	eel mair-**kah**-toh
news-stand	l'edicola	leh-**dee**-koh-lah
post office	l'ufficio postale	loo-**fee**-choh pos-**tah**-leh
shoe shop	il negozio di scarpe	eel neh-**goh**-tsioh dee **skar**-peh
supermarket	il supermercato	su-pair-mair-**kah**-toh
tobacconist	il tabaccaio	eel tah-bak-**eye**-oh
travel agency	l'agenzia di viaggi	lah-jen-**tsee**-ah dee vee-**ad**-jee

Sightseeing

art gallery	la pinacoteca	lah peena-koh-**teh**-kah
bus stop	la fermata dell'autobus	lah fair-**mah**-tah dell ow-toh-booss
church	la chiesa	lah kee-**eh**-zah
	la basilica	lah bah-**seel**-i-kah
closed for the public holiday	chiuso per la festa	kee-**oo**-zoh pair lah **fess**-tah
garden	il giardino	eel jar-**dee**-no
library	la biblioteca	lah beeb-lee-oh-**teh**-kah
museum	il museo	eel moo-**zeh**-oh
railway station	la stazione	lah stat-see-**oh**-neh
tourist information	l'ufficio turistico	loo-**fee**-choh too-**ree**-stee-koh

Staying in a Hotel

Do you have any vacant rooms?	**Avete camere libere?**	ah-veh-teh kah-mair-eh lee-bair-eh?
double room	**una camera doppia**	oona kah-mair-ah doh-pee-ah
with double bed	**con letto matrimoniale**	kon let-toh mah-tree-moh-nee-ah-leh
twin room	**una camera con due letti**	oona kah-mair-ah kon doo-eh let-tee
single room	**una camera singola**	oona kah-mair-ah sing-goh-lah
room with a bath, shower	**una camera con bagno, con doccia**	oona kah-mair-ah kon ban-yoh, kon dot-chah
porter	**il facchino**	eel fah-kee-noh
key	**la chiave**	lah kee-ah-veh
I have a reservation.	**Ho fatto una prenotazione.**	oh fat-toh oona preh-noh-tah-tsee-oh-neh

Eating Out

Have you got a table for …?	**Avete una tavola per …?**	ah-veh-teh oona tah-voh-lah pair …?
I'd like to reserve a table.	**Vorrei riservare una tavola.**	vor-ray ree-sair-vah-reh oona tah-voh-lah
breakfast	**colazione**	koh-lah-tsee-oh-neh
lunch	**pranzo**	pran-tsoh
dinner	**cena**	cheh-nah
Enjoy your meal.	**Buon appetito.**	bwon ah-peh-tee-toh
The bill, please.	**Il conto, per favore.**	eel kon-toh pair fah-vor-eh
I am a vegetarian.	**Sono vegetariano/a.**	soh-noh veh-jeh-tar-ee-ah-noh/nah
waitress	**cameriera**	kah-mair-ee-air-ah
waiter	**cameriere**	kah-mair-ee-air-eh
fixed price menu	**il menù a prezzo fisso**	eel meh-noo ah pret-soh fee-soh
dish of the day	**piatto del giorno**	pee-ah-toh dell jor-no
starter	**antipasto**	an-tee-pass-toh
first course	**il primo**	eel pree-moh
main course	**il secondo**	eel seh-kon-doh
vegetables	**il contorno**	eel kon-tor-noh
dessert	**il dolce**	eel doll-cheh
cover charge	**il coperto**	eel koh-pair-toh
wine list	**la lista dei vini**	lah lee-stah day vee-nee
rare	**al sangue**	al sang-gweh
medium	**al puntino**	al poon-tee-noh
well done	**ben cotto**	ben kot-toh
glass	**il bicchiere**	eel bee-kee-air-eh
bottle	**la bottiglia**	lah bot-teel-yah
knife	**il coltello**	eel kol-tell-oh
fork	**la forchetta**	lah for-ket-tah
spoon	**il cucchiaio**	eel koo-kee-eye-oh

Menu Decoder

l'abbacchio	lah-back-kee-oh	lamb
l'aceto	lah-cheh-toh	vinegar
l'acqua	lah-kwah	water
l'acqua minerale gasata/naturale	lah-kwah mee-nair-ah-leh gah-zah-tah/ nah-too-rah-leh	mineral water fizzy/still
l'aglio	lahl-yoh	garlic
al forno	al for-noh	baked
alla griglia	ah-lah greel-yah	grilled
l'anatra	lah-nah-trah	duck
l'aragosta	lah-rah-goss-tah	lobster
l'arancia	lah-ran-chah	orange
arrosto	ar-ross-toh	roast
la birra	lah beer-rah	beer
la bistecca	lah bee-stek-kah	steak
il brodo	eel broh-doh	broth
il burro	eel boor-oh	butter
il caffè	eel kah-feh	coffee
il carciofo	eel kar-choff-oh	artichoke
la carne	la kar-neh	meat
carne di maiale	kar-neh dee mah-yah-leh	pork
la cipolla	lah chee-poll-ah	onion
i fagioli	ee fah-joh-lee	beans
il formaggio	eel for-mad-joh	cheese
le fragole	leh frah-goh-leh	strawberries
frutta fresca	froo-tah fress-kah	fresh fruit
frutti di mare	froo-tee dee mah-reh	seafood
i funghi	ee foon-gee	mushrooms
i gamberi	ee gam-bair-ee	prawns
il gelato	eel jel-lah-toh	ice cream
l'insalata	leen-sah-lah-tah	salad
il latte	eel laht-teh	milk
i legumi	ee leh-goo-mee	vegetables
lesso	less-oh	boiled
il manzo	eel man-tsoh	beef
la mela	lah meh-lah	apple
la melanzana	lah meh-lan-tsah-nah	aubergine
la minestra	lah mee-ness-trah	soup
l'olio	loll-yoh	oil
l'oliva	loh-lee-vah	olive
il pane	eel pah-neh	bread
il panino	eel pah-nee-noh	roll
le patate	leh pah-tah-teh	potatoes
patatine fritte	pah-tah-teen-eh free-teh	chips
il pepe	eel peh-peh	pepper
la pesca	lah pess-kah	peach
il pesce	eel pesh-eh	fish
il pollo	eel poll-oh	chicken
il pomodoro	eel poh-moh-dor-oh	tomato
il prosciutto cotto/crudo	eel pro-shoo-toh kot-toh/kroo-doh	ham cooked/cured
il riso	eel ree-zoh	rice
il sale	eel sah-leh	salt
la salsiccia	lah sal-see-chah	sausage
secco	sek-koh	dry
succo d'arancia/ di limone	soo-koh dah-ran-chah/ dee lee-moh-neh	orange/lemon juice
il tè	eel teh	tea
la tisana	lah tee-zah-nah	herb tea
il tonno	ton-noh	tuna
la torta	lah tor-tah	cake
l'uovo	loo-oh-voh	egg
l'uva	loo-vah	grapes
vino bianco	vee-noh bee-ang-koh	white wine
vino rosso	vee-noh ross-oh	red wine
il vitello	eel vee-tell-oh	veal
le vongole	leh von-goh-leh	baby clams
lo zucchero	loh zoo-kair-oh	sugar
gli zucchini	lyee dzo-kee-nee	courgettes
la zuppa	lah tsoo-pah	soup

Numbers

1	**uno**	oo-noh
2	**due**	doo-eh
3	**tre**	treh
4	**quattro**	kwat-roh
5	**cinque**	ching-kweh
6	**sei**	say-ee
7	**sette**	set-teh
8	**otto**	ot-toh
9	**nove**	noh-veh
10	**dieci**	dee-eh-chee
11	**undici**	oon-dee-chee
12	**dodici**	doh-dee-chee
13	**tredici**	tray-dee-chee
14	**quattordici**	kwat-tor-dee-chee
15	**quindici**	kwin-dee-chee
16	**sedici**	say-dee-chee
17	**diciassette**	dee-chah-set-teh
18	**diciotto**	dee-chot-toh
19	**diciannove**	dee-chah-noh-veh
20	**venti**	ven-tee
30	**trenta**	tren-tah
40	**quaranta**	kwah-ran-tah
50	**cinquanta**	ching-kwan-tah
60	**sessanta**	sess-an-tah
70	**settanta**	set-tan-tah
80	**ottanta**	ot-tan-tah
90	**novanta**	noh-van-tah
100	**cento**	chen-toh
1,000	**mille**	mee-leh
2,000	**duemila**	doo-eh mee-lah
5,000	**cinquemila**	ching-kweh mee-lah
1,000,000	**un milione**	oon meel-yoh-neh

Time

one minute	**un minuto**	oon mee-noo-toh
one hour	**un'ora**	oon or-ah
half an hour	**mezz'ora**	medz-or-ah
a day	**un giorno**	oon jor-noh
a week	**una settimana**	oona set-tee-mah-nah
Monday	**lunedì**	loo-neh-dee
Tuesday	**martedì**	mar-teh-dee
Wednesday	**mercoledì**	mair-koh-leh-dee
Thursday	**giovedì**	joh-veh-dee
Friday	**venerdì**	ven-air-dee
Saturday	**sabato**	sah-bah-toh
Sunday	**domenica**	doh-meh-nee-kah